Historical Essays
1938–2001

Historical
Essays
{1938–2001}

R.B. McDowell

THE LILLIPUT PRESS
DUBLIN

First published 2003 by
THE LILLIPUT PRESS LTD
62–63 Sitric Road, Arbour Hill,
Dublin 7, Ireland
www.lilliputpress.ie

A CIP record for this title is available
from The British Library.

1 3 5 7 9 10 8 6 4 2

ISBN 1 84351 028 6

The Lilliput Press receives financial assistance from
An Chomhairle Ealaíon / The Arts Council of Ireland.

Set in 10 on 13.5 Sabon
Printed in Middlesex by Creative Print and Design Group

Contents

List of Illustrations
(between pages 112 and 113)

Preface and Acknowledgments

It would be optimistic, indeed presumptuous and futile, to expect to be able to point out a unifying theme in a miscellany of articles written over a stretch of more than sixty years. But it may be hoped that at least some of them deserve to be rescued from what has been described as the 'honoured yet common grave' of a learned periodical, and that the collection as a whole may be of interest as illustrating the varieties of human experience. For instance, that College dons not only engaged in study and teaching but could be strong political partizans and keenly interested in money. Then in the 1790s there were those in Dublin who were meeting weekly to debate earnestly and interminably the reshaping of political institutions on revolutionary lines and others who frequently enjoyed the gossip and glitter of Castle entertainments – both forms of activity being pursued within five minutes walk of one another. Also it is to be hoped that this collection may reflect some important aspects of history – pain, pleasure, success, failure and inconsistency and absurdity.

In preparing this work for publication I am greatly indebted to Professor David Dickson of Trinity College Dublin for most helpful advice and criticism, to Dr C.J. Woods for very useful information, and to Dr E. Boran, Miss K. Dickson and Miss M. Swan for valuable assistance.

I am also grateful to the staffs of the libraries and record offices in which I have worked, and to those acquaintances, colleagues and friends who over the years have instructed and encouraged me and who on occasion have conversationally stimulated me, when we 'tired the sun with talking and sent him down the sky'.

Foreword

An Address to the Kildare Street University Club on the Occasion of R.B. McDowell's Ninetieth Birthday

I must first confess to being here under false pretences. I am not an eighteenth-century historian; I was not a particular pupil of our guest of honour; and I am only an Overseas Member of this Club, who cannot remember that he has to put on a tie in order to eat a solitary sandwich at Daly's Bar. However, this inability about the tie probably stems from the fact that I am of the generation who read history at TCD in the late 1960s and early 1970s – and that does qualify me to speak. Because we were all influenced by the work of R.B., as I'll call him, since he represents that great age of Initials (T.W., F.S.L., R.D. and so on). And that work has remarkably continued right up to now. We may be catching up on him in age, as was brought home to me this afternoon when a solicitous club servant did his best to persuade me to take the new chair-lift up to my room. But he remains ahead in productivity, wit and interests. I have sat beside him tonight discussing – among other things – Joseph Roth's great novel *The Radetzky March*, David Gilmour's new life of Kipling, the history of the Contemporary Club, and the social pretensions of the Marquis MacSwiney of Mashonaglass, a subject he offered to talk on 'all night if necessary'. It was very tempting to take him at his word.

R.B.'s influence on several TCD generations was not only historiographical. A couple of years ago I received a small inheritance, enough to buy a picture with but not more. As it happened, the studio contents of the late Derek Hill were being auctioned in London, and among them was a charming painting of a windblown Trinity scene – the Rubrics, grey stone beyond, a flurry of rain, and a familiar figure exiting, muffler wrapped around him, high pile of books,

leaning back at about 110 degrees: 'Dr McDowell leaving the
Rubrics'. It suggested, irresistibly, an observed moment from my
increasingly distant youth. It was on the cover of Christie's cata-
logue, which should have warned me, but nevertheless off I went to
South Kensington. And found that I was surrounded by half familiar faces of TCD provenance, all of whom looked to have done
rather better in worldly things than I had, and all similarly determined to recapture that moment of their youth. The painting went
for between six and seven times its estimate. I left the saleroom with
a small Wicklow landscape by that underrated painter John Jobson
(whose shares I hope I've talked up a bit tonight) and a healthy
respect for R.B.'s effect on his contemporaries.

That effect was also demonstrated by another echo from the
past. R.B., besides being a legendary History tutor, was an extremely
effective Junior Dean, in charge of disciplining the student body. His
tenure of the post brought him up against the Trinity Internationalists, a hard-line Maoist group from comfortable upper-middle-class
homes, bent on extreme revolution. R.B.'s strictures against them
led to a group of prominent Internationalists dogging his steps bearing a placard 'Junior Dean Explain Your Actions!', which became a
regular part of the Front Square scene around 1968. Cut forward
many years, when a TCD contemporary of mine whom I won't
name had become a commodities broker. He was dealing on the
phone with another representative of unfettered capitalism, talking
up sugar or coffee to some socially unacceptable level, and when the
deal was done they had to exchange names. To my friend's aston-
ishment, his adversary gave the name of one of those long-ago Internationalists. My friend riposted automatically, 'Junior Dean
Explain Your Actions!' There was an appalled pause down the
international line, and then a hissed enquiry: 'Who are you? *Who
are you working for?*' Again, evidence of R.B.'s far-flung effect, and
also perhaps of the paranoia that afflicts ex-revolutionaries.

My own Trinity memories of R.B. are essentially those of an
observer, as I was a Moody person. I'm not referring to a matter of
temperament, but simply that my affiliations were to the great
Theo Moody and his Home Rule special subject. This did not of
course mean, as it would have with Professor Otway-Ruthven, that

I therefore couldn't have anything to do with R.B; simply that my interests lay elsewhere. Not that it stopped some people – a friend of mine came to do a Ph.D on the Volunteers, meaning the body set up before World War I, but TCD in its wisdom decided he must mean the eighteenth-century Volunteers, so he ended up with R.B. as a supervisor – who did very well by him. And I have read, I think, all of R.B.'s remarkable oeuvre. I may even have provoked him to write one book. Twenty-seven years ago I wrote my first academic book review, for *Irish Historical Studies*: it was R.B.'s *The Church of Ireland 1869–1969*. With the testiness of crabbed youth, I took him to task for not dealing with the political allegiances of the C. of I. in Irish life throughout that period; I remember Theo Moody saying to me with a suppressed twinkle, 'I see you have chastised the young McDowell.' Anyway, twenty years later, R.B. answered me with panache, by publishing *Crisis and Decline: The Fate of the Southern Unionists*, to which he added a short but very effective 'memoir' of his own youth, which I recommend to anyone here who hasn't read it.

And there have been many other books, long and short. *Public Opinion in Ireland*; *The Irish Administration*; biographies of Alice Stopford Green and (with W.B. Stanford) Mahaffy; *The Irish Convention*; *Ireland in the Age of Imperialism and Revolution*; *Land and Learning*, a history of two clubs which don't need naming in this company; his history of TCD, written with another great Trinity figure, the botanist David Webb; and only a year or so ago, a life of Grattan which presented a slightly subversive take on him as a sort of proto-Liberal Unionist. A book of essays is now due, from Lilliput, his admirable publishers. He handles, with fluency and high style, institutional history, biography, politics, from the eighteenth to the twentieth century. The books are marked by lucidity, sense, judiciousness and unsentimentality – as well as sharp psychological and social observation. There may be no 'excess of epigram' (Grattan's governing fault, we're told) but there are plenty of sharp shafts. Many occur in my personal favourite, the history of Trinity – an institution balanced, he tells us at one point, like the Dublin of its time, 'between the stodgy and the raffish'. There are reflections which send a long echo. 'Young men dependent on seniority for promotion are always in favour of a retiring age, but for most of them there comes a time in later middle age when they begin to wonder whether the arguments are quite as compelling as they thought.' There are immortal insights into Irish definitions, as where he discusses the statistical fact that so many TCD undergraduates in the 1890s were described as 'the sons of gentlemen'. 'All the term really meant was a man who did not have to get up in the morning if he did not want to. And in Ireland this implied neither great breeding nor very great wealth.' There is the description of Walter Starkie as 'the sort of professor of whom every university ought to have one, but not more than one'. And there are wonderful anecdotes, like Provost Salmon's judgment of Sarah Purser's portrait of Samuel Haughton: 'Excellent, excellent: you can just hear the lies trickling out of his mouth.'

You get the flavour. More seriously, there are aspects of the McDowell oeuvre which were innovatory in their time, and still arrest attention. An interest in the concept of public opinion, and public space, though it wasn't yet called that. An eye for the creation of spurious reputations by historiographical enthusiasms. An understanding of the self-fulfilling dynamics of institutions. A realization of the importance of might-have-beens. An appreciation and wide knowledge of unexpected archives and sources. And above all a fairly merciless hard sense, arising from detachment: the kind of detachment he explains, with honesty and courtesy, in that memoir attached to *Crisis and Decline*. It is history written from a sceptical Belfast boy's point of view, and furthermore, a Belfast boy who read Hobbes – he tells us – 'with delight'.

This can come as a welcome and bracing splash of cold water into the sometimes overheated atmosphere of Irish historical debate – especially as pundits and pop historians colour it up and dumb it down, searching for political angles and revelling in spurious victimhood. The eighteenth-century mentality that R.B. discovered as one of his early subjects, and has returned to repeatedly, includes a dislike of 'enthusiasms' and in his work, I think, this blends with a northern antipathy to 'guff'. 'Semi-assimilation', he has written, may be slightly absurd and have its disadvantages, but it may also 'sharpen the social perceptions and widen the sympathies of the unassimilated and be of benefit to a community that regards variety and a degree of dissension as desirable'.

I'd argue that we could do with that outside view, in an age when 'history' runs the danger of being rewritten as 'collective memory' in a very dubious way. There is always, as R.B. knows, a danger in taking personal empathy too far. The great eighteenth-century historian Lewis Namier, who never wrote about Ireland, once pointed out that we imagine the past in terms of our own experience, and base our ideas of the future upon analogies founded on the past, so we end up imagining the past and remembering the future. When I read this insight I shared it with R.B.'s collaborator, David Webb, who said deflatingly, 'Well I don't see that there's any-thing very new in *that*.' But I persist in thinking that it's an obser-vation with great relevance to the way we see our past in Ireland. Nowadays, here as elsewhere, we're told that history is an élite nar-rative and must be recaptured and reimagined, and indeed replaced, by 'experience' and an 'embrace of ahistoricity'.

History has become therapy, marketed by commemorative jam-borees and by attempts to relive it. The notion that we can access collective memory is sold hard, especially regarding the Famine. Politicians tell us (as I was told at a conference in Virginia on 'Reimagining Ireland') that we involve ourselves in world aid because we 'remember' the Famine. I agree with the leading Famine scholar Cormac Ó Gráda, who believes this is an invention of the 1980s and 1990s, and that Irish involvement in this sphere results much more directly from the Irish missionary tradition. But that is a much less fashionable connection to make. By the end of the Famine celebrations, prosperous politicians born into the upper reaches of the Fine Gael *nomenklatura* were talking as if they remembered a youth with their mouths stained green from eating nettles amid a ravaged and skeletal landscape. Memory and history collapse together into re-enactment. We're promised we can relive the experience by sailing on the *Jeanie Johnston* (if another million euros is poured down her hold) or fighting the Battle of Ballina-muck with plastic pikes, or crouching for ten minutes in a newly constructed mud cabin. What the late great Gerry MacNamara, humourist and social commentator, would have called 'silly makeyuppy history' may provide fulfilment at various levels, but it leads to pretty dubious over-simplifications in the political sphere.

We need the kind of intelligent, analytical and on occasion sceptical history that R.B. has given us – both to understand that we *can't* re-experience the past, and to understand and preserve, for instance, what real and concrete heritage we have. The politicians who enter into communal re-enactments seem less keen on fighting to preserve environmental sites, buildings and archaeological survivals, threatened by irresponsible or corrupt planning authorities – or in funding postgraduate research. It's funny, I think, that on one level we're building interpretive centres and replicas, and on another allowing real historical inheritance to be compromised while we invent 'heritage'. Many of us here, and far outside this Club, have learned far more about our fractured history and its obscure dynamics from the writings of our guest of honour and the generation he so happily still represents. I'd like to propose his health, and cheer him on to his next book. He tells me it's going to be about himself, by himself. No better subject; no better man.

ROY FOSTER

Historical Essays
1938–2001

1 The Court of Dublin Castle

The viceroy, the monarch's representative in Ireland, performed two roles. He was the official head of the Irish civil service and the army, and even when, as was frequently the case after 1800, the chief secretary had more political weight and the commander-of-the-forces in Ireland handled most military matters, the viceroy could significantly influence policy. While the chief secretary had to spend the parliamentary session in London, the viceroy was in Dublin continually and so played an important part in the routine administration of the country. Secondly, the viceroy personified the 'dignified' aspect of the government, maintaining a court which, with its officers, ceremonies and pageantry, expressed the majesty and beneficence of the state and which attracted men of position, power and property (and their ladies), concerned to demonstrate by due deference their allegiance to the Crown and eager to bask in the splendour and gaiety of a court.

A court must have its head, its *roi soleil*, its seat, its officers and its ceremonial and social pattern. The viceroy, known from 1700 as the lord lieutenant, should, according to Disraeli, have united in himself rank, character, some degree of popular talent (particularly the gift of speech), considerable wealth, and freedom from strong religious partisanship.[1] As regards rank, the sixty-two lords lieutenant who held office between 1700 and 1922 were all peers, including fifteen dukes, five marquesses and twenty-eight earls. Twenty-seven (including two prime ministers) attained Cabinet rank; two (Cornwallis and Wellesley) were governors-general of India; one (Dudley) became governor-general of Australia; four (Ormonde, Townshend, Cornwallis and French) commanded armies in the field; and Anglesey commanded the cavalry at Waterloo. Some were remarkably able; all were competent, conscientious and apparently self-confident. Moreover, a number had that useful attribute, usually possessed by a landed magnate – *gravitas*.

Of course, viceroys in their temporary elevation were exposed to criticism: for instance, Lord Buckingham was criticized for being over-conscientious. 'He greatly enjoyed', it was said, 'being surrounded by papers and setting as many people at work at a time as he possibly could.' As a result, he was extremely well-informed but his verbosity in communicating what he knew earned him in the 1780s 'the fashionable appellation of a bore'. Lord Londonderry favoured short, fast meals, so that at one of his castle dinners, 'if you happened to talk you would get nothing to eat'. (A vicereine once remarked that one of the disadvantages of Irish dinners was that 'the amusing talkers all told *strings* of stories'.) Lord Aberdeen knew nothing about racing and his wife was frankly bored by the subject. Denigration was maximized by Bernal Osborne when he wrote, 'Lord Wodehouse's assumption of dignity is more damaging to his office than Lord Carlisle's want of it.'[2]

But on the whole, viceroys seem to have performed their ceremonial and social duties at least adequately – indeed, in some instances with considerable éclat – and the respect and interest lords lieutenant aroused is evinced topographically. In Dublin alone there were named after viceroys thirty streets, four terraces, a quay, a fever hospital, a lunatic asylum, a hospital for the treatment of venereal disease and four bridges (Carlisle, Essex, Richmond and Whitworth). In addition, Sarah's Bridge at Islandbridge was named after Lady Westmorland who laid the foundation stone in 1796. Three lords lieutenant – Buckingham, the first Grand Master of the Order of St Patrick, Eglinton and the seventh Earl of Carlisle – were commemorated by statues and a fourth, Rutland, by an elaborate drinking fountain in Merrion Square. The last architectural commemoration of a viceroy seems to have been the Aberdeen Hall in the Gresham.

Ideally the lord lieutenant was above party affiliations, symbolizing, amongst other things, unity of feeling in the country. Unhappily, at times when party feelings were running strongly, the viceroy was identified by fervent partisans with the government of which he was a member. When Mulgrave, the Lord Lieutenant in a Whig administration (which Irish Conservatives believed was intent on altering the balance of power and patronage between Protestants and Catholics), made his state entry into Dublin riding on a showy charger, he found as he passed along the north side of Merrion Square that all the blinds were down. But if he saw a curious lady peeping out, he bowed deeply. A number of persons of rank refused to attend his levees and drawing-rooms, which, it was said, were the smallest ever known. Still he had, according to a critical Aide-de-Camp (ADC), a brilliant household and his after-theatre parties were much appreciated.[3]

Forty years later, in 1893, when the debate on Home Rule was rising in vehemence, Lord Houghton, the Liberal Viceroy, noticed 'the pre-arranged absence of the landed classes with very few exceptions from his drawing-rooms and levees'. He regretted that they had failed to pay their respects to Her Majesty's representative, implying that when they had attended the levees of his two Conservative predecessors they had done so 'as an act of attention to a political ally'. The Queen regarded the question with mixed feelings. She agreed that it was 'uncivil of the Irish gentry not to have attended the courts held by her representative'. But she appreciated that, as Houghton was a member of the government, attendance might be construed as support for its measures.[4]

A unionist, dwelling on the 'boycott', noticed the absence of 'quality' at Houghton's drawing-rooms; there were, he remarked, only a few ladies whose trains were not made at home. But it had to be admitted that the St Patrick's Day ball was one of the best attended and most cheerful of the season and that 'the smart hunting set', though standing aloof from the castle, went readily enough to a point-to-point arranged by the Viceroy.[5] Near the end of Houghton's term of office a very disturbing rumour ran through the Irish fashionable world: if, as was expected, the Duke and Duchess of York came to stay at the Viceregal Lodge during Punchestown, only those who had attended a levee or drawing-room during the past year would be invited to meet them.[6]

Unionists complained that Houghton on his arrival had refused to receive addresses from the Dublin Chamber of Commerce and the Methodist Conference because they contained references to the maintenance of the Union (an address from Trinity was only received after negotiations over its phraseology). Furthermore, it was stated that later, on his tour of the south and west, he received addresses containing expressions in favour of Home Rule – 'a one-sided' and unconstitutional attitude. Houghton's defenders pointed out that he had depreciated such allusions.[7] The next Liberal Viceroy, Lord Aberdeen, seems, at first, to have had reasonably amiable relations with the unionist world, but when it became clear that the Home Rule bill was going to be pushed through, the unionist landlords and their families absented themselves from the Castle; undoubtedly diminishing, Lord and Lady Aberdeen declared, 'the brilliance of our balls and dinners'.[8]

Dublin Castle provided by the middle of the eighteenth century a fit setting for the viceregal court. A medieval castle begun in the early thirteenth century, with four strong towers and curtain walls, it was situated on comparatively high ground at the north-east corner of the city and was strong enough to resist Irish enemies and rebellious lords. By the age of Vauban it was obsolete as a fortress but already, at the close of the seventeenth century, 'new houses, buildings, rooms and other necessary edifices' had formed a convenient place of residence' for the viceroy and 'his train or household'. There followed a long sequence of repairs, renovations, refacing, rebuilding and decorating. From about 1730 a considerable amount of work was undertaken, with the result that the Upper Castle Yard became a large, well-proportioned, sedate square, containing the viceroy's private apartments, the grand staircase, state rooms, and the Throne Room, which, according to Queen Victoria, was 'quite like a palace'.[9] By the beginning of the twentieth century the castle housed not only the viceregal court but also a variety of government departments. In Upper Castle Yard, the quarters of the chamberlain, the state steward and the usher, the state apartments and the Office of Arms rubbed shoulders with the offices of the Prisons Board and of the Inspector of Lunatics. In Lower Castle Yard the viceregal ADCs and the verger of the Chapel Royal were lodged amongst a number of police and military officers.

Wishing to escape from a close-packed urban environment (the Castle at the beginning of the seventeenth century was described as 'noysome'), viceroys had, from the mid-sixteenth century, a rural residence: first Kilmainham Priory and then, from early in the seventeenth century, a house called the Phoenix in a large park north of the Liffey. Both Ormonde and Essex when viceroys had to fight off efforts by the Duchess of Cleveland (a keen property developer) to obtain from the Crown a grant of Phoenix Park. Essex, expostulating, declared that the Park was the only diversion 'this place affords'. Deprived of it the viceroy would be like a prisoner: 'the Castle being one of the most incommodious dwellings I ever came on and there is no place of pleasure belonging to it nor house to retire to for a little air upon occasions of sickness'. Also, the viceroy would no longer have 'the command of a buck for his table nor grazing ground for his horses'. Ten years later Clarendon emphasized that the house at Chapelizod was 'the cheapest that has been built, and nothing has been laid out that was not absolutely necessary to make it habitable'.[10] Eighteenth-century viceroys seem to have occasionally rented a country house near Dublin and in 1782 parliament voted £25,000 for the purchase of the ranger's house in Phoenix Park for the lord lieutenant. From early in the nineteenth century viceroys tended to spend most of the year at the Lodge, coming into residence at the Castle for the Dublin season. In the 1860s a viceroy's young son found the Lodge 'a really very jolly country house with the imitation purple assumed for state ceremonies', but an English visitor to the Lodge at the beginning of the twentieth century was struck by 'the tremendous ceremony', noting that 'everything was very regal'.[11]

The origins of the viceregal household are to be found in the officers surrounding a great medieval or renaissance magnate. Towards the close of the Tudor era Sir John Perrot, the Lord Deputy in 1585, had a steward, a comptroller, a treasurer, a secretary and gentlemen of the horse. By the beginning of the seventeenth century his successor, Mountjoy, had two gentlemen ushers. To these officers should be added Ulster king-of-arms, responsible for approving claims to arms and for investigating and certifying pedigrees; to assist him he had Athlone pursivant and ultimately three other pursivants.

Wearing their sumptuous tarbets, the officers of arms added to the picturesque splendour of the viceregal court on state occasions.[12]

In the early seventeenth century Wentworth, when opening parliament in style, was attended, in addition to the state officers, by his steward, comptroller, gentlemen ushers, a gentleman of the horse, pages carrying his train and Ulster king-of-arms and pursivants.[13]

After the Restoration the viceregal court was enlarged to embrace the pleasures of life. The office of the master of the revels and masques had been created by Wentworth. However, the first holder, John Oglivy, who brought over actors and musicians and opened a theatre in Dublin, was ruined by 'the calamities of the times'. In 1661 his patent was renewed and with his fellow patentee, Thomas Stanley, he formed a theatrical company in Dublin. In 1670 the performance of Beaumont and Fletcher's *The Loyal Subject* in their theatre was attended by the newly arrived Viceroy, Lord Berkeley, who pronounced that it was 'a very good play, very well acted'. It was unfortunate that the actors were badly dressed, 'but His Excellency's bounty and the advantage they will have by his countenance will soon make them and the scenes very fine'. Until the close of the eighteenth century the master of the revels supervised the Dublin theatres, but in 1786, consequent on the Theatrical Licensing Act, he lost his powers over the Dublin stage and in 1831 the office was abolished.[14]

Another post-Restoration innovation was the beginning of what was later known as the State Music by the appointment of six trumpeters and a kettle drummer. In 1783 Lord Temple, having discovered that the members of the band were living in England, suggested that it should be reorganized and enlarged and, by the end of the century, it comprised, in addition to the kettle drummer and trumpeters, seven violins, two French horns, two hautboys, four bass viols and a dulcimer.[15] Another post-Restoration official connected with amusements was the groom porter, first appointed in 1678, who was empowered to license bowling-alleys, tennis courts and other games in Ireland. This office was abolished in 1745.[16]

Shortly after the Restoration, the corps known as the Battle-axes, the viceroy's bodyguard, seems to have been formed. At the close of the eighteenth century the corps was credited with a highly romantic origin, it being suggested that its first members were gallowglasses from western Scotland. More prosaically, the Duke of Ormonde had in 1662 a guard of halberdiers – a captain, lieutenant and sixty-two rank and file. Ten years later he referred to the Battle-axes and in 1676 Lord Essex complained that the 'guard of Battle-axes' was shabbily clad. Wearing a uniform resembling that of the yeomen of the guard and armed with swords and partisans, the corps, composed of respectable Dublin citizens, very much part-time soldiers, provided a decorative escort for the lord lieutenant on state occasions. When in the early 1830s it was decided to disband the corps (the Battle-axes having purchased their situations, probably in some cases as a form of annuity), it was felt that posts in the Battle-axe Guards 'should be abolished as they fell in'.[17]

At the beginning of George III's reign the viceregal household comprised a state steward and a comptroller (both with white staffs), two gentlemen ushers, two gentlemen of the bedchamber, four gentlemen at large, Ulster king-of-arms and his pursivants, the master of the horse, the master of the revels, ADCs, a private secretary and pages. The state steward, 'a gentleman of rank' (sometimes in the nineteenth century a peer), was responsible for the viceroy's domestic arrangements, 'house and table'.[18] The comptroller checked accounts and paid bills, kept the viceregal residences in order and saw to the comfort of the viceroy's guests. Keeping the accounts was an exacting task, as can be seen from Lord Anglesey's comptroller's papers, a bulky collection, covering expenditure on multifarious items – provisions, clothes, charitable donations, payments to the minor Castle officials (for instance, the scavenger of the Castle Yard and the water pumper) and servants' wages. In 1828 there were at least forty-eight domestics in viceregal employment – cooks, grooms, postillions and maids (ladies', still-room and laundry).[19] One Comptroller, Lord Pirrie (1907–13), aroused widespread admiration. Well-versed in the construction of Atlantic liners, he modernized the Castle kitchens and sanitary arrangements.

At the end of the 1820s a well-informed observer pointed out that the functions of the state steward and the comptroller overlapped, and that sometimes 'the Steward was the man that did the work, the Comptroller more assisting in the pageantry of the Court, but very often the Comptroller was the man conversant with business and the roles should be reversed'.[20] In fact the balance tilted in favour of the comptroller, and the state steward, though the senior officer of the household, was in the end merely responsible for ordering processions and settling the lists of guests for state dinners. When there were two ushers, the first attended on the lord lieutenant, the second on the lady lieutenant, with the first being responsible for birthday nights.[21] At some date between 1764 and 1778 the two ushers were replaced by a gentleman usher and master of ceremonies and a chamberlain. The gentleman usher regulated levees and was expected to know 'who could properly be introduced to the Lord Lieutenant'. The Chamberlain regulated drawing-rooms and balls and c. 1780 to c. 1820, he had the assistance of 'the attendant at balls', described as 'a gentleman'.[22] Since one of the holders of the post was a dancing master it may be assumed that his duty was to regulate the more formal dances. The gentlemen of the bedchamber preceded the viceroy on state occasions. The gentlemen at large 'had nothing to do nor a great deal to receive': they waited behind the lord lieutenant at dinner and enjoyed a free meal afterwards.[23] The master of the horse was responsible for the stables. Probably the best-known master of the horse was Robert Jephson, the eighteenth-century playwright and poet. He held the post for almost thirty years and would have welcomed promotion. Unfortunately, the two household offices to which he could aspire were those of steward and of comptroller but the holders of these posts were expected to preside at household dinners – a duty, Jephson explained, for which 'I am very much disqualified by my constitution requiring the strictest temperance.'[24] There was also from c. 1715 a master of the riding school who gave lessons in horsemanship to members of the household.

Ulster king-of-arms in addition to his four pursivants had, after the creation of the Order of St Patrick in 1783, the assistance of two heralds, Dublin and Cork. In the eighteenth century the viceroy had six ADCs; in the nineteenth, twelve – six paid and six unpaid. (Undoubtedly the most outstanding of the viceregal ADCs was Arthur Wellesley [1787–93].) In the nineteenth century it was one of the ADCs' duties to arrange the sitting at viceregal dinners – an exacting business because, except at state banquets, the table of precedence was not strictly observed when placement was being considered.[25] There were four pages – two for the lord lieutenant, two for the lady lieutenant. During the eighteenth century the viceroy was expected to provide for his pages by obtaining for them commissions in the army, but at the close of the century he paid each of them £75 a year towards their education.[26]

The private secretary was a very useful if comparatively inconspicuous member of the viceregal staff. By the close of the seventeenth century the secretaries who were part of the viceregal entourage had evolved into what has been termed 'the Irish secretariat', an essential part of the Irish administrative machine.[27] If the secretary of state became virtually a sinecure, the chief secretary, the principal member of the secretariat, became in time the effective head of the Irish administration. Naturally, then, the viceroy required a personal assistant, a private secretary, to look after his correspondence, to help him keep in touch with Irish life and to tackle a number of minor but tiresome tasks. In short, the private secretary was 'to be never in the way and never out of it'.[28] For instance Yates Thompson, Private Secretary (1870–1), noted in his diary that he helped his chief, Lord Spencer, to draft a memorandum on Irish land law, investigated Irish education when making a tour of the west and north, moved energetically in Dublin social life and arranged hotel accommodation for an Indian prince visiting Dublin.[29]

Obviously, since each viceroy sought a congenial private secretary, the private secretaries varied considerably in background and character. During the eighteenth century the private secretary was frequently one of the viceregal chaplains. (Ironically, at the close of the seventeenth century Jonathan Swift had been denied the post of private secretary to a lord justice on the grounds that it would be improper for the holder to be a clergyman.)[30] Laymen who were private secretaries in the eighteenth century included John Lees, private secretary to Townshend, who went on to occupy important roles in the Irish administration; Scrope Bernard who became a British MP; and Sackville Hamilton, later under-secretary in the civil department. The nineteenth- and twentieth-century private secretaries included

relations of the lord lieutenant, four clergymen, a dozen army officers, a few Irish civil servants, two men (Courtney Boyle and
Stephen Tallents) who had successful careers in the British civil service, two young peers (Plunket who became governor-general of
New Zealand and Herschell, the son of a Liberal lord chancellor),
Arthur Magenis, who became minister in Lisbon, Yates Thompson,
famous for his collection of illuminated manuscripts, and the gifted
Basil Blackwood. One private secretary, Henry Ponsonby, attained
the pinnacle of his profession. Private secretary to the lord lieutenant in 1855, in 1870 he became private secretary to the Queen,
whom he served with the greatest skill and tact for the next twenty-
five years.

In addition to the household officers who have just been discussed, there were the ecclesiastical and medical households. In the
eighteenth century the lord lieutenant was accompanied from England by two or three chaplains who were supposed to have a claim
on 'his goodness for preferment'[31] – in some instances the claim
being strengthened by the first chaplain acting as the viceroy's private secretary. Indeed, the tendency for viceregal chaplains to reach
the episcopal bench inspired George II to declare that 'all the bishoprics ought not to be given to chaplains'.[32]

In the nineteenth century things changed. The last chaplain from
England to be placed on the Irish Bench was Hardwicke's private
secretary Charles Lindsey, who in 1804 was appointed Bishop of
Kildare. When he died in 1846 he was said to be 'enormously
wealthy'.[33] About 1816 Lord Whitworth appointed a number of
Church of Ireland clergymen, including several dignitaries as viceregal chaplains (unpaid).

From medieval times there was in the Castle a chapel which, it
has been proved, was not a viceregal chapel but a Chapel Royal[34] –
though of course attended by the viceroy – in the eighteenth century
with 'pages, gentlemen of the bed chamber, Gentlemen at Large and
other officers'.[35] When the Castle chapel was destroyed by fire in
1684, it was replaced by a simple structure at the south-east
corner of the Castle. At the beginning of the nineteenth century a
much more impressive building was erected: an early and bold
example of Gothic revivalism, with high cliff-like walls and a richly

ornamented interior, the glass and panelling carrying the arms of successive viceroys in all the colours and contortions of heraldry.

The new chapel was opened in 1814 and a new office, that of the dean of the Chapel Royal – with precedent over the chaplain of the Chapel Royal – established. The dean was also chaplain to the household and sometimes first chaplain to the lord lieutenant. Amongst the deans were Bissett, Bishop of Raphoe; Singleton, private secretary to Northumberland (Lord Lieutenant 1829–30) and the addressee of Sidney Smith's celebrated *Letters*; Graves, distinguished in mathematics and Celtic scholarship; William Conor Magee, afterwards Archbishop of York; and Herculus Dickinson, well known in Dublin as a wit.

After Disestablishment the cost of the chapel, clergy and choir continued to be carried on the estimates. In 1892, when Lord Aberdeen was viceroy, two leading Irish Nationalist MPs asked if there was any legal obstacle to holding a Presbyterian service in the Chapel Royal, and would it be taken into account when the present dean's successor was to be appointed 'that all viceroys in the future' might not belong to 'the Disestablished Church'. John Morley, the Chief Secretary, answered that the Chapel was vested in the dean and that it would be difficult in a single appointment to provide for all the possible theological contingencies that might arise.[36] When in 1921 a Catholic viceroy, Lord FitzAlan, was appointed, the Pope granted him the privilege of having a private chapel in which Mass could be celebrated; at the same time it was made known that there would be no change in the Chapel Royal.[37] When the dean, Charles Mease, who had held office from 1913, died in 1922, the office remained unfilled, and in 1943 the Chapel was handed over to the Catholic Church. It should be added that though the Castle had its own chapel it was in the parish of St Werbugh's, with its impressive parish church. The lord lieutenant occasionally attended St Werbugh's, which had a viceregal gallery at its west end.

The medical household comprised of a state physician (first appointed in 1684); a state surgeon (from 1776); a state dentist (from 1822); a state apothecary (from 1784), a post not filled after the early 1880s; and a surgeon oculist (from the early 1880s). There was also from the late 1830s a surgeon to the household. From the mid-nineteenth century the medical men denoted 'state' were instead termed 'in ordinary'. From 1903 there were two honorary physicians, an honorary surgeon, and an honorary surgeon oculist to the King in Ireland.

The viceregal household reached its apogee at the close of the eighteenth century and by the early 1830s a pruning process had set in. The Battle-axe Guards, the state music and the post of master of the revels were abolished. The number of gentlemen of the bed-chamber was reduced to one and of gentlemen at large to two, and in the mid-nineteenth century they were replaced by three gentle-men-in-waiting who 'afforded general assistance at levees'. About 1907, the posts of gentleman usher and gentlemen-in-waiting were abolished, the offices of state steward and chamberlain were united and the post of master of the horse taken over by an ADC. During the War the number of ADCs was reduced to four, and after the 1917 death of the State Steward and Controller, Sir Anthony Weldon, the post was not filled. Finally, the household became severely functional – reduced to a comptroller and his assistant, a military secretary, a financial secretary and four ADCs.

Household posts were filled by the lord lieutenant and their holders might be replaced when a new viceroy took office. But some members of the household enjoyed a fairly long, uninterrupted term of office – after all, experience counted and an incoming viceroy might not have an appointee in mind. Moreover, household posts scarcely rated very highly as patronage. The salaries paid to the senior household officials, though certainly adequate, were not lav-ish – for instance, in 1791 the steward was paid £411, the comp-troller £309, and the gentleman usher £234. In 1900 the state stew-ard received £506, the comptroller £414, the gentleman usher £200 and the private secretary £829, together with a residence in the grounds of the Viceregal Lodge. In addition, the five senior mem-bers of the household had 'a furnished residence in Dublin Castle'. The household officers' salaries were met out of the concordatum fund until in 1793 they were placed on the civil list. Later in the early 1830s they were transferred to the civil estimates.

Supported by his entourage, the viceroy endeavoured both to perform the 'dignified' functions inherent in his office and to make his court the centre of the country's social life. Even in the sixteenth and seventeenth centuries, when the viceroy was frequently engaged in campaigning or in leading punitive expeditions, ceremonial and official entertaining were not neglected. For instance, viceroys were installed with considerable attention to form and pageantry. In 1556, two days after the Earl of Sussex arrived in Dublin as viceroy designate, he attended a service at Christ Church along with St Leger, the viceroy in office. When it was concluded, Sussex's patent was read by the master of the rolls to the viceroy, 'kneeling before the altar'. St Leger then surrendered the sword, the symbol of royal authority, to Sussex who took the oath on a Mass book held by Athlone Pursivant. 'That done the trumpets sounded and the drums beat.' The next day the new viceroy, 'nobly accompanied and under a canopy', attended a *Te Deum* at Christ Church. Fifteen months later when Essex left Ireland, the lords justice (the Lord Chancellor and Sir Henry Sidney) went to Christ Church and were received by the dean and clergy in copes. After Mass the sword was delivered to them and a *Te Deum* sung.[38]

With the Reformation the religious aspect of the ceremony altered, as can be seen from an account of the installation of Lord Falkland in 1622. After his arrival in Dublin he went with the Council from the Castle to Christ Church where the Bishop of Meath (James Ussher) preached a learned sermon which aroused some controversy – his text was 'bearth not the sword in vain', his theme that more attention should be paid to the enforcement of the recusancy laws. With the Council seated at the communion table, Falkland delivered his patent, was sworn and received the sword. He knighted two gentlemen and departed to the Castle 'in solemnity of state'.[39] His successor, the imperious Wentworth was, as he explained, careful on the morning of his installation to visit the lords justice in their own homes. Because, being still 'a private person', he wanted to set an example of how to behave to the supreme governor. In the afternoon he took the oath and received the sword from the lords justice in the Council chamber.[40] From then on the installation ceremony seems to have been held in the Castle. The viceroy designates would approach the Council chamber, the gentleman usher or Ulster king-of-arms would knock on the door and announce his presence, and on being allowed to enter, the incoming viceroy would find privy councillors seated round the table with their hats on. His patent would be read, he would be sworn in and receive the sword. The councillors would uncover, and he would take his seat at the head of the table.[41]

The sword, 'the emblem of sovereignty', 'the impersonation of royal power', which figured so prominently in the installation ceremony, was also carried before the viceroy in sixteenth- and seventeenth-century progresses, at the opening of parliament, at Castle functions (including in the nineteenth century, somewhat incongruously, state balls, when it was placed on a bracket behind the throne). Once, in 1590, it was nearly employed in a very practical manner by its bearer, the redoubtable Sir George Carew, when the Viceroy was confronted by mutinous soldiery in Dublin Castle.[42] When George IV arrived at the Castle on 17 August 1821, the Viceroy surrendered the sword to the King who immediately returned it to him. On future royal visits to Dublin the sword does not seem to have been surrendered to the monarch, probably because it was agreed that during a royal visit the legal position of the viceroy should be 'unaffected and that he would continue to have the same powers and duties as usual'.[43] But when George V spent a few hours in Belfast in 1921, the sword was tendered to the King by the Viceroy who then carried it before the King at the opening of the parliament of Northern Ireland. After the Restoration the Established Church's prayer for the lord lieutenant supplicated that he might use the sword which 'our sovereign lord the king hath committed into his hands with justice and mercy'. In the eighteenth century the phrase 'in justice and mercy' was replaced by 'in faith and fear', the form employed by the Church of Ireland in the revised prayer book of 1875.[44]

Until the 1860s and before his installation, the viceroy would have made his state entry into Dublin. But in 1869 Lord Spencer made 'a flying visit' for his installation, then, having returned to England, shortly afterwards made his state entry, a precedent henceforth often followed. The Duke of Ormonde's entry in 1662 was, Carte asserted, 'an epitome of what had lately been seen in London'. Unfortunately he does not go into details, but we do know that when Ormonde returned to Dublin from England in 1665 he was met by the nobility and gentry on horseback, by a troop of 'the bachelors of the town' and by the Lord Mayor and Corporation. Three 'pageons' (tableaux) were set up in the streets and a great 'foundary' ran with claret. At night there were bonfires, fireworks and artillery salutes.[45] Though in later days this baroque exuberance was dispensed with, it was customary for the new viceroy to ride in procession to the Castle through streets lined with troops. When it became the practice for the incoming viceroy to come up to Dublin from Kingstown by rail he would be greeted at Westland Row by the lord mayor and Corporation who would offer him the city keys. This ceremony was last performed in May 1882. When the next Viceroy, Lord Carnarvon, a Conservative, arrived in July 1885 the Dublin Corporation refused to take part in his ceremonial entry. *The Times* pointed out that the Lord Mayor was not a free agent, being a publican 'with a heavy stake in his business'. However, though there was no recognition of the 'Queen's imperial sceptre' by the Corporation, there was an extraordinary display of military splendour.[46] From then on, the arrival of a new viceroy was ignored by the Dublin Corporation, but the viceroy was often welcomed by the Kingstown municipal commissioners.

The last state entry was made by Lord Wimborne in 1915. According to *The Times*, whose correspondent detected 'a reaction from the frugality and Puritanism' of the Aberdeen regime, his reception was excellent. A senior civil servant thought the crowds apathetic but not hostile.[47] Wimborne's successors, Lord French and Lord FitzAlan, arrived in Dublin unobtrusively.

One display of state pageantry was fortunately called for only once after the close of the seventeenth century – a viceregal funeral. In the summer and autumn of 1787 the Duke of Rutland had made a strenuous tour of the north and west, commenting perceptively on social habits and the scenery. At Westport he caught 'a violent cough' which developed into a fever; on his return to Dublin, though he strove to perform his duties, he sank rapidly and on 24 October he died at the Lodge in Phoenix Park. From 13 November he lay in state in the Great Committee Room of the House of Lords under a large canopy, decorated by great black plumes. On 17

November the Duke's body on a hearse drawn by eight horses was taken by a circuitous route – St Stephen's Green, Parliament Street, Essex Street, Mary Street – to the North Wall, in the midst of a vast procession which included cavalry, artillery, five battalions of infantry, military bands, mourning horses caparisoned in black, the lord lieutenant's household, the judges, the nobility, members of the House of Commons, the Corporation of Dublin, Trinity College, the choirs of the two cathedrals, the boards controlling civil service departments, and the Battle-axe Guards. Bells tolled, minute guns resounded and military bands provided 'a most affecting combination of plaintive harmony'. When the coffin reached the waterside it was hoisted by a crane on to a great barge which conveyed it to a yacht; the vessel set sail that afternoon for England. The whole ceremony, a tribute to a popular viceroy, which vividly illustrated the functions and power of the Irish governmental system, seems to have been well organized. There were only two discordant notes. The Dublin bell-ringers tried, apparently unsuccessfully, to obtain from the chief secretary's office quintuple wages for tolling the church bells; and the military were accused of being heavy-handed when dealing with the crowds attending the lying in state.[48]

Until the close of the eighteenth century viceregal pageantry was most impressively displayed when the viceroy visited parliament to open the session, for a prorogation or to signify the royal assent to bills. Wentworth, believing in being 'thorough', before holding his first parliament consulted the Earl Marshal on the forms which should be observed, with the result, he complacently noted, that the meeting of parliament in 1634 was marked by 'the greatest splendour and civility that Ireland ever saw'.[49] In the eighteenth century the lord lieutenant went to parliament in considerable state, attended by 'guards on horseback, the principal officers of the household with their wands, and the pages in their liveries, paddling through the mud, with grooms of the chamber and footmen.'[50] On the last day of the Irish parliament, 2 August 1800, Cornwallis in a House of Lords 'where all was or looked courtly and free from vulgar emotion',[51] congratulated both Houses for 'maturing and completing the great measure of legislative union'. He was convinced that 'under the protection of Divine Providence, the United Kingdom of Great Britain and Ireland' would 'remain in all future ages the fairest monument to His Majesty's reign'.

The semi-official social side of the viceroy's life was well established by the sixteenth century. In 1586 Sir John Perrot, the Deputy, in accordance with precedent, maintained two tables at which he entertained daily: his own table for twenty of the 'nobility, council and gentlemen'[52] and his Steward's table for eighteen 'officers, strangers and gentlemen'. Twenty years later another viceroy, Sir William Russell, noted in his diary that on the anniversary of the Queen's accession he was 'wonderously attended on by five bishops, the counsellors and divers earls and lords', and the following day there were 'divers shows', riding at the ring and jousting.

A year later, visiting Galway, Russell was met by the Mayor and aldermen in scarlet gowns who presented him with the keys of the town gates and a Latin oration. He heard a sermon from the Bishop of Kilmacowe in English and Irish, dined with the Mayor and attended 'a mask' presented by 'the noblemen and captains'. In Dublin in January 1596 a masque was performed by 'certain lords and gentlemen' before the Viceroy who 'honourably feasted' the performers.[53] It is perhaps worth noting that this devotion to the drama was accompanied by the arrival at the Castle of the heads of executed rebels, sent to Dublin by the commanders in the field. In the seventeenth century another viceregal diarist, Lord Clarendon, recorded that he 'commonly received people at dinner and in the withdrawing room'. Indeed 'every creature from the highest to the lowest had access to him'. In 1686 he made the King's birthday a 'state day' in the Castle. Twenty persons were at his table, besides ladies who were with his wife and there was another table for the household. On 6 January, being 'a state day, I dined in public – the Lord Chancellor and most of the lords in town dined with me'. He also noted a piece of local etiquette. The Lord Chancellor called at the Castle 'to bid me welcome though I was only a few days away' – at a race meeting at the Curragh.[54]

At the beginning of the eighteenth century Wharton – in Swift's angry opinion 'the most universal villain I have ever known' (Wharton was a vehement Whig) – when lord lieutenant, made Dublin Castle the centre of Irish fashionable life, 'the day was for council,

the night for balls, tables [gaming] and other diversions'. Amongst
these was music, Wharton inviting to Dublin Thomas Clayton, a
pioneer in England of Italian opera. Wharton was supported by his
wife, a Loftus by birth, who welcomed at the Castle the wives of
aldermen and citizens with the 'humanity and easiness which
adorned all the actions of her life'.[55] From then onwards there
emerged the pattern of functions which made up the social routine
of Dublin Castle. The King's and Queen's birthdays were celebrated
by the performance to music of an ode – a banal and stilted expression of unexceptionable sentiments along with a reception and a
ball. There were levees for the men and drawing-rooms for the
ladies and their male escorts.

About mid-century the programme was a heavy one. In a winter
when parliament was not sitting Lord Harcourt held four drawing-
rooms, two balls; on the Queen's birthday, an ode, a ball and a supper; on the King's birthday a levee, an ode and a state dinner. During a parliament winter there were eleven drawing-rooms, ten
assemblies held by his daughter-in-law (who acted as his hostess),
seventeen balls, together with, for the Queen's birthday an ode, a
levee and a supper for numerous ladies.[56] In the 1730s Mrs Delany,
attending a drawing-room, was impressed by the size of the rooms
and observed how the Vicereine, the Duchess of Dorset, after she
'received and made her compliments to the company', sat down to
basset. Quadrille parties were made up and the idle picked up
acquaintances to talk to. About a year later the Duchess provided
what would now be called a buffet supper (Mrs Delany, fascinated,
explains the arrangements in some detail). When the doors of the
supper-room opened 'the hurly burly was not to be described;
squawling, shrieking, all sorts of noise, some ladies lost their lappets, others were trodden upon'.[57] Another experiment was more
successful. Lady Carlisle in 1781 gave 'an exceedingly pretty ball'
and a supper to 'all the young dancing people' which just filled,
'without a crowd', a circular room in one of the castle towers.[58]

After the Union, the political and social importance of the
viceregal court may have somewhat declined but, according to the
first post-Union Viceroy, Hardwicke, there was no diminution in
the numbers attending Castle functions.[59] If many Irish peers and

some great landowners, eager for contact with power and fashion, preferred London to Dublin, many county families were content with the less expensive and for them probably more sociable, Dublin season. A house agent about 1850 asserted that in Dublin rents were raised by country gentlemen coming to the city in the winter and spring to meet their friends and 'introduce their daughters'.[60] Also Dublin was a garrison town, and had a large and growing professional world and many substantial businessmen, merchants, bankers and brewers, who could scarcely be dismissed as 'being in trade'. The circles from which those eligible to attend court functions were drawn tended to expand – for instance, in 1861 the Gentleman Usher remarked that 'at a time not so remote, attorneys were not received at the viceregal court', but he added, 'I am glad to say such exclusiveness no longer exists.'[61] Of course the tendency towards greater inclusiveness was bound to annoy some with an acute sense of the social niceties – about 1910 a member of the household deplored the appearance of reefer coats and brown boots at Castle functions; and a writer brought up in the heart of the old regime complained that under the Aberdeens 'the rag, tag and bob tail of Dublin' went to the Castle. Their court, he wrote, was popular only with the middle classes who liked to dress up in feathers and trains and strut in rarely worn court suits. However, 'the chemistry of time' inevitably corrodes social barriers and dissolves coteries.[62]

After the Union, the pattern of official functions at the Castle was two levees and two drawing-rooms, early in the year, during the Dublin season which ran from December to St Patrick's Day. At a levee, a long sedate procession (it might number a thousand) of officers, officials and gentlemen in uniform or court dress passed deferentially before the lord lieutenant in the Throne Room. Only on one occasion was the solemnity of the occasion seriously marred. In April 1885 when a levee was held by the Prince of Wales there were traffic problems inside and outside the Castle. In spite of the efforts of the police, the long lines of carriages converging on the Castle became inextricably intermingled with trams and carts and many of the occupants had to get out and walk. Inside the Castle a series of barriers had been set up which caused unprecedented 'inconvenience and disorder'. One small door afforded ingress and egress to the Throne Room, and a crowd of soldiers, judges, civil servants, clergymen and gentlemen, 'huddled and crushed together', battled to get in or get out. Fortunately, the Prince was quite unaware of 'the loyalty at high pressure' displayed by those presented to him.[63]

It was laid down in the 1830s that the rules governing presentation at Dublin Castle 'shall assimilate as closely as possible to those at the court of St James'. At a levee, noblemen and gentlemen had to be presented by a person who himself had already been presented and the same rule applied to ladies at drawing-rooms, ladies being presented by a lady who herself had been presented. The fact that these rules had to be republished in the later nineteenth century suggests that they were not always strictly observed. Indeed, in 1887, Ulster King-of-Arms proposed that occasionally the rule that a lady presenting should herself have been presented might be waived, so that the presentee might have as her sponsor a lady of some distinction. The Lord Lieutenant concurred. In the following year the Lord Chamberlain's department informed Ulster King-of-Arms that 'blameless' ladies who had divorced their husbands for a breach of the matrimonial vow could be presented. In 1903 and 1911 when the King held a levee and the Queen a drawing-room in the Castle the rules were relaxed, it being permitted that presentations could be made by the viceroy and the vicereine.[64] At a drawing-room ladies wore lappets and feathers and gentlemen could attend only if accompanying the ladies of their family. From after 1760 until shortly before 1883 it was customary for the lord lieutenant to kiss on the cheek all ladies attending a drawing-room. Thenceforth he kissed only those presented. Finally in 1902 Viceroy Lord Cadogan, with the King's permission, dispensed with kissing.[65]

A vivid and detailed account of a drawing-room, held in February 1882, was penned by George Moore, in his third novel, *A Drama in Muslin*, written while he was still in his naturalist phrase.[66] He starts by describing the long line of carriages, each with its 'silken cargo', converging on the Castle about 9.30 p.m. After disembarking and advancing up the great staircase with its walls decorated with rifles and stars of swords, the young presentee and the lady who was to present her found themselves pushed and crushed in an atmosphere compounded of gas fumes, the dusty odour of *poudre de riz*, the acidities of perfume and the smell of perspiration. At last, after a struggle 'almost like a battle', they arrived at the Throne Room, 'the smooth lustre of marble columns and the opulently twisted candelabra ... evoking the grandeur of a cathedral'. The presentee's train having been skilfully manoeuvred by an ADC, she found herself facing the Viceroy and Vicereine (Lord and Lady Cowper), 'long and sad legs in maroon breeches' and 'teeth and diamonds', backed up by a semi-circle of soldiers in scarlet and 'ladies of honour in silk and tull'. She curtsied, was kissed by the Lord Lieutenant and passed on to St Patrick's Hall, 'a vast congregation watching the ceremony with devout collectiveness'. In the Hall there was a great crowd of ladies, soldiers and civilians in velvet and 'two strange creatures in long garments', dons from Trinity. People vigorously demanded crème ices, champagne or claret cup and there was plenty of cheerful conversation.[67]

Moore's account of the drawing-room is spiced with malice. This is understandable. The theme of his novel was that young women were the slaves of convention which dictated that they should make a good match. Presentation at court was obviously an important move in the hunt for a suitable husband. Also, Moore was incensed by not receiving the invitation he had requested to a state dinner. As he explained to a court official, he was writing a book dealing with the social and political power of the Castle and he wanted his picture to be as complete as possible. 'A passionless observer' is scarcely likely to be the most desirable of dinner-table companions so it is not surprising that Moore was informed that the dinner lists were full. He sent the correspondence relating to this rebuff to a nationalist newspaper, thereby probably demonstrating his unsuitability in the eyes of Castle officialdom to receive a dinner invitation. However, it should be added that in the following year Moore referred rather favourably to a Castle function. 'I have been', he wrote, 'at a state ball in the Castle and I have I confess found it grand and imposing.' If 'the Catholic lot' seemed 'low, common place and uneducated', he had the satisfaction of securing several attractive partners.[68]

Coincidentally, a year after Moore's heroine was presented, a visitor to Dublin recorded her impression of a Castle drawing-room at which she acted as a lady-in-waiting – the vicereine could have as many as ten ladies in attendance. It was, for the visitor, a strenuous evening. She had to dress twice because she could not attend the pre-drawing-room dinner in her train. When the household procession arrived at the Throne Room, Lady Spencer, the Vicereine, took her seat on the throne with her train gracefully spread round her by her small pages. But the ladies-in-waiting were 'ready to sink' as they stood throughout the ceremony with their trains over their arms. At the conclusion of the presentations they hoped to get something to eat in St Patrick's Hall, but there was such a crowd of hungry people that three ladies-in-waiting had to divide 'a glass of sherry and a slice of cake between them'.[69]

Other Castle functions were state dinners and balls, the trooping of the colour on St Patrick's Day in Upper Castle Yard and in March 1897 a tattoo in Upper Castle Yard. At a state dinner the room was 'a blaze of scarlet, gold, lace and diamonds, the table filled with Switzer's most expensive frocks and black coats, coruscating with stars and orders'.[70] Some balls had special features. On St Patrick's night the state ball would start with 'the time honoured country dance'. In 1858 Lord Carlisle gave a juvenile ball to which parents and children were invited. In 1876 the Duke of Abercorn gave a fancy dress ball. One quadrille was 'the Eastern question', showing the advantages of purchasing the Suez Canal, the key to India. Ladies represented the Nerva, Constantinople, the Mediterranean and the Suez Canal. The lady representing the Canal wore the most rich costume which included a cloth of gold robe with wavy bands of azure satin, typifying the Mediterranean waves passing through the sands of the desert and a red satin under-skirt representing the Red Sea; at her girdle was a golden key, labelled Suez Canal, £4,000,000. The choreography is not easy to conceive. Duke and Duchess Abercorn, anxious to be comprehensive in their entertaining, in addition to balls gave afternoon parties, 'especially for the non-dancing part of the community'.[71]

Keeping the Court machinery running smoothly demanded that rulings should be made – often by Ulster king-of-arms or the gentleman usher – which both preserved decorum and enabled individuals to relax in comfortable conformity with convention. The rules for court mourning and half mourning, dress and duration, were published in the *Dublin Gazette*. In 1844 the Queen dispensed with court mourning for the Prince of Saxe-Coburg-Gotha, 'to avoid injury to the trades people of Dublin', and in 1900 she ruled that only court officials should go into mourning for the Duke of Teck. There were questions of costume, which dress – full dress, undress, 'blue evening dress' plain clothes – should be worn on particular occasions. Then, what civil servants were entitled to wear civil service uniform?[72] Could the consul for Liberia (a Dublin merchant) appear at a levee in evening dress? The answer, based on advice from St James, was no. The chairman of the Belfast Harbour Commissioners who wished to attend a levee in his official uniform, and a private in a volunteer corps who requested permission to attend in the uniform of his rank, were both informed that they must wear court dress. In February 1865 the Gentlemen Usher was perturbed when a Captain Lalor appeared at a levee in Confederate uniform; the Gentleman Usher doubted if he should have been admitted and suppressed his designation in the newspapers.[73]

A few years earlier the Gentleman Usher had had a disagreeable encounter with the Chief Justice of the Common Pleas. The Usher explained to him 'respectfully and civilly' that he should not be in the Throne Room when ladies were being presented. The Chief Justice declared that a gentleman-in-waiting had indicated that he should enter. When the Usher asked him to point out the gentleman, the Chief Justice retorted, 'I won't point him out. He may go to Hell and you with him.' Some days later the Chief Justice admitted to the Viceroy that he regretted an expression he had used and the Viceroy decided that the matter should be dropped.[74]

Another wider problem arose in the 1870s. It was observed that at Castle balls 'distinguished ladies' had not been taken into supper by the gentlemen assigned to escort them, who seemed to be occupied elsewhere. Members of the household were reminded that they 'must be devoted to the furtherance of the enjoyment of the guests'.[75]

During the same decade the Crown Prince Rudolf of Austria's visit to Dublin created difficulties for the Lord Lieutenant, the Duke

of Marlborough. The Prince arrived on 23 January 1878. The
Viceroy arranged for him to be met and invited him to a Castle ball
that evening. At the ball the Prince's suite appear to have been
annoyed that he was not provided with a *fauteuil* and when the
Viceroy invited the Prince to dinner he wanted to know if he would
take precedence over his host. Marlborough made it quite clear that
as representative of his sovereign he was entitled to the first place.
In 'the most friendly spirit' the idea of a dinner was abandoned, and
the Viceroy and the Prince simply exchanged visits. Marlborough's
attitude was commended in England: Ponsonby, the Queen's private
secretary, pointing out that if it were thought that the lord lieutenant could alter the rules governing precedence it might handicap
the Viceroy of India when dealing with Indian princes. The Queen's
solution was to give the lord lieutenant the privilege of yielding 'the
first place' to imperial and royal visitors. For instance, when going
into dinner, the visitor could now take in the lord lieutenant's wife,
the lord lieutenant following. But this concession would not apply
to state ceremonies – only to levees and drawing-rooms.[76]

Besides maintaining the ceremonial and social routine associated
with the Castle, viceroys were assiduous in encouraging worthy
institutions, good causes and sporting events. For instance, Trinity
men were offered premiums in 1732 by Lord Dorset for the best
verses on Her Majesty's birthday, and in 1764 by the Duke of
Northumberland for 'exercises' celebrating the conquest of
Canada.[77] Four years later in March 1768 Lord and Lady Townshend, 'willing to encourage every scheme for public utility',
attended St Andrew's when a sermon was preached by Dr Thomas
Leland on behalf of a charitable fund for seamen's children, and at
the close of the year Lord Townshend, visiting Cork, gave £50 to
each of the city infirmaries. In 1791 Lord Westmorland laid the
foundation-stone of the Westmorland lock on the Grand Canal, and
five years later Lord Camden opened the Canal's floating and graving
dock at Ringsend; the Viceroy entered the dock on a yacht accompanied by a number of highly decorated boats filled with 'beautiful
women'. He knighted the chairman of the company, and 1200 persons breakfasted in tents, the whole ensemble producing 'a glow of
pleasure'.[78] About the same time, Camden laid the foundation-stone

of the new buildings at Maynooth. Later viceroys were indefatigable in visiting benevolent and educational institutions, opening bazaars, and attending major race meetings. A viceroy sponsored very up-to-date activities on at least two occasions: in 1895 Lord Houghton took the chair at the Irish Tourist Development Association, and in 1903 Lord Cadogan attended the Dublin Cycle and Motor Show – unfortunately only one motor-car was on display.[79]

A very good impression of this side of a viceroy's life is provided by the diary of Lord Wodehouse (Lord Lieutenant 1864–6). A conscientious and perceptive man, he visited and invigorated a wide range of institutions (his tart comments on much of what he saw being confined to his diary). He attended the Dublin Cattle Show ('speeches too long and tedious'), and dined at the Literary Club ('a bad dinner') and with the Catch Club ('too long an affair to be pleasant'). He went over to Trinity College and visited the Royal Hibernian Academy ('had to buy two pictures by Irish artists as a way of patronizing native art'). He went to a ball for the Academy of Music ('a cold and comfortless affair'), to a lunch at the Kingstown Regatta ('a most tiresome and useless function'), and to the Trinity College sports ('a pretty sight, crowds of people'). He attended 'a ridiculous function called a *converersazione* for the St Vincent de Paul charity', and a lecture 'able but ill delivered' given by Archbishop Trench at the YMCA. He visited Glasnevin Gardens ('fine palm houses'), Maynooth College ('the building very handsome'), the Marlborough Street Model Schools where he listened to teachers being examined, and to two large schools, the Baggot Street Convent of Mercy and St Columba's College ('it looks Puseyitish which I suspect is the true cause why it does not thrive').

He also inspected the Meath Hospital, Mountjoy Prison, two female penitentiaries (one Protestant, the other Catholic), a farm worked by convicts at Lusk, two reformatories (one at Glencree and the Protestant one in Cork Street), the Richmond Asylum, two private asylums, and the RIC depot in the Phoenix Park (where 'the Board of Works had managed to combine 'extravagance, incompleteness and inconvenience with marvellous skill'). During his time in Ireland, Wodehouse visited Kerry (twice), Limerick, Clonmel (where he attended a cattle show, a banquet and a ball), Portlaw (where he inspected the factory), Drogheda, Derry (where he saw the sights 'at railroad speed'), and Belfast, where he inspected the principal institutions 'at a gallop'.[80]

Wodehouse was admirably supported by his wife, a grand-daughter of the first Earl of Clare (at the outset she maintained she 'did not fancy being a vice-queen'). It is worth noting that the vicereine was often an energetic and influential patroness of good causes in her own right. In the late 1870s, at a time of agrarian distress, the Duchess of Marlborough set up a relief fund. In the following decade Lady Carnarvon was active in organizing the Irish contribution (lace and needle work) for the Edinburgh Industrial Exhibition; Lady Zetland was eager to found a hospital for consumptives; Lady Dudley was keen to establish district nurses; Lady Aberdeen was intensely involved in efforts to combat TB and worked hard to promote Irish industry and women's organizations. Even a not very friendly critic had to admit that Lady Aberdeen's 'activity was enormous; some of it was undoubtedly beneficial'.[81]

At this point it is desirable to refer to a very practical – some would have felt crude – question, viceregal remuneration and expenditure. At the beginning of the seventeenth century Mountjoy, estimating his income for two years at £10,379 and his expenses at £13,314, believed he would return to England 'a mere beggar'.[82] When, seventy years later, Lord Berkeley was viceroy, his secretary declared Berkeley's 'vast expense, which must a little be measured according to the greatness of his heart', would make Ireland 'a hard province' for him if the King did not come to his financial assistance.[83] In the next century Chesterfield, near the end of a short period of residence in the 1740s, complained that he would be £5000 out of pocket by 'this campaign, not from any ridiculous profusion but from the excessive price of everything here'.[84]

At the beginning of George III's reign in 1762, the House of Commons – without apparently any official prompting – taking into account that 'the entertainments and appointments of the Lord Lieutenant … [are] inadequate to the dignity of that high office', raised his salary to £16,000 per annum. Then, in the euphoria that followed legislative independence, parliament decided that the lord lieutenant should receive £20,000 per annum. It should be added that the first viceroy to receive the new salary (Temple, afterwards Marquess of Buckingham) informed a successor (Rutland) that in addition to his salary he would have to spend at least £15,000 out of his private means.[85] But a well-informed observer, Lewis O'Beirne, referring to both Temple and Rutland, drew attention to a factor which might easily be overlooked. It was essential for a viceroy, he pointed out, to have a good house steward; Portland (Viceroy in 1782) had as his house steward 'the best, most honest and intelligent man in that office I have ever known', so that Portland 'after living sumptuously' saved from his salary a few hundred pounds.[86] 'By not attending to this the Duke of Rutland was plundered to an enormous extent and even the parsimonious Lord Buckingham, I have good reason to know, dipped into his private means.' Westmorland, in the early 1790s, according to an unreliable source, was said to have saved a considerable sum while in Ireland. But Cornwallis, though living as 'a general officer with his staff in boots and uniform', 'without form or ceremony', and entertaining very meagrely, found his official income scarcely sufficient for his 'retired mode of living'.[87]

In 1810 the government proposed that the lord lieutenant's salary should be raised to £30,000 (£27,000 British), it being noted that the Duke of Richmond and his immediate predecessor, the Duke of Bedford, had spent almost as much as their salary out of their own private resources. Tierney, a leading Whig, rather ungraciously remarked that Richmond could 'well afford that expense', but the government's proposal was accepted. However, in 1830 in a cost-conscious era, the lord lieutenant's salary was adjusted to £20,000 per annum. At the close of the nineteenth century it seems to have been accepted that a viceroy would have to spend annually between £15,000 and £20,000 in addition to his salary – though Salisbury thought 'it might be done for less'. On the other hand Eglinton, it was said, went to Ireland in 1852 with the intention of spending not only his whole official salary but all his private income – he became a very popular viceroy.[88]

In estimating the viceroy's remuneration, it should be taken into account that from the sixteenth century a viceroy on assuming office was granted 'equipage money', defined in 1921 as 'an outfit allowance', amounting to £3000 from the seventeenth century. Two viceroys early in the reign of George III, Bristol and Weymouth, both of whom resigned very shortly after being appointed, collected their equipage grant without ever setting foot in Ireland.[89]

Since the viceroy's remuneration was so large, it may seem strange that holders of the office had to draw on their private resources to support their position. The explanation is simple. The viceroy was expected to maintain semi-regal state and to entertain generously in a world contemptuous of anything savouring of cheese-paring. Towards the close of the eighteenth century an incoming viceroy was informed that during the parliamentary session there was a great increase in expense because in addition to the Board of Green Cloth, the table at which the senior household officials dined, and at which a considerable amount of wine was drunk, extra tables had to be provided – a table for pages, a table for the Battle-axes, a table for the soldiers on guard. On occasion wine was given to the household officers and servants. The senior officers of the household also received coal, candles and stationary (almanacs and pocketbooks) from the viceroy. And at the end of the 1820s the gardens at the Lodge in Phoenix Park, 'one of the best gardens in the world', cost Lord Wellesley a large amount in addition to what was spent by the Board of Works.[90]

At the beginning of the nineteenth century Lord Hardwicke (1801–6), emphasizing how inadequate his salary was, listed a number of charges he had to meet. He had to pay four pages (he implied they should be on the civil list); he was expected to make supplementary payments to the Battle-axes for attending Castle functions; and he had to pay for the King's plate at the Curragh. Then there were charitable donations, 'the greater part of which are scarcely optional', amounting to £1348, and heating and lighting (coal and candles) costing £3000. Needless to say, the viceregal cellars had to be well-stocked. In 1751 the Duke of Dorset sent over in advance a consignment of wine. The Archbishop of Armagh, having organized a tasting, pronounced that nothing but the claret was any good. The champagne sealed with red was 'too bad for an election dinner', the burgundy was equally bad, but the champagne sealed with yellow might 'go off at balls'. In the early

1760s, during a short parliamentary session, 1400 dozen of rare wines were consumed at the lord lieutenant's table. Twenty years later the Duke of Rutland (1784–7) arranged for the wine he needed in Dublin to be purchased by an agent in France who obtained for him 500 bottles of Sillery champagne 'of the very best quality', 300 of Hauteville champagne, 'the growth preferred in Paris', and 300 bottles of St Georges 'from the very cellars of the chapter of Nuits'. The agent also arranged for the Duke's cook to work for two months in the Duke of Orleans' kitchen, which is 'the best school of his trade in Paris'. Rutland presumably agreed with the contemporary dictum that the viceregal cook 'was one of the most effective ministers of the Irish government'.

With the setting in of an age of retrenchment in the 1830s and the viceroy's residence for three-quarters of the year at the Viceregal Lodge, some of the perquisites enjoyed by the household officers disappeared. Nevertheless the expenses of the viceroy – maintaining a great nobleman's establishment magnified – remained on a high level. For instance, in the 1860s those who had been present at a drawing-room drank 300 bottles of the viceroy's sherry, and it was said in the 1890s that during the season the viceregal kitchens consumed two tons of coal a day.[91]

It is easy to dismiss the viceregal court, its officers, rules and ceremonies as of very marginal historical importance. Advanced nationalists saw it as an expensive and offensive symbol of foreign oppression, a magnet for those who betrayed their country's cause. Even some of those who accepted the general political framework regarded the viceregal court with mild contempt. The no-nonsense Archbishop Whately in a momentary outburst of irritation told a senior court official, 'you silly man, you don't even know your own silly business';[92] and, much earlier, Lord Lieutenant Chesterfield spoke of 'the silly forms and ceremonies I have been obliged to go through'.[93] For Victorians with a satirical turn of mind, the viceregal court was an obvious target. Thackeray regarded Dublin Castle as 'the Pink and pride of snobbishness' with 'a very high life below stairs look', and referred (in a passage which delighted a literary-minded Chief Secretary) to how many of those attending viceregal functions 'lived by their boluses or their briefs'.[94] An Irish country gentleman who had been called to the English Bar poked fun at the 'make belief court at the Castle', with its 'cringing abject deferential tone' and its long-serving courtiers solemnly taking it seriously.[95] An eloquent Irish MP, Richard Lalor Shiel, declaimed against this 'mimetic institution', this 'glittering superfluity', 'a mere scenic machine for the representation of royalty on a very provincial stage'. An English radical MP attacked the viceregal court for creating 'heart burnings'; going to Castle functions, he asserted, did not depend on worth or wealth, but 'on intrigue and the mere *ipse dixet* of a certain underling'. Another MP strove to amuse the House of Commons by quoting from a Dublin newspaper a tailor's advertisement offering gentlemen's court dresses on hire, half a crown a day, 'secresy observed'.[96]

It is scarcely surprising then, that in an age of retrenchment and reform, the lord lieutenant and the viceregal court should come under fire. A pertinacious advocate of economy, Joseph Hume, on three occasions between 1823 and 1844, moved in the House of Commons that the Irish lord lieutenancy should be abolished and a similar motion was made by an outspoken radical, John Roebuck, in 1857. In the late 1840s Lord John Russell decided that the Irish viceroy should be replaced by a secretary of state, and in 1850 a government bill abolishing the office of lord lieutenant received a second reading in the House of Commons.[97] But the bill failed to make further progress, partly because its supporters could not agree on whether or not a secretary of state for Ireland should be created. The abolition of the lord lieutenant was urged on the grounds that it would save money and promote administrative efficiency and the social unity of the British Isles, and abolitionists in passing referred contemptuously to the viceregal court as 'a mimic representation of royalty which brought royalty itself to contempt'.[98] In defence of the court at Dublin Castle it was pointed out that it discouraged absenteeism and benefited Dublin economically. Moreover, it was said that the behaviour of all classes was improved by their mingling together at court. Disraeli characteristically saw the Irish viceroyalty as an institution possessing a valuable mystic. Would they, he asked the House of Commons, put an end to all ceremonies and pageantry? 'Reduce government to a much more rude and simple form', he argued, and they would discover 'they had destroyed all the sources of authority'.[99] After the 1850s the threat to the Irish viceroy and his court receded. There were more important questions to be debated, the viceroyalty seems to have been taken for granted, being in Lecky's opinion, 'one of the few institutions in Ireland which nobody *seriously* dislikes'.[100] Incidentally Lecky was against the suggestion, occasionally aired, that the monarch might be represented in Ireland by a member of the royal family.[101]

Undoubtedly the viceregal court encouraged cohesion and confidence amongst the Irish ruling world and important – in their own eyes the most important – sections of Irish society. Court functions with their pageantry, traditional forms, the boast of heraldry, the pomp of power, blending the majesty of the state with courtesy and chivalry, stirred the feelings and fortified the convictions of those participating. There was another side to the court. For a number of prominent and well-established Irish people, especially if they were living in Dublin, who met, conversed, dined and danced at Dublin Castle or the Lodge, the viceregal court represented a series of exhilarating, dignified, pleasantly deferential and enjoyable occasions. A vivacious and intelligent young woman, who from the early 1880s 'lived, laughed and loved' in Dublin society, was sure that 'we were almost as magnificent as Buckingham Palace at our toy court and much more amusing' – society in Dublin being much less cliquish than in London.[102] Pleasure is an important component of life, and the influence of the viceregal court as a social centre was not confined to those who attended its functions. Middle-class suburban and provincial party givers and goers, often upwardly mobile, eager to observe the manners and rules of good society (to quote the title of a widely read work), had patterns provided by the well-reported activities of the viceroy and his consort. This sort of imitation can be dismissed as snobbish, but snobbery can be a civilizing force.

On occasion the viceroy's brilliance was eclipsed when royalty itself arrived in Ireland. The first monarch to visit Ireland in the modern age was the dethroned James II. Preoccupied with military problems, he had little time for ceremonial functions. According to a very unsympathetic observer, he entered Dublin with 'far less splendour than the Lord deputy was used to do', his base-born sons riding on either side and Tyrconnell carrying the sword. Eight months later he was attended 'very meanly' when he went to Mass at Christ Church. He put his court into mourning on the death of the Dauphin and (something no viceroy could aspire to) he touched for the King's evil – though it was pointed out that 'all that were touched brought their own money'.[103] James finally left Dublin on 2 July 1690. Three days later William III reached the neighbourhood of the capital. 'He did not come onto the city but stayed in the field with his army'. But on Sunday 6 July he attended a great service at St Patrick's and for the next few days he received petitions and issued proclamations.[104]

The next royal visit occurred 130 years later when in 1821, shortly after his coronation, George IV came to Ireland for three weeks. The King, as a man and a monarch, had well-publicized weaknesses, but he had imagination, charm, a flair for public relations, and an obvious pleasure in playing the leading role on ceremonial and social occasions. Irishmen seem to have been grateful for a gesture which emphasized their country's place in the empire. Protestants and Catholics joined in welcoming the visit, the Irish public, according to *The Times*, 'looking forward to an occasion of vigorous festivals … unmixed by [sic] party feeling or acrimony'.[105] Early in August it was reported that seventy-four royal servants had arrived in Dublin and that the King's baggage filled an array of wagons and carts.[106] Visitors from the provinces and across the water poured into Dublin and it was said that it was difficult to get post horses from the south of Ireland and that the price of lodgings in Dublin had doubled, hotels demanding £1 a night. Amongst the visitors were two secretaries of state, Castlereagh and Sidmouth (the latter according to very malicious gossip was never sober during the visit), and Prince Esterhazy, a Hungarian magnate who took twenty-eight rooms in the Hibernian.[107] The streets were filled with elegant equipages and 'so thronged as to be nearly impassable' – 'You can hardly get a shopkeeper', it was said, 'to open his shop or a labourer to work in this metropolis.'[108]

Amongst the early arrivals from England was the King's secretary, Sir Benjamin Bloomfield, a Tipperary man, who with the State Steward, planned the details of an elaborate programme. On 12

August the King landed from a steam packet at Howth; as Castlereagh who was in attendance pointed out, the elements had determined that he should 'land on his birthday in the land of Saints and
scholars which is also the anniversary of the battle of Aughrim
which closed the prospects of the Stuarts in Ireland'.[109] After landing, the King drove to the Viceregal Lodge where he was to stay for
most of the visit, accompanied by a cavalcade of mounted gentlemen, whom he thanked, promising to drink their health in 'a
bumper of good Irish whiskey'.[110] He then spent some days in seclusion, in accordance, as he put it, 'with decorum and decency',[111] his
estranged wife having died on 7 August.

On 17 August he made his state entry into Dublin. At the top of
Sackville Street he was met by the Lord Mayor and Corporation at
a triumphal arch representing the city gates, inscribed 'A hundred
thousand welcomes' in Irish. A great procession was formed,
including cavalry, the Corporation, guilds, citizens and about 200
carriages (Ulster King-of-Arms had issued detailed regulations naming the points at which carriages should assemble).[112] The streets
were crowded and houses 'over-laid with spectators'. On arrival at
the Castle, the King received numerous addresses. The next day
there was a review in Phoenix Park and the King went to a three-
hour service at Christ Church, joining in the choral part of the service.[113] During the following days he held a levee attended by 3000
and a drawing-room at which 1000 ladies were presented and
kissed, 'the most juvenile female … feeling ease and confidence'
from the King's 'gracious and condescending manner'.[114] He visited
the Linen Hall, the Bank of Ireland – where a banquet with 'every
delicacy and the choicest wines'[115] was provided in the old House of
Lords – and the Theatre Royal, where two of Sheridan's plays, *The
Duenna* and *St Patrick's Day*, were performed, the packed audience
singing 'God Save the King' three times.[116] The city dinner for the
King, attended by 400 diners, was served in a room built for the
occasion, the circular courtyard of a Moorish palace, 'lighted by a
vast circle of light, hung by invisible wires', the whole 'gay, graceful
and grand'.[117] The Royal Dublin Society gave a *fête champêtre*,
erecting a noble marquee surrounded by fifty tents.[118]

After inspecting the Society's museum, the King drove at 'a

spanking pace' (10 miles an hour) to Slane Castle, the residence of
Lord and Lady Conyngham. The cheering peasantry lined the route
and the houses round Slane were illuminated. The King and Lady
Conyngham rode along the banks of the Boyne and attended service
in Slane church. They gave a dinner party, which Croker, an experienced judge, found 'the pleasantest I was almost ever at', the King
in excellent spirits asking the Attorney General could he stay in Ireland, sending the Lord Lieutenant as viceroy to England.[119]

Back in Dublin the King attended a dinner held in Trinity in the
public theatre. Before the dinner there was a reception in the library
to which the scholars were invited. Ladies watched the dinner from
the theatre gallery – it was regretted that they were not better supplied with refreshments. The dinner was 'handsome', the wines very
good and the music excellent – an anthem beginning, 'Welcome!
Welcome noble King! Joy to Erin's Isle you bring', being sung.[120]

The King also attended an installation dinner of the Knights of St
Patrick in the Castle, displaying his 'suavity and conversational powers', and a ball, given by the knights in the Rotunda, decorated to
resemble 'a magic structure in an Oriental romance'.[121] Towards the
end of his visit he went to the Curragh for a day to watch the races.
The Turf Club, it was said, had spent £3000 on a royal stand, and
had taken care to provide adequate sanitary facilities for the King –
a matter on which Lady Glengall dilated so frankly that Creevy felt
unable to reproduce her account in full.[122] Also, marquees were
erected in which the local people were regaled with beef, porter and
whiskey. Finally, the King attended a banquet at Powerscourt at
which Thomas Moore's 'The Dark Days Are Over' was sung. From
Powerscourt he drove to Dunleary (thenceforth Kingstown), and on
5 September embarked for Wales. 'I leave you', he declared to the
Irish public, 'with a heart filled with sorrow. God bless you all.'[123]

George IV's visit to Ireland inspired Byron's scarifying poem,
'The Irish Avatar', a powerful condemnation of the welcome given
by an enslaved and impoverished people to a 'glutinous monster'.
But Byron's fellow poet, Thomas Moore, though he denounced
Irishmen for knowing 'no medium between brawling, rebellion and
foot-licking idolatry', pronounced that the King had acted 'wisely
and sensibly'. Byron, indeed, when indulging with full poetic licence

in vehement indignation, had disregarded the Irish upper and middle classes, vigorous and fairly prosperous, who responded with alacrity to the royal visitor. The King's gushing enthusiasm – he was reported to have said, 'My heart has always been Irish,' and that he never felt himself so perfectly a King as when he came to Ireland – accorded well with the exuberance and sentimentality readily expressed by large sections of Irish society.[124]

Queen Victoria paid four visits to Ireland, the first being in 1849, though she had been anxious to come earlier. She arrived with Prince Albert at Cove on 3 August and paid a short visit to Cork, where she found the people 'noisy, excitable and very good humoured' and 'the beauty of the women remarkable'. After cruising along the south and east coast, she arrived at Kingstown. According to a young, very able Irish Whig peer, 'it was a beautiful sight, the sun was just setting behind the Wicklow mountains, there was not a ripple on the water and thousands of people crowding upon the pier ... the populace shouted ... the drums played, the yachts hoisted all their colours and I felted it a fine thing to be a Queen.' En route to the Viceregal Lodge the Queen was met by the Lord Mayor, and at an arch erected in Baggot Street the keys of the city were presented to her. She held a levee and a drawing-room in Dublin Castle and a review in Phoenix Park. She and the Prince visited the Bank of Ireland, Trinity College, the Zoo and the Marlborough Street Model Schools where they were received by Dr Murray, the Catholic Archbishop.

The Prince also visited the Royal Irish Academy, the Royal College of Surgeons and the Irish Constabulary Depot. The Queen and the Prince visited Carton, seeing the students as they passed Maynooth College and watching the country people dancing jigs, 'which was very amusing', quite different from the Scottish reel. Embarking at Kingstown on 10 August, they sailed for Belfast. 'It was', the young peer who has just been quoted wrote, 'a sweet, calm, silent evening, and the sun just setting behind the Wicklow mountains, bathed all things in golden floods of light. Upon the beach were crowded in thousands the screaming people filled by love and devotion for her ... surging to and fro like some horrid sea, and asking her to come back quick to them, and bidding her God-speed.' 'I [do] not like', he added, 'popular demonstrations of applause; generally speaking there is something terribly humiliating, I think, in the sight of an enthusiastic mob.' But he thought that the Queen must have wondered whether it should be written in history hereafter that in *her* reign and under *her* auspices, Ireland first became prosperous and her people contented.

In Belfast, where the reception was 'very hearty', the Queen and the Prince visited the White Linen Hall, the Queen's College, the Botanic Gardens and the Deaf and Dumb Institute. The Queen's spontaneous delight and the Prince's ability when visiting institutions to put 'questions *en savant*' made a most favourable impression. To the Prince, the visit seemed a continuous jubilee and he believed it had brought people of all parties together.[125]

The primary object of the next visit (1853) was to encourage the Industrial Exhibition of Ireland, held near Merrion Square in a 'minor crystal palace', as the Prince was convinced that such exhibitions promoted peace and the advance of civilization. At Westland Row Station the city keys were presented and Dublin was illuminated. The day after their arrival the Queen and the Prince visited the exhibition where 16,000 people were present. During the next few days they toured the exhibition several times, making a number of purchases. They also attended a review in the Park and paid a call on William Dargan, the great Irish railway promoter who had organized the exhibition. Though the weather was wretched, the Queen was sorry to leave, 'having spent such a pleasant, gay and interesting time in Ireland'.[126]

In August 1861 the Queen and the Prince Consort spent a few days in Dublin, the visit 'being conducted with an entire absence of ceremonial'. The Prince of Wales was training on the Curragh, so naturally the principal event was a review and field day in Phoenix Park. The Prince Consort visited the new Kildare Street Club building, Dublin prisons, the RDS, the Fine Art Society exhibition and Trinity College. The Queen took drives in the country and through Dublin – 'The streets and buildings', she noted, 'are really very fine.' From Dublin the royal party went to Killiney where the Queen was 'enchanted' by the scenery which reminded her of 'the dear Highlands'.[127]

It was forty years before the Queen visited Ireland again. After the Prince Consort's death in December 1861 she lived a comparatively secluded life, her travels usually being for health and relaxation. But at the end of the century, full of admiration for 'the fighting qualities' displayed by her 'brave Irish soldiers',[128] she decided on an Irish visit. With the Queen, who had now reigned for over sixty years being a great symbolic figure, the forthcoming visit aroused intense interest, great enthusiasm and some controversy. W.B. Yeats and George Moore wrote letters of protest; Maud Gonne MacBride wrote articles denouncing the visit in the *United Irishman*; and Amy Parnell (Parnell's sister), declaring that indifference was not enough, called for immense crowds to assemble, dressed in black, and sing ditties praising the Boers. These protests may have been historically significant but seem to have made little immediate impact. Unionists, and probably many others, revelled in Percy French's good-humoured welcoming poem, 'The Queen's After-Dinner Speech as Overheard by Jamesy Murphy', and the Dublin Corporation decided by 39 votes to 22 to welcome the Queen – the Lord Mayor, Thomas Pile, arguing that Home Rulers would not weaken their case by greeting the head of the state.[129]

The visit was intended to be comparatively informal – though fourteen carriages, forty-three horses and thirty-five grooms were sent over from the royal mews.[130] It began with a long drive from Kingstown to the Viceregal Lodge through lavishly decorated streets. The Queen received 'a wildly enthusiastic greeting', the mood of the day being caught by one of the mottoes displayed – 'Well played – 63 not out'.[131] The Corporation met the Queen at Leeson Street Bridge where a facsimile of the front of Baggotrath Castle had been erected to represent a city gate. When Athlone Pursivant demanded entrance for the Queen, the gates jammed, but two sturdy life guardsmen quickly forced them open and the Lord Mayor presented the city keys.[132] During the following three weeks the Queen held a review in the Park; inspected a gathering of 52,000 school children, 'their cheering being quite over powering'; received at the Lodge a number of addresses (levee dress being worn); met a number of Jubilee nurses; saw a practical demonstration of lace work in the Lodge drawing-room; and visited the Royal

Hospital, the Adelaide and Meath Hospitals, two convents, a Masonic school and the zoo – admiring the lions. She gave a dinner party at the Lodge, with Cardinal Logue amongst the guests – 'unassuming and pleasing in manner though hardly in looks' – and drove in her pony chair in the large gardens greeted by 'the people outside singing God Save the Queen'. She also took a number of drives through the adjacent countryside, making an excursion to Clondalkin to see 'one of the curious old Irish towers'. On the day she left Ireland she reflected it was sad that 'this eventful visit' had 'like everything else in this world' come to an end. She was, she added, very tired but she could never forget 'the enthusiasm and affectionate loyalty' displayed by 'this warm and sympathetic people'.[133]

Her successor, Edward VII, paid seven official visits to Ireland, four as Prince of Wales and three as King. Early in 1865 the Prime Minister Lord Palmerston, with Fenianism gathering strength, thought that the loyal section of the Irish population should be gratified by a royal visit – moreover, he pointed out, the Irish in general 'are of an impulsive temperament and are very sensitive to kindness or the reverse'. The Prince himself agreed with the Lord Lieutenant that he should go over and open the Dublin International Exhibition, as 'a great deal depends on the popularity of the crown there [Ireland]'. In May the Prince spent four days in Dublin and opened the exhibition held in Earlsfort Terrace, addressing an audience estimated to number 10,000. Having toured the exhibition, 'stopping before several pictures', he attended a ball that evening at the Mansion House. *The Times* correspondent considered it was inconveniently crowded and the Viceroy thought there were five times as many people present as could comfortably stand in the room. But the Prince danced a good deal and stayed until 2 p.m. He also attended a review and a ball in the Viceregal Lodge and visited the recently restored St Patrick's. With Lincoln's assassination in mind, the Viceroy was very nervous about the St Patrick's visit but except for some hissing in the streets all went off well, though at the Cathedral the mob was 'somewhat uproarious in their greeting'. The Viceroy (Wodehouse) was very satisfied with the visit, summing up his royal guest as self-indulgent and non-intellectual but sensible and pleasantly disposed to those with whom he came in contact.[134]

Three years later, after the Fenian disturbances, the Irish executive, anxious that the Prince should again visit Ireland, suggested he
could enjoy a day or two at 'a place', Disraeli wrote, 'with the
unfortunate name of Punchestown'. The Queen greatly regretted
'that the occasion for the Prince's visit should be *races*' – racing, she
pointed out, had ruined many a young man and the Prince's attendance at Punchestown would contribute to the opinion that his
chief aim in life was amusement. But Disraeli insisted that there was
in Ireland 'a great yearning for the occasional presence and inspira-
tion of royalty', and the Prince explained that Punchestown was 'a
kind of annual national festival'. A compromise was arrived at. It
was agreed that the main reason for the Prince's visit would be his
investiture as a Knight of St Patrick.

In April the Prince and Princess arrived for a ten-day visit to
Dublin. It included the 'grand ceremony' of the investiture to which
the *Annual Register* devoted four pages, and for the Prince, two visits to Punchestown. 'The *coup d'oeil*', he wrote, 'was very pretty.'
The Prince and Princess visited Trinity College, where the Prince
unveiled a statue of Edmund Burke, the Adelaide and Mater Hospitals, the Hibernian Academy, the Catholic University, and the
RDS Cattle Show. They also went to two balls, the Lord Mayor's
which the Prince pronounced a great success – 'very full and very
hot' – and the Citizens Ball, where there were 4000 present, 'the
Prince plunging into the eddies of the waltz with the gay company'.[135]

Three years later, in 1871, the Prince was back in Ireland. He
had obviously enjoyed the 1868 visit, and Spencer, the Viceroy,
strongly believed in the value of a royal visit. Personal influence, he
was convinced, was of great importance in Ireland. When the Irish
people saw the person, or the nearest representative of the person,
to whom they owed allegiance, their good feelings and loyalty were
drawn out and developed. The Prince arrived on 15 April and was
met at Westland Row by the Lord Mayor and Corporation; he visited the RDS show grounds and spoke with genial competence at
the Agricultural Society's banquet. He attended an investiture of
two Knights of St Patrick in St Patrick's Hall. 'The religious element',
The Times pointed out, had been eliminated from the ceremony
'in accordance with the liberal spirit of the times', but a series of

processions and martial music gave a dramatic character to the
event with Sir Bernard Burke 'acting as the Prospero of the scene'.
Installed as a patron of the Masonic Order in Ireland, the Prince
stressed that as masons they had no politics. The Prince also visited
the Model Schools, the Horse Show, and two hospitals, and
attended a review and two balls.[136] The visit went smoothly except
for some hissing in the streets, but there was an unfortunate appendix. With what an English Liberal MP condemned as 'bad taste and
timing', it was decided to hold a meeting in Phoenix Park to
demand the release of the Fenian prisoners on 6 August, the Prince's
last night at the Viceregal Lodge. The Irish administration forbade
the meeting, drawing attention to the fact that the Park was Crown
property, and the efforts of the police to disperse the crowd led to
an ugly clash.

The Prince's next visit to Ireland, which included not only a stay
in Dublin but visits to the south and Ulster, met at some points a
strident hostility – an unusual experience for Victorian royalty.
Towards the close of 1884 Spencer, Viceroy for a second term and
coping with agrarian agitation and Parnellism, thought a royal visit
would bring the loyalists 'to the front',[137] and when the visit was
rumoured, nationalists saw it as an attempt to use the Prince to bol-
ster up an unpopular government. The Parnellite party declared that
the attitude of the Irish people to the royal visitors should be one of
'dignified neutrality', avoiding discourtesy but doing nothing to
suggest that they would relinquish their claim to self-government.[138]
Dublin Corporation decided by 41 votes to 17 not to present an
address of welcome, and the Lord Mayor stated he would lower the
flag on the Mansion House the day the Prince landed in Ireland.
Loyalists (including many moderate nationalists) were put on their
mettle and the Prince and Princess, on arrival at Westland Row,
were met by representatives of a city welcome committee and on
their visit to the Spring Show greeted by 'salvoes of cheering'.[139]
The Prince laid the foundation stone of the Museum of Science and
Art and the Princess, visiting the docks, named a new basin the
Alexandra Basin. The Prince held a levee (the Queen's reluctance to
the Viceroy being superseded having been overcome) and the
Princess held a drawing-room. They both visited Trinity and the

Royal University and on Sunday the 12th were to have attended
Evensong at St Patrick's but did not 'seem equal to the ordeal' after
a very long morning service in the Chapel Royal.[140] Reflecting contemporary concern with working-class housing, the Prince visited
the Coombe, inspecting model dwellings and decayed tenements.

After a week in Dublin, the royal visitors departed for Cork. At
Mallow, while the Prince was being received by local dignitaries on
the down platform, bands playing nationalist airs were removed by
the police from the up platform. In Cork there was cheering and
hissing. The Prince opened the Crawford School of Art and visited
the Convent of the Good Shepherd where he was received by the
Catholic Bishop of Cork, Dr Delany, who had reminded his clergy
of 'the respect and devotion due to those of exalted rank' and of
their duty to welcome their future ruler.[141] At the new Church of Ireland cathedral, packed to the doors, the Prince and Princess met
with a reception 'magnificent in its cordiality' but a visit to University College was abandoned because of the possibility of a hostile
undergraduate demonstration. On leaving the city at Parnell Bridge,
the Prince and Princess had 'a hostile and offensive reception' –
John O'Connor MP raising his umbrella or stick to lead the groan-
ing or threatening attitude of some 300 to 500 people – and at one
point a coffin on a car was driven against the royal carriage: 'the
Princess did not like it'. To Arthur Ellis, an equerry, the Cork visit
was a nightmare – streets filled by 'the lazzaroni of Cork' with 'their
sullen, hideous countenances, hissing and grimacing into one's very
face'. Since there seems to have been loud cheering from the loyalist sections of the population, Ellis' opinion probably reflects the
shocked surprise of a courtier at royalty meeting anything short of
profound respect.[142]

In Killarney the royal visitors enjoyed a hearty welcome and
good weather. On the return journey, at the terminus of the Kerry-
Limerick railway, a rush towards the royal train was checked by the
police – 'the booing of a Kerry rabble', it was remarked, 'is an exe-
crable noise'.[143] At Listowel bands played nationalist airs; at
Abbeyfeakle black flags were displayed. At Limerick the station was
filled by the gentry and the loyal inhabitants of the city and county,
and the Prince and Princess attended a luncheon there. Back in

Dublin they met in the Phoenix Park 8500 Church of Ireland Sunday-school children, went to Punchestown and to the Citizens Ball in the RDS Hall, where there were tea rooms, a supper room in which 1500 persons could be served at a time and where 'bright uniforms and costumes mingled in vivid splendour'.[144]

The next day the royal visitors started by train to the north, and from Dundalk they met with an enthusiastic welcome – near Lisburn, linen in a bleaching field was arranged in the shape of the Prince of Wales' feathers.[145] In Belfast addresses were presented in the Ulster Hall, and the Prince visited two linen factories, and a printing works; later the Prince and Princess were greeted by 20,000 Protestant Sunday-school children in the Botanic Gardens. After visiting Londonderry and Baronscourt they left for England. The Lord Lieutenant thought that, on the whole, the visit had been a great success. Loyalist enthusiasm had been very marked, especially in Ulster. In Dublin scarcely any hostile feeling had manifested itself. In the South a few MPs had tried to arouse demonstrations against the Prince and Princess, but these had obtained no support from respectable people. The Lord Lieutenant could not speak too highly of the courage and good sense of the Prince, 'who took the unpleasant incidents in the right way and made no sweeping condemnation of the Irish'.[146]

This was the last visit paid by the future Edward VII to Ireland while still Prince of Wales. But in the 1890s the Duke and Duchess of York (later George V and Queen Mary) twice came and spent some time in Ireland. During the 1897 visit they received addresses at the Castle and presented colours to three regiments. The Duchess, indefatigable when it came to sight-seeing, visited Trinity College, the Bank of Ireland, the National Museum and Alexandra College. Together they attended a textile exhibition, a flower show, a garden party and the Leopardstown races (twice). Having visited Valentia, they travelled across the country via Cavan and Baronscourt to Belfast, where they attended a garden party. Two years later the Duke and Duchess were again in Ireland: when in Dublin they attended Punchestown (twice), Leopardstown, and a ball at the King's Hospital. They visited the Curragh camp, the Guinness Brewery and the Spring Show. They then stayed at Kilkenny with the Marquess of Ormonde, the Duchess visiting country houses and the Duke fishing on the Blackwater. On Sunday when they attended morning service at St Canice's Cathedral, 'the whole congregation broke spontaneously into the National anthem'.[147]

Edward VII, as King, paid no less than three visits to Ireland, the first in July 1903. At the outset he displayed his well-known tact by associating himself with the mourning for Leo XIII who had died the day before the King landed at Kingstown. From there, the King and Queen drove to the Viceregal Lodge through eleven miles 'of bunting and cheering crowds growing denser and more vociferous … a prolonged roar, blare, glare, glitter and glamour of two variegated, agitated, sonorous hours' – to quote Wyndham, a high-spirited Chief Secretary with a romantic approach to politics.[148] During the next few days the King and Queen visited Trinity College, Maynooth, Alexandra College, the Guinness Trust buildings and Corporation housing for the poor. The King held a levee, received addresses at the Castle, was presented at a review in the Phoenix Park where, again to quote Wyndham, 'the Phoenix monument was a pyramid of mad humanity, screaming, blessing, waving hats and handkerchiefs, and so on down an interminable lane of frenzied enthusiasm'.[149] The Queen held a drawing-room attended by 600 debutantes. St Patrick's Hall was decorated with 8000 roses and electric fans were installed in the Hall and in the King's supper room.[150] Proceeding to the north, at Strangford the royal visitors heard a selection of Irish airs – 'Brian Boru's March' particularly appealing to the King.[151] They visited Belfast and Londonderry – where the King referred to 'the great missionary of the west', St Columba, and the Catholic bishop took part in the royal procession.[152] From Buncrana on Lough Swilly, the royal party travelled by yacht along the west and south coasts, landing from time to time to drive inland (the King using a 24 horse-power Daimler weighing two tons, with an average speed of 25 mph).[153] The visit ended with a day in Cork, where they received 'a right, royal welcome', to see the Cork International Exhibition.[154]

The next year (1904) the King and Queen spent nine days in Ireland, arriving on 26 April. In Dublin they attended Punchestown, Leopardstown and a command performance at the Theatre Royal where the Beerhohm Tree Company performed scenes from *Richard II*, *The Last of the Dandies*, and *Trilby*. The King laid the foundation stone of the new College of Science in Merrion Street; then with the Queen he travelled to Lismore, visited Kilkenny and Waterford, receiving addresses from the corporations and visiting agricultural shows.

The last visit in July 1907 was very short. The Lord Lieutenant, Lord Aberdeen, was very keen on a royal visit but his wife was conscious of problems – if the King and Queen stayed in the Lodge, furniture would have to be moved from the Castle, and since 'we cannot go to unlimited expense', she thought that the principal viceregal entertainment should be a garden party 'to which we can ask all Ireland'. She added, 'I know the King cannot abide me though he tolerates Aberdeen.'[155] Fortunately contact between the royal guests and their viceregal hosts was diminished by the King and Queen remaining on the royal yacht from which they went to Leopardstown and to a garden party at the Lodge, attended by 'a large and brilliant company'. The King and Queen also visited the Dublin International Exhibition in Herbert Park, where a verse was appended to the national anthem:

> Come back to Erin and Ceud míle fáilte.
> Welcome our King to Hibernia's green shores,
> True hearts will greet thee and brave hands will meet thee
> Come back to Erin and welcome galore.[156]

The last state visit to Dublin before the Great War was paid by George V and Mary in July 1911; they stayed for five days in the Castle. During the visit the King opened the College of Science, held a review in Phoenix Park and a levee at the Castle.[157] The King and Queen visited Trinity College, Maynooth, and a TB clinic. They attended Leopardstown and the Phoenix Park races. There was an investiture of two Knights of St Patrick, one of whom was a well-known Kerryman, Lord Kitchener, and the Queen held a drawing-room, there being in attendance, in addition to the viceregal household, great household officers from England, the gentlemen-at-arms, and the yeomen of the guard. It was the last and possibly the greatest Castle occasion of the old regime.

Four years later the state apartments were to be converted into a military hospital. The viceroys who succeeded Aberdeen, though on occasion they attended functions such as an investiture, a military parade, a polo match or a race meeting, spent much of their time, in what was a period of growing tension, in comparative seclusion. The last display of the Irish viceregal state was in Belfast on 22 June 1921 when the Lord Lieutenant, Lord FitzAlan, and Ulster King-of-Arms and his officers were in attendance on the King during his visit to Belfast to open the parliament of Northern Ireland. FitzAlan remained Viceroy until early December 1922, but made few public appearances after the installation of the provisional government on 16 January 1922. His departure from Dublin went almost unnoticed.

FitzAlan's successor in Dublin was Timothy Healy, the first Governor-General of the Irish Free State. When, just after his appointment, he was asked whether there would be any viceregal ceremonial he replied, 'I hope not', his wish being for 'simplicity itself'.[158] Ironically, the acerbic Beatrice Webb, visiting Dublin in 1930, commented severely on 'this pretence of a court', 'their excellencies [James McNeill, then Governor-General and Mrs McNeill] and the splendour of the viceregal establishment (27 indoor servants and 15 gardeners) seem an expensive anachronism for such a small country'.[159]

To those who focus on the development of Irish nationalism, that potent force, the royal visits that have just been described, were of slight and ephemeral significance – their importance was merely that they stimulated the more advanced nationalists by providing them with occasions for protest. The protests against Queen Victoria's 1900 visit have already been mentioned. A few years later, when it was suggested that the Dublin Corporation should present an address to Edward VII on his 1903 visit, there was a stormy meeting in the council chamber. The gallery was packed, Mrs Maud Gonne MacBride and Edward Martyn were greeted with boisterous cheers, 'A Nation Once Again' was sung, and (according to *The Irish Times*) 'mob law' prevailed. The council adjourned, and at a meeting ten days later it was resolved by 40 votes to 37 not to present an address. The size of the minority shows that the nationalist members were divided between those who believed that the Nationalist party was emphatically a constitutional one which respected the monarchy, and those who held that presenting an address to the King implied that the Irish people were satisfied with the political status quo.

The debate on the address is imprinted on Irish literature. A group of minor municipal politicians drinking stout in a dingy committee room discussed the issue. An advanced nationalist spoke of the honour of Dublin being dragged in the mud to please a German monarch. An older man, a constitutional nationalist, asked, 'Are we going to insult the man when he comes on a friendly visit?' and when it was suggested that 'King Edward's life you know, is not the very ...', he goes on to say, 'Let bygones be bygones ... I admire the man personally. He is just an ordinary knockabout like you and me. He is fond of his glass of grog and he's a bit of a rake perhaps but he is a good sportsman. Damn it, can't we Irish play fair?'[160]

When early in 1911 it was announced that George V would visit Dublin, the Corporation in April resolved by 42 votes to 9 not to present an address – because Ireland was still deprived of its parliament; the Lord Mayor, a nationalist, was in favour of an address, and shortly before the visit a special meeting of the Corporation was summoned to consider rescinding the April resolution. A private meeting of the nationalist members of the Corporation decided against the address by 24 votes to 4, and the special meeting collapsed owing to the absence of a quorum. Outside the City Hall a crowd of protestors, opposed to an address, scuffled with the police (Countess Markievicz was conspicuous among them). After the special meeting adjourned, a gathering in the council chamber with Councillor Cosgrave (the future president of the executive council) in the chair, protested against the conduct of the police. However, the Lord Mayor, wearing his civic chain, attended a viceregal garden party given in honour of the royal visitors. Also, it should be added that both in 1903 and 1911 citizens' reception committees – representative of solid, prosperous, conservative Dublin (unionist and moderate nationalist) – were organized and presented loyal addresses.[161]

Successive royal visits seem to have aroused, at least in some quarters, intense if momentary enthusiasm. Conservative journalists and courtly politicians may have exaggerated the degree and depth of the loyalty displayed – Queen Victoria reflected in 1897 that though her three visits to Ireland 'went well', they 'did not produce a lasting effect' (although she seems to have been happier after her fourth visit a few years later).[162] However, for many Irish men the monarchy was a venerable and valued institution, an impressive and personal symbol of the state that some had served at home and abroad, and the monarchs who visited Ireland performed their public functions superbly, combining dignity with affability. Public-spirited people were gratified by the cachet conferred on institutions with which they were associated by a royal inspection. Those present at the festivities in either the Castle or at the Viceregal Lodge were bound to be exhilarated; Dublin trade received a fillip and the crowds who mustered on the pavements seem to have been delighted by the pageantry, the cavalry and carriages, the bands, the troops lining the streets, and the lavishly decorated buildings (the usual royal routes went through strongly loyalist areas). Even a fervent nationalist might exclaim, 'Still I cheered – God forgive me – I cheered with the rest.'

NOTES

1. S. Lee, *King Edward VII*, i (1925), p. 233.
2. C. Sheridan to R. Fitzpatrick, 30 December 1782 (BL, Add. MS 47582); *Charlemont MSS*, HMC, i, p. 157; Lady Fingall, *Seventy Years Young* (1937), p. 102; A.C. Benson, *Edwardian Excursions* (1981), p. 47; M. Headlam, *Irish Reminiscences* (1947), p. 40; A.I. Dasent, *John Thodeus Delane*, ii (1900), pp. 163–4.
3. P.H. Bagenal, *Life of Bernal Osborne* (1884), p. 23; A. Ponsonby, *Frederick Ponsonby* (1942), p. 220.
4. *Letters of Queen Victoria*, 3rd series, ii, pp. 222–3; A. Ponsonby, *Frederick Ponsonby*, p. 220.
5. *Vanity Fair*, 1893, pp. 82, 131, 148; 1894, pp. 142, 170; 1895, pp. 115, 196.
6. *Irish Society*, 27 Jan. 1894.
7. *Hansard*, 4th series, xiii, p. 1680; xiv, p. 540, 1276–80; xv, pp. 273–96.
8. Lord and Lady Aberdeen, *We Twa*, vol. ii (Edinburgh 1925), p. 179.
9. Queen Victoria, *Leaves from the Journal of our Life in the Highlands* (1868), p. 183.
10. *SPI 1615–29*, xxviii–xxxii, *Ormonde MSS*, HMC, NS IV, p. 152; *SPI 1603–6*, p. 381; *SPI 1509–73*, pp. 55, 106; *Essex Papers*, ed. O. Airy, i (1890); (Camden Society, NS, xlvii), pp. 57–8, 68–9, 71.

11. E. Hamilton, *Forty Years On* (1922), p. 123; Lady Cynthia Asquith, *Diaries 1915–18* (1968), pp. 61, 126.

12. *SPI 1586–90*, p. 113; *SPI 1600–01*, p. 316; *SPI 1601–03*, p. 400; *Lib. Munerum*, i, pt. 2, p. 85; J. Barry in *A Guide to the Genealogical Office* (1998), pp. 57–76; S. Hood, *Royal Roots: The Survival of the Office of Arms* (Dublin 2002).

13. The Earl of Stafford, *Letters*, ed. W. Knowles, i, (1739), pp. 282–5.

14. *Lib. Munerum*, i, pt. 2, p. 92; *SPI 1669–70*, pp. 122–3, 416–17.

15. Lord Temple to Treasury, 12 Feb. 1783 (BL, Add. MS 40177).

16. *Lib. Munerum*, i, pt. 2, p. 93.

17. *SPI 1666–69*, pp. 58–9; C.C. Lawson, *A History of the Uniforms of the British Army* (1961), p. 42–3; J. Walker, *Historical Essay on the Dress of the Ancient and Modern Irish* (1788), pp. 124–9; *Army Hist. Rev.*, iv, p. 80, xvii, pp. 144–5, xxviii, p. 122; *Irish Sword*, iii, pp. 166–9, xv, 29; *Hansard*, 3rd series, vi, p. 932; *Selections from the Correspondences of Arthur Capel, Earl of Essex*, ed. C.E. Pike, 3rd series, xxiv (Camden), p. 83.

18. For the viceregal household see *House of Commons Jnl Irl.*, xix, pp. xxxviii–xxxix; *Dublin Gazette*, 17 Jan. 1764; Standing orders viceregal household staff, 5 July 1895 (NLI, G.O. 339); *Harcourt Papers*, ed. F. Harcourt, ix, pp. 18–19; *Select Committee on Civil Government Charges Evidence*, H.C. 333, iv (1831); *The Civil Establishment of Ireland ... Jan. 1773* (BL, Add. MS 30214); *Watson's Dublin Directory*.

19. PRONI, D 619/33/1A1.

20. *Select Committee on Civil Government Charges: Evidence*, p. 21.

21. Duke of Richmond, 20 April 1813 (NLI, G.O. 321, ii).

22. *Watson's Dublin Directory*.

23. *Harcourt Papers*, ix, p. 19.

24. R. Jephson to —, 11 Nov. 1780 (BL, Add. MS 34417).

25. *Nineteenth Century*, lx, p. 561; C.A. Cameron, *Autobiography* (1921), p. 114.

26. *Cal. Home Office Papers 1770–72*, p. 240; W.W.M. 28/55.

27. *Handbook of British Chronology*, 3rd edn (1986), p. 125.

28. T. Jones, *A Diary with Letters* (1954), p. xx.

29. Yates Thompson diary (NLI, MS 25593).

30. Jonathan Swift, *Miscellaneous and Autobiographical Pieces*, ed. H. Davis (1969), p. 195.

31. *Harcourt Papers*, ix, p. 18.

32. *Stopford Sackville MSS*, HMC, i, p. 177.

33. *Gentlemen's Magazine*, NS, xxvi, p. 422.

34. H.J. Lawlor, 'The Chapel of Dublin Castle', in *RSAI Jnl*, liii, pp. 34–72; lviii, pp. 44–53.

35. *Harcourt Papers*, iii, p. 131.

36. *Hansard*, 3rd series, pp. 106–7.

37. *The Times*, 8 Aug. 1921.

38. *Cal. Carew MSS*, i, pp. 257–8. 278–9.

39. *SPI 1615–28*, pp. 5–6; *The Whole Works of James Ussher*, ed. C. Elrington, xv (1864), pp. 180–1.

40. Earl of Stafford, *Letters*, i, p. 97.

41. M. Headlam, *Irish Reminiscences* (1947), p. 74; NLI G.O. MS 311, p. 241.

42. NLI G.O. MS 337, p. 21; *Nineteenth Century*, lx, p. 564; *RSAI Jnl*, lxii, p. 39; *SPI 1666–9*, pp. 205, 208; *Cal. Carew MSS*, ii, p. 32.

43. *Letters of Queen Victoria's*, 3rd series, iii, p. 517.

44. *The Book of Common Prayer According to the Use of the Church of England and Ireland* (Dublin 1666); *The Book of Common Prayer* (Dublin 1753). The historian J.R. Green, hearing on a visit to Dublin in 1859 the prayers for the Lord Lieutenant, remarked it was 'a raw-headed and bloody bones way of teaching loyalty' (*Letters of J.R. Green*, ed. L. Stephen (1901), p. 35.

45. Thomas Carte, *Life of James Duke of Ormonde*, iv (1851), p. 114; *SPI 1663–5*, p. 651.

46. *The Times*, 8 May 1882; 6, 8 July 1882.

47. *Ibid.* 4 April 1915; Headlam, *Irish Reminiscences*, p. 74.

48. *Rutland MSS*, HMC, iii, pp. 423–6; *Walker's Hibernian Magazine*, Nov. 1787; *Dublin Chronicle*, 3 Nov. 1787; *Hib. Chronicle*, 19 Nov. 1787; *DEP* , 15, 17 Nov. 1787.

49. Earl of Strafforde, *Letters*, i, pp. 259, 274, 282–5.

50. *Harcourt Papers*, iii, pp. 117–18.

51. De Quincey, *Collected Works*, i (1889), pp. 221–3.

52. *SPI 1566–88*, p. 113.

53. *Cal. Carew MSS*, i, pp. 224–5, 229, 238–40.

54. Lord Clarendon, *State Letters* (1765), i, pp. 40, 263; ii, 174–6.

55. *Memoirs of the Life of the Late Marquess of Wharton* (1715), pp. 58–69.

56. *Harcourt Papers*, iii, pp. 139–41.

57. *The Autobiography and Correspondence of Mary Granville, Mrs Delany*, 1st series, i (1861), p. 290.

58. *Carlisle MSS*, HMC, pp. 532–3.

59. Hardwicke to Addington, 22 July 1802 (BL, Add. MS 35708).

60. *Hansard*, 3rd series, cxlvi, p. 1077.

61. F.W. Willis to B. Bushe, 11 Feb. 1861 (NLI, G.O. 321, ii).

62. N. Wilkinson, *To All and Singular* (1926), p. 295; C. Dickinson, *Dublin of Yesterday* (1929), p. 17.

63. *The Times*, 10 April 1885.

64. *Dublin Gazette*, 16 Jan. 1836, 16 Jan. 1877, 6, 10 March 1885, 16 June 1903, 3 March 1911; NLI G.O. 338.

65. *Nineteenth Century*, lxi, p. 563; *Irish Society*, Feb. 1903; NLI G.O. 337.

66. When republished in 1928 Moore entitled it *Muslin*.

67. G. Moore, *A Drama in Muslin*, book ii, chapter 3.

68. J. Hone, *Life of George Moore* (1936), pp. 107–9.

69. Mrs C. Roundell, 'A Diary at Dublin', in *Nineteenth Century*, lx, pp. 539–75; NLI G.O. 337.

70. *The Times*, 9 April 1900; Wilkinson, *To All and Singular*, p. 38.

71. *Irish Society*, 30 March 1895; NLI, G.O. 311; *Annual Register*, 1876, pp. 27–8; Lord and Lady Aberdeen, *We Twa* (1925), ii, p. 179.

72. NLI G.O. 337.

73. NLI G.O. 311.

74. *Ibid.*

75. NLI G.O. 337.

76. *Ibid.*

77. *Dublin Gazette*, 9 March 1768, 11 March 1732, 14 July 1764, 19 March, 12 Nov. 1768.

78. *Hibernian Magazine*, April, May 1796.

79. *Irish Society*, 27 April 1895; *Variety Fair*, 21 Jan. 1897.

80. *The Journals of John Wodehouse, First Earl of Kimberley 1862–1902*, eds A. Hawkins and J. Powell (Camden, 5th series, ix [1997]), pp. 144–91.

81. *Ibid*. p. 143; *Irish Society*, 29 Jan. 1894; BL, Add. MS 60830; *The Times*, 19 Aug. 1939.

82. *SPI 1601–03*, pp. 248–9; *SPI 1600–01*, p. 174.

83. *SPI 1669–70*, p. 119.

84. Chesterfield, *Letters*, ed. B. Dobrée, iii (1932), p. 665.

85. *Rutland MSS*, HMC, iii, p. 73.

86. T. O'Beirne to Fitzwilliam, Sept. 1794 (Wentworth Woodhouse muniments, 29/7).

87. *DEP*, 2 Sept. 1794; *The Diary of Sir John Moore*, ed. F. Maurice, i (1904), pp. 308, 327; Fortescue MSS, HMC, iv, p. 369; Hardwicke Papers, 7 Nov. 1803 (BL, Add. MS 35704).

88. Disraeli, *Derby and their Contemporaries*, ed. J. Vincent (1978), p. 71; S. Lee, *King Edward VII*, ii, p. 161.

89. *SPI 1599–1600*, pp. 448–9; *SPI 1666–69*, p. 258; W.H. Lecky, *History of Ireland*, ii (1913), p. 78; *Hansard*, 5th series, cxliv, p. 912.

90. T. Ramshay to Fitzwilliam, 9 Dec. 1794 (Wentworth Woodhouse muniments, 28/57); *Report of the Select Committee on Civil Government Charges*, appendix (H.C., 1831, iv).

91. Stopford Sackville MSS, HMC, i, p. 170; *Rutland MSS*, HMC, iii, pp. 345, 363; F. Hamilton, *The Days Before Yesterday* (1920), p. 80; F.E. Rose, *Historical Reminiscences of Dublin Castle* (1896), p. 69; G. Brenan, *A History of the House of Percy*, ii (1902), pp. 446–7; C. Spencer, *Althorp: The History of an English House* (London 1998), pp. 81–2.

92. P. Fitzgerald, *Recollections of Dublin Society and Dublin Castle* (1902), p. 31.

93. Chesterfield, *Letters*, iii, p. 659.

94. W.M. Thackeray, *An Irish Sketch Book*, chapter 12; A. Birrell, *Things Past Redress* (1937), p. 198.

95. P. Fitzgerald, *Recollections ...*, p. 7.

96. *Hansard*, 3rd series, cxi, p. 1452; cxlix, p. 715; lxxiv, p. 845.

97. H.Greville, *Memoirs*, ed. H. Reeve, new edn, vi (1888), pp. 82–7.

98. *Hansard*, 3rd series, lxxiv, p. 845.

99. *Ibid*. xxiv, 570; cxlvi, 1097–9.

100. W.H. Lecky, 'Memorandum on the Proposed Abolition of the Viceroyalty', in TCD Library.

101. *Letters of Queen Victoria*, 2nd series, i, pp. 313, 576; ii, p. 192; S. Lee, *Life of Edward VII*, pp. 232–3; ii, p. 112.

102. Fingall, *Seventy Years Young*, pp. 69, 84.

103. *Ormonde MSS*, NS, HMC, viii, pp. 362–3, 373, 382.

104. G. Story, *An Impartial History* (1691).

105. George IV's visit was reported in some detail in the *Annual Register*, *The Times*, the *Dublin Evening Post*, and *Saunder's Newsletter*. Also, J.W. Croker wrote an account in his diary (*The Croker Papers*, ed. J.L. Jennings (1884), i, pp. 199–207).

106. *The Times*, 21 Aug. 1821; *DEP*, 7 Aug. 1821.

107. *The Times*, 4 Sept. 1821; *DEP*, 9 Aug. 1821; *The Creevy Papers*, ed. H. Maxwell (1904), ii, p. 31.

108. *The Creevy Papers*, ed. H. Maxwell, ii, p. 29; *Letters of Harriet Countess Granville*, ed. E.L. Gowen (1894), i, p. 211.

109. Londonderry to Sidmouth, 10 Aug. 1821 (BL, Add. MS 38289).

110. *Annual Register, 1821*, pp. 129–32; *The Times*, 11 Aug. 1821.

111. W. Knighton, *Memoirs* (1858), i, p. 144.

112. *Saunder's Newsletter*, 16 Aug. 1821.

113. *DEP*, 21 Aug. 1821.

114. *Saunder's Newsletter*, 21 Aug. 1821.

115. *Ibid.* 24 Aug. 1821.

116. *Ibid.* 23 Aug. 1821.

117. *The Croker Papers*, i, p. 205; the new 'circular room' cost £8000 (*Cal. of the Ancient Records of Dublin*, ed. Lady Gilbert, xvii (1916), pp. 397, 404–5.

118. *Saunder's Newsletter*, 25 Aug. 1821.

119. *Ibid.* 27, 31 Aug. 1821; *Croker Papers*, i, pp. 206–7.

120. *The Times*, 3 Sept. 1821; *Saunder's Newsletter*, 28 Aug. 1821; Croker Papers, i, p. 207.

121. *Saunder's Newsletter*, 29 Aug., 3 Sept. 1821.

122. *The Times*, 9 Aug., 4 Sept. 1821; *Creevy's Life and Time*, ed. J. Gore (1937), pp. 144–6.

123. *DEP*, 4 Sept. 1821; *Saunder's Newsletter*, 4 Sept. 1821.

124. *Saunder's Newsletter*, 4 Sept., 22 Aug. 1821; *The Times*, 17 Aug. 1821.

125. A. Lyall, *Life of the Marquis of Dufferin and Ava*, i (1905), pp. 57–8; A.T. Dasant, *John Thadeus Delane*, i (1908), p. 92; T. Martin, *The Life of the Prince Consort*, ii (1876), pp. 208–13.

126. *Annual Register, 1853*, p. 60; *The Times*, 31 Aug.–2 Sept. 1853; Martin, *Life of the Prince Consort*, ii, pp. 504–5.

127. *The Times*, 24 Aug 1861; Queen Victoria, *Leaves from the Journal of our Life in the Highlands*, pp. 316–18; *Martin, Life of the Prince Consort*, v (1886), pp. 378–84.

128. *Letters of Queen Victoria*, 3rd series, iii, p. 493.

129. *The Collected Letters of W.B. Yeats*, ed. J. Kelly, ii; *The Times*, 15, 20 March 1900.

130. *The Times*, 28 March 1900.

131. *Ibid.* 5 April 1900.

132. *Ibid.*

133. *Letters of Queen Victoria*, 3rd series, iii, pp. 521–44.

134. Lee, *Life of Edward VII*, i (1925), pp. 225–6; *Letters of Queen Victoria*, 2nd series, i, pp. 250–1; *Journal of John Wodehouse, First Earl of Kimberley*, pp. 159–60; *The Times*, 11 May 1865; *Annual Register, 1865*, pp. 56–60.

135. *Letters of Queen Victoria*, 2nd series, i, pp. 513–15, 522; Lee, *Life of Edward VII*, i, pp. 227–9; G.E. Buckle, *Life of Benjamin Disraeli*, v (1920), p. 14; *The Times*, 17–23 April 1868.

136. Lee, *Life of Edward VII*, i, pp. 231–2; *Letters of Queen Victoria*, 2nd series, ii, p. 215; *Hansard*, 3rd series, ccviii, pp. 1491–514, 1773–837.

137. Lee, *Life of Edward VII*, i, p. 236.

138. *The Times*, 7 June 1885; *Annual Register, 1885*, pp. 196–8.

139. *The Times*, 10 April 1885.

140. *Ibid.* 13 April 1885; Lee, *Life of Edward VII*, i, p. 226.

141. *The Times*, 10 April 1885.

142. P. Magnus, *Life of Edward VII* (1964), p. 189; Spenser to W.E. Gladstone, 24 April 1885 (BL, Add. MS 44312); Spencer to H. Campbell-Bannerman, 17 April 1885 (BL, Add. MS 41228).

143. *The Times*, 21 April 1885.

144. *Ibid.* 24 April 1885.

145. *Ibid.*

146. Spencer to Gladstone, 24 April 1885 (BL, Add. MS 44312).

147. *The Times*, 24 April 1899.

148. J.W. Mackail & G. Wyndham, *Life and Letters of George Wyndham* (1924), ii, p. 461.

149. *Ibid.* ii, p. 464. By the Phoenix Monument he probably means the Wellington Monument. The royal visit to Trinity College is commemorated by plates affixed to two of the large chairs used by the Caput at Commencements.

150. *The Irish Times*, 24 July 1903.

151. *Ibid.* 15 Aug. 1903.

152. *Ibid.* 29 July 1903.

153. *Ibid.* 2 Aug. 1903.

154. *Ibid.* 3 Aug. 1903.

155. Lady Aberdeen to Campbell-Bannerman, 30 May 1907 (BL, Add. MS 41210).

156 *The Irish Times*,11 July 1907.

157. The College of Science façade (now Government Buildings) displays the royal monogram carved in stone close to the Taoiseach's office.

158. *The Times*, 6 Dec. 1922.

159. B. Webb, *Diaries, 1920–32* (1956), p. 250.

160. *The Irish Times*, 4 April, 4, 13 July 1903; James Joyce, *Dubliners* (1914), 'Ivy Day in the Committee Room'; *The Collected Letters of W.B. Yeats*, eds J. Kelly and R. Shuchard, iii (1884), pp. 346, 377–8.

161. *The Irish Times*, 4 April, 6, 12 July 1911; *Freeman's Journal*, 1, 5, 6 July 1911; the Earl of Meath, *Twentieth-Century Memories* (1924), pp. 62–3, 200.

162. *Letters of Queen Victoria*, 3rd series, iii, p. 198.

11 Trinity College Dublin and Politics

Throughout its history Trinity College (much as some of its members might have wished it) has never been an insulated institution, a Laputa, peopled by highly intelligent, unworldly dons. For over three centuries from its foundation it was closely linked to the Irish ruling world, continuously in touch with power and privilege. Moreover, during the nineteenth century the Trinity community – staff, undergraduates and graduates – was overwhelmingly conservative and unionist. Devotion to sound scholarship and pure science was accompanied by political convictions and commitment; and the College was a rallying point in the South of Ireland for opposition to Irish nationalism, reflected in a number of movements, including Repeal, Young Ireland, the Land Agitation, Home Rule, Sinn Féin, and the Gaelic Revival. Standing in the middle of Dublin, its severe, reserved, classical front embodied both the academic virtues and an assured, unyielding defiance of popular enthusiasms. But, from the 1920s, survival demanded an unhurried adaptation to striking changes in the social and political environment and a politic conciliation of the new powers that be.

Trinity College Dublin was founded towards the close of a tumultuous century, during the great struggle between the Reformation and the Counter-Reformation, and when the whole of Ireland was, with much vigorous campaigning, being brought under the control of the Crown. With the advance of royal authority, sustained efforts were made both to promote the Elizabethan ecclesiastical polity and the spread of English law, language and manners. As Bacon, the great humanist, declared, 'Ireland, the last of the

daughters of Europe', was being reclaimed from 'savage and barbarous custom' to 'humanity and civility'.[1]

The cultural conflict went back to the Middle Ages, the Gaelic
tradition showing remarkable resilience in spite of intermittent
attempts by English monarchs and the English colony to encourage
the English language, manners and apparel. But during the sixteenth
century the Gaelic tradition was fatally weakened by the determination of the Crown and the more zealous colonial officials to
establish English law and English institutions in the areas brought
under royal authority, and by the inevitable loss of prestige that
accompanied the defeat of its champions. However, the general situation was complicated by the emergence of a great religious divide.
Many of those who prided themselves on their loyalty to the Crown
and English speech and custom obstinately refused to renounce
papal supremacy in religious matters. Even in Dublin, the bastion of
English power in Ireland, there were aldermen who would not conform to the Established Church.

One way of dealing with this contempt of the religion professed
by the monarch and the state,[2] this preference for 'the superstitious
idolatry of anti-Christ', was coercion.[3] But it was realized that in
what was essentially a battle for hearts and minds, force must be
supplemented by persuasion, and that 'the swarms of titular bishops and seminarians, Jesuits, priests and friars' must be countered
by a 'learned ministry'.[4] Not only landlords and farmers, but
preachers too, had to be planted. But unfortunately it was difficult
to obtain an adequate supply of clergy from England. The ecclesiastical organization recognized by the state, the Church of Ireland,
was in a perilous condition, its revenues misappropriated, its
benefices poor and often in disturbed areas, and its churches in bad
repair or in ruins with small or non-existent congregations. In 1552
Archbishop Crammer wrote that 'though he knew many men in
England meet for Irish' bishoprics, he 'knew few willing to go
thither', and Queen Elizabeth, with homely force, scornfully
referred to those Englishmen who, rather than striving in Ireland,
preferred to stay at home, 'holding their noses over the beef pots'.[5]

Obviously a local source of supply for clergymen ready to work
in Ireland was needed. Moreover, with the new learning making

men conscious of the European cultural heritage, and the Pale
expanding, a serious lacuna in Irish intellectual life, the absence of
a university, was painfully apparent. In 1577 the Queen was
informed that with the Pale growing more prosperous, there was a
growing desire there for university education, 'some of the principal
gentlemen' sending their sons to continental colleges, in which
'Your Majesty is rather hated than honoured'.[6] It must too have
been observed that Scotland by the 1580s had four universities, one
of which, Aberdeen, having amongst its objectives the education of
the rude and unlettered Celtic inhabitants of the north-east.

From the middle of the sixteenth century it was being urged that
a university should be founded in Dublin, 'a lively trope to call that
barbarous nation from evil to good', and 'in place of wilful stub-
bornness bringing civil obedience'.[7] Browne, the first Anglican
Archbishop of Dublin, in 1547 thought of employing the revenues
of St Patrick's to endow a university.[8] At the beginning of Elizabeth's
reign the Irish Act of Supremacy listed amongst those obliged to
take the Oath of Supremacy, the graduates of any university 'that
hereafter shall be within this our realm'. Ten years later the Lord
Chancellor declared that a university was the best means of preserving peace in the realm.[9] Then in 1584 the English Privy Council
directed Sir John Perrot, the Deputy, to take steps towards the foundation of a university. Again it was thought that the revenues of St
Patrick's might be used to fund the new institution, a suggestion
which aroused the ire of Adam Loftus, a formidable pluralist, Archbishop of Dublin and Dean of St Patrick's, who asserted that St
Patrick's was the only place in Ireland for the maintenance of good
and godly preachers. In the ensuing conflict between the Archbishop and the Deputy the university project floundered.[10]

Some years later a group of Dublin citizens, including Henry
Ussher, later Archbishop of Armagh, and Luke Challoner, a schoolmaster, persuaded the City Corporation to grant the buildings and
grounds of All Hallows, a dissolved Augustinian house lying a short
distance to the east of the city, as a site for a college. Backed by the
then Deputy and Loftus (the threat to St Patrick's being out of the
way), the group obtained from the Queen a charter for the new
foundation and the essential financial underpinning was soon

provided. During the first half-century or so of its existence the College secured substantial benefits from the Crown – annual grants from the Exchequer, exemptions from quit rents, a grant of two 'superstitious houses' (Franciscan friaries) seized by the Crown in 1630, the advowsons of a number of valuable Ulster livings, for which at Disestablishment it received a large sum in compensation, and above all, very large grants of lands derived largely from the great confiscations in Munster and Ulster – in 1900 the College possessed nearly 180,000 acres worth over £40,000 per annum.[11]

The value of the new institution to the Irish state was soon recognized. The very vigorous Deputy, Arthur Chichester, having emphasized the great importance of 'breeding and bringing up scholars who must be this kingdom's reformers (for without learning and understanding barbarous customs will never decay)', went on to suggest that part of the peace dividend available at the end of the O'Neill wars might be used to found scholarships in Trinity.[12] In 1623 his master James I, a keen intellectual, declared that the main object of the College (which, understandably, he pointed out, he had 'plentifully endowed') was 'bringing up the natives of Ireland in civility, learning and religion' – and he suggested that a number of Irish-speaking clergymen, who had studied 'the grounds of religion' in Trinity, should be placed in livings amongst the mere Irish. Six years later his successor, Charles I, liked 'wonderously well, Bedell's foundation of an Irish lectureship'.[13]

Bedell's scheme soon lapsed and later efforts during the seventeenth and early eighteenth centuries to provide tuition in Irish for divinity students were short-lived.[14] It has been pointed out that evangelization through the medium of Irish would not contribute to spreading English civilization.[15] However, it was probably assumed that converts to Protestantism or their offspring would soon become English-speaking. It was almost certainly assumed that with the predominant classes in Irish society Protestant and English-speaking, the whole community would become Anglican and anglicized. It may be added that another ambitious scheme for using Trinity to strengthen Protestantism in the Irish landed world failed. In the early seventeenth century it was suggested that royal wards should be imbued with English habits and religion by being educated in Trinity. But owing to Catholic resistance and defects in the system for supervising the wards, few of them came to Trinity.[16]

However, the hopes of Trinity's founders and early protectors that the College would provide a supply of fit persons to serve in Church and State were to some extent realized. From soon after the foundation of the College a trickle, which after the Restoration swelled into a flood, of Trinity-trained divines were installed in Church of Ireland parishes. In another sphere, the first Trinity man to be placed on the judicial bench, James Barry, was appointed a Baron of the Exchequer in 1634, and between that date and the close of the seventeenth century, thirteen Trinity men became judges (about a quarter of those appointed).

In the partnership between Trinity and the State, College, of course, was bound to be the junior partner. When in 1613 a number of new parliamentary boroughs were created with the aim of increasing the Protestant interest in the House of Commons, Trinity became a borough, with the provost, fellows and scholars forming the electorate. The College was expected to return government supporters and in 1634 (and probably in 1639), Wentworth named the candidates whom College was to elect. Less than a year after Wentworth arrived in Ireland as deputy, his friend William Laud was elected chancellor of Dublin University. Believing that 'religion and civility ... much depend upon the reformation of that place [Trinity College]', Laud, though 'overlaid with business', set to work to obtain a new charter for the university and new statutes for the College. Challenging the Puritanism of Trinity's early days, Laud strongly supported the choice of William Chappel as Provost, condemning attempts to discredit him by using that 'great bugbear called Arminianism'.[17] During the Commonwealth, Trinity was under Puritan control and in 1651 parliamentary commissioners insisted that Trinity undergraduates should be educated in the knowledge of God and the principles of piety, since if learning was 'attained before the work of grace upon the heart, it serves only to make a sharper opposition against the power of Godliness'. Four years later the provost and fellows were directed to advance learning and piety by prayer, preaching and 'private Christian meetings', and to rebuke those members of the College who were swearers,

gamblers or tavern haunters.[18] The Commonwealth authorities
encouraged the College by granting it the property of Christ Church
and St Patrick's, property which the College had to disgorge at the
Restoration. With the Restoration, Trinity again became Episco-
palian. But throughout all these changes it remained Protestant and
pro-English, continuity being assured by the ease with which some
of the fellows adapted themselves to successive regimes.

The Restoration marked the beginning of a stable, happy relationship between Trinity, the State and the Established Church,
which lasted (with a short parenthesis between 1687 and 1690) for
two hundred years. For the first half-century or so of this long era,
Trinity was dominated and protected by the Dukes of Ormonde,
great magnates in England and Ireland, who epitomized the Church
and Cavalier tradition. Each duke in turn was chancellor and took
a keen interest in the College, exemplified by the part they played
when a provost had to be appointed. The College in return elected
to the first Restoration parliament, two of the first Duke's sons, 'the
gallant Ossory' and his brother, Lord John Butler, dissolute even by
Restoration court standards.

Of the thirteen MPs returned for Trinity between 1661 and
1714, in addition to the Duke's two sons, seven others (including
William Molyneux) were at some stage in their careers connected
with the house of Ormonde. It may be added that of the thirteen,
nine were officials (including Richard Aldworth, a Whig, appointed
chief secretary in 1695), two lawyers (John Coghlan and Marmaduke Coghill, a fellow of Trinity (John Elwood) and an army
officer (Lord John Butler). Six of the thirteen had been Trinity
undergraduates.

For a short time (during the parentheses that has been mentioned) the university was severed from its chancellor. In 1689
Ormonde was one of the first peers to swear allegiance to William
and Mary, but Ireland remained under the control of Tyrconnell,
James II's Lord Lieutenant, and in March 1689, James himself
arrived in Dublin. Trinity shared the apprehensions of the Protestant community and the intellectual agonies of conscientious Anglicans, long committed to the doctrines of Divine Right and passive
obedience. The fellows waited on James when he arrived in Dublin,

presenting him with an address in which they declared that their principles of loyalty were those of the Church of England, and that though they persevered in their religion, they 'could never forego our allegiance',[19] and the College returned to the parliament summoned by James' two MPs, Sir John Meade and John Coghlan, a barrister. Both, feeling it 'scandalous to be in such company', soon withdrew from the House.[20] The College resisted an attempt to install a fellow by royal mandate and tried to smuggle the College silver over to England. After an English expeditionary force landed in the North, the fellows and students were expelled, the College, 'a ruined and devastated seat of learning', becoming a barrack and a prison for Protestants. This disastrous period ended when William III arrived, his solicitude for the reviving College being shown by a grant to its library of 'all books belonging to forfeiting papists'.

After experiencing Jacobitism – Irish Jacobitism – in power, the overwhelming mass of Irish Protestants to whom William III seemed a providential deliverer, heartily supported the Revolutionary Settlement and were thoroughly averse to popery and the Pretender. However, strange as it may seem, a few Trinity graduates continued to adhere to political ideals which were fast becoming archaic – Dodwell, an erudite non-juror, who in the end conformed to the Established Church, Thomas Sheridan, Chief Secretary when James II was in Ireland and an upholder of the English interest against Tyrconnell, Charles Leslie, a pugnacious and versatile controversialist, a strong Church of England man and Jacobite propagandist, and his son Robert Leslie much involved in Jacobite dissension and dubbed a madman by his critics.

At the close of the Stuart period, with, in the opinion of High Churchmen, the Church threatened by Presbyterian fanaticism, and with the Duke of Ormonde prominent in the Tory leadership, there was bound to be a Tory party in Ireland. Exaggerated and excitable Toryism could mutate into Jacobitism and a few sensational episodes suggest that at the opening of the eighteenth century some members of the College were hostile to the Revolutionary settlement and the Hanoverian succession. When in 1708 the Board decided to deprive Edward Forbes (an Aberdeen graduate who at a College feast had insulted the memory of King William III) of his *ad eundem* MA, there was opposition in the Senate. But the deprivation was confirmed by 76 votes to 6.[21] As a result the House of Commons, impressed by the steady adherence of the College to 'the late happy revolution', 'for the encouragement of good literature and sound revolution principles', granted £5000 towards the erection of a new library.[22]

At the close of Queen Anne's reign, political feeling in Ireland ran high. In 1712 Richard Hartley was suspended from scholarship for three days for, in defiance of the Senior Lecturer, retaining in an oration he delivered on the anniversary of the outbreak of the rebellion of 1641, a phrase thanking the Queen for installing Tory ministers in office; and in 1714 it was observed that the College had 'taken the example of Parliament and the city and has fallen into great heats and divisions'.[23] At a crowded meeting of the Senate an attempt was made to reverse the sentence on Forbes. But the Vice-Provost and senior fellows, by withdrawing from the hall, brought proceedings to an abrupt close. An undergraduate, Theodore Barlow, was expelled for toasting the Pretender, and a junior fellow, William Thompson (elected 1713), was accused of proposing an offensive toast equating William III with Oliver Cromwell. It was also said that he was instilling seditious principles into 'young boys' whom he entertained in his chambers and in taverns. However, in time he was to become a senior fellow, and he ended his days as a County Fermanagh rector.[24]

Later in the year there was a series of incidents with political undertones in which members of the College were involved. Attempts by undergraduates to deface the statue of King William in College Green, led to scuffles with the watch, arrests, committals for trial and the expulsion from College of three undergraduates. A scholar was rusticated for saying that William and Mary were usurpers, a seditious pamphlet, *Nero Secundus* (George I) was circulated, Ormonde's birthday was riotously celebrated, and the singing of Jacobite songs (including 'Will ye no come back again') in the squares long after midnight could be heard in Dame Street – the fellows ensconced in their chambers seemed to be deaf.[25]

How far these manifestations of Jacobitism reflected deep, well thought-out loyalties, a doctrinaire refusal to surrender outmoded concepts, the opposition of some 'young masters'[26] to the senior fellows, a wish to *épater le bourgeois* (stolid Irish Protestants) or undergraduate rowdiness, is hard to say. But at two exciting meetings of the Senate the supporters of the Revolutionary settlement triumphed by very substantial majorities, and it may be safely asserted that Trinity Jacobitism never advanced beyond singing political ballads and drinking toasts.

Understandably, however, the authorities were alarmed and on the advice of the Under-Secretary Eustace Budgell, a minor literary man, who was greatly exhilarated by his novel administrative duties, a royal letter was issued suspending the election of fellows and scholars.[27] The visitor of the College, William King, a sagacious ecclesiastical statesman and a strong upholder of the Protestant succession was also dismayed at seeing Trinity, which he regarded as 'a seminary of divines to supply the Church of Ireland', becoming 'a nest of Jacobites'.[28] Clear-headed and energetic, he exerted himself to prevent Forbes's sentence being reversed and when Ormonde was attainted in August 1715, he emphatically urged that he should be replaced as chancellor by the Prince of Wales. Choosing a candidate 'disagreeable to the Court', King stressed, might be of 'fatal consequence to the society'. After all, the College might become the subject of a parliamentary enquiry.[29] King ensured that two influential senior fellows, John Elwood and Robert Howard, should be present when the Board was selecting a chancellor, rebuking Howard for lingering in England (admittedly 'the centre of business and information') when he had 'an outpost of great importance' committed to his care.[30]

In March 1716 the Board elected George, Prince of Wales, as chancellor. A deputation from the College; the Provost, Benjamin Pratt, and two fellows, Robert Howard and George Berkeley, accompanied by 'all the persons of quality and distinction from Ireland at this time in London', presented the Prince with the 'instrument' of his election in a gold box. Pratt, in an elegant and fulsome address, explained that the University of Dublin was seeking a head equal in birth and virtue to its generous foundress. Pratt dwelt on the qualities of 'the greatest and best of kings', George I, 'valiant, just and magnanimous', a defender of English liberty and

Protestantism, qualities which he said were faithfully copied in the Prince of Wales. Finally in a glowing peroration, he exclaimed: 'Descend then most mighty Prince to give us laws. Ireland submits its harp into your royal hands. Rule, instruct and nourish the attending Muses. Make them the envied subjects of your present care, and the lively image of a happy people.' The German courtiers and the Prince and Princess of Wales, a majestic blue-stocking, who was to become Berkeley's patron, all seem to have been suitably impressed.[31] Berkeley himself, who a few years before had preached in favour of a carefully qualified passive obedience, now thought it 'inconceivable what a show of an advantage an Irish protestant could fancy to himself from the success of the Pretender'.[32]

The inauguration of the Prince of Wales was followed by the removal of the inhibition on the election of fellows and scholars and in 1717, by a second parliamentary grant towards the building of the library – the College in its petition to the House of Commons sedulously pointing out that it was resolved to educate the youth in its care 'in principles of zeal and affection to the constitution in Church and State'.[33] By then King was engaged in easing out the Provost, who he thought had not his heart in his work and was a poor disciplinarian. Pratt was willing to leave College if offered a bishopric. King considered that the deanery of Derry, worth a few hundred per annum more than the provostship, was all he deserved and he let Pratt know that if a visitation was held the question of how far the Provost's visits to England had been licensed might be raised.[34] On Pratt's accepting the deanery, Baldwin became Provost and if any Jacobitism lingered on in College – and what Archbishop Boulter thought was Jacobitism may merely have been dislike of Baldwin's autocratic ways – it soon faded away.[35]

During the eighteenth century Trinity was a very important part of the established order – the university of the Irish ruling world. Amongst its graduates were the bulk of the Church of Ireland parochial clergy, numerous lawyers (of those who attained the judicial bench, forty-six out of a total of seventy-four were Trinity men), many country gentlemen, and a substantial number of MPs, including almost all of those conspicuous in Irish political life, and a few who played a part on a wider stage – Burke, Barré, Lord George

Germain. Indeed, in about 1724 it was suggested that there should be in Trinity a school of laws, history, and eloquence, in which young noblemen and others of rank and fortune might be instructed 'in the springs of action' and 'causes of great events', and learn how to debate, not by making set speeches but by speaking *ex tempore* or from short notes.[36] Though the school was not set up, Chairs of History and Oratory were founded and sections of the undergraduate course – classical works relating to history and rhetoric, writings on what may be termed political science and perhaps logic – provided a useful preparation for political life.

During the eighteenth century the state, which in Great Britain and Ireland restricted itself to a limited range of activities, generally speaking left the universities to their own devices. So far as Trinity was concerned, the provostship was a royal appointment and royal letters were required for the amendment of the statutes. But the provosts appointed (with one startling exception, the persevering and politically adroit Hely-Hutchinson) were all respected senior fellows and the royal letters issued had been requested by College. There was, however, a sphere in which the state intervened in College affairs, with what may truly be called spectacular results. Between 1698 and 1790 the Crown and parliament granted Trinity £75,000 for building. No other academic institution in the British Isles received government support on this scale, but College, 'half a bow-shot' from the Parliament House, was well-placed for lobbying. Fortunately too, one of its MPs for thirty-six years was Philip Tisdall, the Attorney General, and two of its fellows, William Clement and Francis Andrews, were prominent members of the House of Commons. Well-endowed and munificently assisted by the state, the College was built in the grand manner, and the gratefully named Parliament Square reflects in its aloof sweep the ideals of the eighteenth-century ruling world – balance, proportion, clarity, self-assurance and imperial sway. It perhaps should be added that one intelligent and influential don, Arthur Browne, towards the close of the eighteenth century, asserted that the government had been 'inattentive' to Trinity, an institution that 'particularly merited the name of a whig university', professing the most generous principles of freedom and displaying ardent loyalty to the Crown. He urged the government to encourage the College – about half of whose graduates went into orders – by the use of ecclesiastical patronage; implying that from time to time fellows should be placed on the episcopal bench.[37]

Towards the close of the eighteenth century the College honoured two of its graduates who were outstanding in public life, Grattan and Burke. Henry Grattan had won widespread acclaim for the achievement of legislative independence in 1782 and the Board arranged for his picture to be painted and hung in the hall. Some years later it was rumoured that Grattan was so popular with the younger men that he might stand for Trinity, but it was said he would not be elected because his approach to the tithe question had 'rendered him obnoxious to the Fellows'.[38] In 1798 when Conservatives suspected him of sympathizing with treason, his picture was taken down. Later, when his essential conservation was appreciated, it was rehung. In 1790, very shortly after the publication of the *Reflections*, Burke was given an honorary LLD as 'the powerful advocate of the constitution, as the friend of public order and virtue and consequently of the happiness of mankind'. And in 1795 the Board requested him to sit for a portrait destined to be hung in College.[39]

Burke's honorary degree was both a belated tribute to his literary genius and an indication of the attitude of the governing body of the College to the great conflict of ideas which was agitating Europe. But in this tumultuous era when fundamental principles and vital Irish issues, parliamentary reform, Catholic Emancipation and Anglo-Irish relations were being vigorously debated, College opinion was bound to be divided. Two of the fellows, both laymen, were conspicuously active in rather different spheres of public life. Arthur Browne, barrister and essayist, was a leading Irish Whig, a strenuous defender of civil liberties and, as befitted a university MP, of the tithe system. Whitley Stokes, a man of many generous enthusiasms, whom Wolfe Tone pronounced would make an excellent Irish Minister of Education, was a member of that well-known radical club, the Dublin Society of United Irishmen, for which he prepared a carefully-devised scheme of parliamentary reform, premising that 'Liberty is only a good as a means to virtue and happiness.'[40] In 1795 Stokes published a refutation of Paine's *Age of Reason*,

addressed to Trinity undergraduates. A year earlier John Burke had
been expelled from College for airing Unitarian views and a few
years later, a grinder, William Corbett (a future French general), was
said to have recommended Paine's works. The Professor of Chemistry explained that Corbett was in fact expounding the doctrine of
philosophic necessity as modified by Dr Hartley; to which the visitor, Lord Clare, retorted that however modified it would lead to
deism and atheism. Though Irish radicals greatly admired Paine's
politics, they had little respect for his theological ruminations and
in Trinity Christian orthodoxy was not seriously challenged, even
by the radically minded.

But political feeling ran strongly. In April 1795, when the fellows
and scholars were proceeding to the Castle to present an address of
welcome to the newly-arrived Lord Lieutenant, the scholars (or
some of them) broke away and, assembling at Hyde's Coffee House,
voted an address to Grattan thanking him for supporting Emancipation and reform. Grattan replied effusively, referring to the College as 'Thou seat of science and Mother of Virtue'.[41] The Board's
response was to post up 'a programme' (notice) expressing its
strong disapproval of student political meetings as 'being foreign
from the object of academic institutions', and in the following year
it admonished four students for attending political meetings outside
College.

In the same year, 1796, a number of patriotic undergraduates
created a problem for the authorities by offering to form a yeomanry corps. A pamphleteer deplored the suggestion that students
should lay aside the academic 'garb and manners' characteristic of
'the sons of science' for 'the fantastic pageantry of mimic warfare',
and three of the fellows opposed the project 'as leading to idleness
and the relaxation of academical discipline'.[42] But a number of their
colleagues thought it would demonstrate the loyalty of the College,
especially when undergraduates went down to the country in the
vacation. Clare, the Lord Chancellor, though he appreciated the
undergraduates' spirit, declared 'that such an association is so
abhorrent from academical institutions that he could not think of
it'.[43] The Archbishop of Dublin, however, supported the proposal
and by the end of the year a corps of about 240 strong had been

formed, officered by fellows who were not in orders – one of them, Arthur Browne, being so keen that he published a drill book. 'Literary men', he wrote, 'will view the military art, not with the eye of the mere common soldier … but as a branch of general knowledge'.[44]

Two fellows (William Magee and Thomas Elrington) and a sometime fellow (William Hamilton, rector of Clonvaddock in Donegal), fought the revolution with intellectual weapons. Magee, an eloquent preacher, denounced 'the savage ferociousness of uncontrolled equality' and eulogized the constitution for protecting 'mental and personal freedom'.[45] Thomas Elrington published an annotated edition of Locke's essay on government, the principal object of the notes being to deprive 'modern democrats' of Locke's powerful assistance by establishing a distinction between their theories and his.[46] Hamilton, a geologist and clinologist, published in 1793 *Letters on the French Revolution*, 'with a view to the instruction of the middle and lower ranks of his countrymen'. An energetic JP, he was murdered in 1797.[47]

From about the middle of the 1790s there were ebullient manifestations of radicalism in College. A medical graduate tore down a proclamation at the Front Gate and was promptly expelled from the corps. It was reported that United Irishmen's societies were meeting in number 5 and number 26. Ardagh, a scholar and BA, had a party in his rooms in number 24 at which a series of incongruous toasts, including 'Grattan', 'Lord Moira', 'the French fleet', and 'Citizen Bonaparte' were drunk. Later in the evening Ardagh and an undergraduate, David Power, were heard shouting in the courts, 'Long live the Republic.' Summoned before the Board, they pleaded that they 'had drunk a good deal' but were expelled – three of the senior fellows, Hall, a future provost, Arthur Browne, and Thomas Elrington voting for two years' rustication. Shortly afterwards, an undergraduate, Purcell O'Gorman, wrote a fiery letter to the *Press*, a radical newspaper, regretting the expulsions of Ardagh and Power and attacking a recent graduate, Arthur McCartney, for saying that he, O'Gorman, had given information against the United Irishmen in College. McCartney, a strong Conservative, who had himself informed the Board about sedition in College, challenged O'Gorman to a duel. The meeting did not take place owing to a dispute over where it should be held and McCartney in a letter to the *Dublin Journal* branded O'Gorman a coward.

The dispute spread to the yeomanry corps, John Browne, a Belfast man, who privately referred to the corps as 'a rascally corps', trying to get McCartney expelled.[48] But Arthur Browne refused to allow the corps to become a debating society. The Board expelled O'Gorman for his letter to the *Press* and for assaulting McCartney's second, and rusticated McCartney.[49] O'Gorman in later life became a QC and assistant barrister (county court judge); McCartney was for many years a County Antrim rector, and Browne was in April 1798 expelled by the visitors. Three undergraduates were reprimanded for, in the course of an angry discussion on commons, calling a scholar an informer and a liar; they complained he had called them United Irishmen; he reported he had merely said they were disaffected.[50] A year or so later one of the three supplied the government with information on sedition in Munster.[51]

These ebullitions led to one of the most dramatic events in College history, the two-day visitation held in April 1798 by Lord Clare and (to the annoyance of some of his colleagues) Professor Patrick Duigenan. The proceedings were dominated by the senior visitor, Clare, the Lord Chancellor. Severe and very self-assured, with flashes of sardonic humour, he conducted a series of dialogues with fellows and students on politics in College. Yielding to 'the prejudices of young minds', he 'omitted enquiring into names' – he already had, he pointed out, plenty of information about individuals and he seems to have established a rapport with those assembled. When he sharply rebuked a radical student there was a 'great clap'. The outcome of the investigation was that Arthur Browne was severely censured for criticizing the Board's disciplinary decision in the case of Ardagh and Power when chatting with undergraduates. Stokes, though he stated that he had 'been strictly a neutral man' from 1792 until he joined the yeomanry, was suspended from tutorship for two years. One graduate and eighteen undergraduates (five of whom were scholars) were expelled.[52]

How strong was Trinity's radicalism in the late 1790s? In addition to the list of those expelled at the visitation, there is in the College archives a list in Clare's hand, headed 'List of the committee of the United Irishmen'. Taking these two overlapping lists together with the names of those punished by the Board, mentioned during the visitation or referred to in other sources, a consolidated list of avowed or suspected supporters of the United Irishmen can be compiled. It amounts to about fifty names but undoubtedly many of them scarcely deserve to be included on a roll of radical students. Undergraduates are often volatile, and alarmed Conservatives were likely to mistake reckless talk, expressive of immature enthusiasms, for dangerous sedition. The later career of one of the undergraduates who figures on Clare's list reinforces his assertion that he never attended a meeting of United Irishmen. He was to be a junior Tory minister, a very influential conservative journalist and a pertinacious opponent of parliamentary reform. Clare frankly apologized to another undergraduate whom he had listed in error. Of those named as being present at the party in Ardagh's rooms, Sandes (a future bishop) left before the toasts, Russell fell asleep and Keating heard only one 'exceptionable' toast, and that was explained away. Two students who had attended radical meetings in College refused to take the United Irishmen's oath and a third withdrew from the United Irishmen when he realized that their objectives extended beyond parliamentary reform.

Even Thomas Robinson, a scholar, whose College rooms were a centre for radical activities and who proved to be such an unsatisfactory witness at the visitation that Clare snapped at him, 'If your memory is so short you had better give up science,' declared that he had withdrawn from the United Irishmen (this did not save him from expulsion). Thomas Moore, a bright youth, who thoroughly enjoyed Trinity, remained on the fringe of the radical movement. He admired the eloquent Robert Emmet and joined a small society that debated politically daring topics, contributed anonymously to the *Press* a rhetorical essay addressed to Trinity students (annoying Emmet who thought it might alert the authorities) and carried himself with dignity at the visitation. But after the visitation, absorbed in his translation of *Anacreon* (published in 1800), suffering from bad health and impressed by a kindly warning from his tutor, he withdrew from politics. He retained all his life a passionate, if pacific, Irish nationalist outlook; living in England and moving happily in Whig circles.

The committed radicals in College around 1798 probably numbered between thirty and forty – a handful compared to those
enrolled in the yeomanry corps. Throughout the country the number
of Trinity radicals was very small compared to the size of the College, more especially when it is taken into account that radicalism
had an undoubted attraction for intellectuals and that Trinity was
the only Irish university.

At the visitation of 1798, Clare not only purged the College, he
also urged its members, both senior and junior, to cultivate the academic virtues. They should devote themselves, he emphasized, to
study and abstain from meddling in politics. He frowned on the
yeomanry corps as 'an innovation totally inconsistent with college
discipline' and he was shocked by the suggestion that an Orange
society should be formed in Trinity. 'Consider yourselves', he said,
'as associated only in a learned seminary.' He directed the fellows to
ensure that their pupils worked steadily and he asked the undergraduates to realize that 'by attending to the duties of this place they
may arrive at the highest situations' – they need only look at the
episcopal bench. This advice was very acceptable to many in
authority in College. John Kearney, in a powerful sermon preached
in 1798 on an important academic occasion, exhorted the College
yeomanry corps to lay aside their arms and return to their studies
once insurrection had been defeated. Two years later as provost, he
told the fellows that the government wished them to abstain from
politics, adding that in his opinion a fellow who asked a student to
sign a political address was committing a breach of academic discipline.[53] 'Removed by our academical situation from political pursuits', the senior fellows were anxious to avoid 'the discussions to
which they inevitably lead' and when attacked by their colleague
Arthur Browne for not expressing their sentiments on the Union,
they defended themselves by saying they were 'setting a good example to the subordinate members of the university'.[54] Browne, himself
a moderate liberal reformer, frustrated by 'the madness of democracy', voted for the Union; his fellow university MP, George Knox,
opposed it. The fellows were also divided on the issue; three were
'indifferent', five were pro-Union, and the rest (fourteen) against.[55]

Protestant Ireland was divided on the other major political issue of the time, Catholic Emancipation, and Trinity, in Browne's phrase, exhibited 'a great diversity of opinion'.[56] When at the close of 1812 Thomas Elrington, recently appointed provost, attempted to obtain the signatures of the fellows and scholars on an address he had prepared against the Catholic claims, to his dismay he discovered that, if he persisted, a counter-address would be promoted.[57] However, in 1813 and 1819 the Board, on behalf of the fellows and scholars, approved of an anti-Emancipation address to the Regent. On the latter occasion the address was approved by 5 votes to 3, the minority including Phipps, who thought the government was not in favour of the address, Nash, who believed that Emancipation was the best means of conversion and Prior, who admitted that over the past twenty-five years he had frequently changed his opinions.[58] Of the seven MPs who represented Trinity between 1790 and 1830, five, Browne, Francis Hely-Hutchinson, George Knox, Plunket and Croker, supported Emancipation. In 1793 Browne thought that indulgences should be granted 'in proportion to increasing knowledge and increasing charity in the Catholic'. Three years later he declared that it was 'just as impossible to prevent Catholics from coming into Parliament as to stop any of the natural laws of gravity'. Francis Hely-Hutchinson said in 1793 that it was wise to adopt 'a new system of politics' based on 'a generous confidence in the great body of the people'. Croker in 1819 explained that he supported Emancipation 'not on the Catholics' own claims or merits but out of my anxiety for the Protestant establishment which I look upon as more endangered by their exclusion as it could be by their admission'.[59]

In 1829 the College did not petition against Emancipation but some 400 to 500 Trinity students signed a Dublin petition against it. George Moore, who presented the petition, declared that it showed that 'the rising youth of Ireland were as much opposed to further concession as those of more mature age'. John Henry North criticized those who had taken the opportunity of 'infusing into the tender mind the deadly virus of party strife', and Croker, remarking that the student signatories were persons 'pursuing the elements of education', pointed out that they were only one-sixth of the student body. It is of course impossible to say what proportions of the remaining five-sixths were pro-Emancipation or simply apathetic.

At this point it is convenient to consider the MPs returned by Trinity during the Georgian era – a group that reflected opinion in College and made some impact on parliament. The electorate, as has been said, was composed of the provost, fellows and scholars. The provost, as returning officer, was by the beginning of the eighteenth century disabled from voting and it was decided in 1791 that scholars who were minors should not have a vote – in spite of the argument that 'those who had made a singular proficiency in learning' should be enfranchised.[60] Trinity was an independent constituency with the electorate influenced by a variety of considerations: family ties, friendship, career prospects and the characters of the candidates. Politics on a national scale do not seem to have played much part in the constituency. Loyalty to the Church might be taken for granted in a constituency in which a substantial proportion of the electorate were in orders or intended to be ordained. Though Swift, when recommending Alexander MacAulay, a barrister, to the constituency in 1739, emphasized that 'he was zealous for the liberty of the subject'; what probably counted in Swift's opinion even more was that MacAulay had upheld the rights of the clergy during the tithe controversy.[61] Also, though MacAulay was an eloquent supporter of an Irish Septennial Act, one of the reasons why he favoured it was that it would incline landlords, especially in the South, to choose Protestant tenants. Where in 1761 Tisdall, the Attorney General, refused 'to explain himself on limited parliaments', some of the scholars, led by John Scott (the later Lord Clonmel), 'put up' Robert French of Monivea, a sometime MP. Faced with this opposition Tisdall yielded and stated that he would support an Octennial bill. He was returned, receiving 56 votes to 19 for French, William Clement topping the poll with 68 votes.[62] But it is remarkable that in the voluminous evidence given on the Trinity election petition of 1791, amongst the welter of references to promises and pressures only one witness stated he voted for a candidate (Parsons) because he thought he would promote the interests of the country. Indeed W.C. Plunket (MP for Trinity 1812–27) specifically declared on the hustings in 1812 that he 'imposed upon himself a perfect silence on politics and always would in that place'.[63]

Between 1714 and 1832, when the size and composition of its electorate greatly changed, nineteen MPs were returned by Trinity, including Elwood and Coghill who sat in Queen Anne's last parliament. All but two (Hopkins and Knox) were alumni. Three were fellows (Arthur Browne, John Elwood and William Clement). Browne and Elwood were both *jurists*. Browne was an elegant essayist and an effective parliamentary debater. Elwood, as he was respected by Swift and Archbishop King, must have been a strong churchman and his reputation as a *bon vivant* probably did not damage his prospects as a candidate.[64] William Clement, a *medicus* and holder of numerous College offices, was, if his bust in the College Library is to be trusted, forcible and irascible. Elected to the first parliament of George III with the support of Provost Andrews (himself a county MP), Clement tended to side with the opposition and, presumably because he had lost the backing of the Provost, did not stand in 1768. But he did not quit politics. At a Dublin by-election in 1771 he was supported by 'the free and independent electors' against Benjamin Geale, the 'altermanic candidate', and was returned by 1521 votes to 1079. Five years later it was reported that Andrews' successor as Provost, Hely-Hutchinson, had deliberately arranged for the College election to be held on the same day as the election for the city so as to deny Clement the opportunity to vote in College. But at a breakfast given to Clement by his city supporters, Napper Tandy, the celebrated city radical, rose and proposed that Dr Clement be requested to leave so that he could vote in College. Clement departed 'amidst acclamation'. Certainly not 'a remote and ineffectual don', he continued to sit for the city until his death in 1782.[65]

Two of the College MPs were office-holders – Edward Hopkins and John Wilson Croker – though Croker was also distinguished as a man of letters. Hopkins, an English MP 'eminently distinguished', it was said, 'for parts, politeness and amiable qualities',[66] was appointed chief secretary when a Trinity seat was vacant owing to Samuel Dropping's death. It was extremely convenient for the government to have the chief secretary in parliament and very probably it was Provost Baldwin, a man of drive and a keen Whig, who secured his election. Hopkins ceased to be chief secretary in 1724 and there was the possibility that College would have an absentee MP until his death in 1736, but there was a general election in 1727 on the death of George II at which Hopkins, naturally, did not stand.

Seven of the College MPs were very active members of the Irish Bar: Marmaduke Coghill, Philip Tisdall, Walter Hussey Burgh, John Fitzgibbon, Arthur Browne, John Leslie Foster, William Conyngham Plunket and Thomas Lefroy. Tisdall at the time of his election was judge of the prerogative court and later became attorney general; Hussey Burgh, a brilliant orator, became Chief Baron; Fitzgibbon gave the College a taste of his abilities when he appeared for the petitioner against the return of Richard Hely-Hutchinson; on Hutchinson being unseated and Tisdall, the petitioner having died, Fitzgibbon was returned in 1778 for Trinity. But Fitzgibbon, a very busy lawyer, was not suited temperamentally to be a member of an assertive constituency, so in 1783 he preferred to be returned for a small borough. Foster became a baron of the exchequer, Plunket was appointed lord chancellor in 1830 and Anthony Lefroy, who at the end of the pre-reform age was elected for Trinity, remained a university MP until 1841 when his party, at last in power, was able to put him on the bench. It should be added that Tisdall, Hussey Burgh and Lefroy all inherited very large landed estates.

Seven of the representatives of the university were country gentlemen – Samuel Dopping, Samuel Molyneux, Sir Capel Molyneux, Archibald Acheson, Laurence Parsons, Francis Hely-Hutchinson and George Knox. Dopping, the son of a Bishop of Meath, was the highly esteemed friend of Swift. Samuel Molyneux, son of William Molyneux and sometime MP for the university, was an astronomer and had valuable connections at court. He died in 1728 shortly after his election. Forty years later his cousin Sir Capel Molyneux was elected MP for Trinity. He sat for the university for eight years (1768–76) but at the general election of 1776 he preferred to contest County Armagh.[67] He was not elected and thereafter sat for a small borough, Cloger. Another County Armagh landowner, Archibald Acheson, was more fortunate. Elected for the university in 1741 at the age of twenty-three, having held the seat for twenty years, he was returned for County Armagh in 1769 and ultimately received a peerage. Another young country gentleman, Laurence

Parsons, a man of strong and original intellect, after representing the College for eight years (1782–90) was unseated by Francis Hely-Hutchinson, son of the Provost, who had mastered 'the mystery of electioneering' (that is to say not to be too blatant in using his influence) since his failure to return a son in 1776.[68] Parsons was consoled by being elected for King's County in 1791. Francis Hely-Hutchinson married an heiress and obtained a senior revenue appointment. In 1797 he did not stand for Trinity, his father, the Provost, having died in 1794.

George Knox was the younger son of Thomas Knox, a County Tyrone landowner who had acquired a peerage in 1791 and a step up in 1791 when he was created Viscount Northland. His sons, Thomas, who secured an Irish earldom and a United Kingdom barony, and George, a barrister, a man of promise, able and charming, a sparkling letter-writer and amusing companion, were both ambitious young men who hoped to inspire their relation the Marquess of Abercorn to play a decisive role in Irish politics. Trinity was included in their schemes; Thomas Knox suggested that Abercorn might be the next chancellor and, for a fleeting moment, that he himself might be the next provost (Hutchinson's appointment having set a precedent). Later, he suggested that Abercorn should back the fellows in their efforts to secure as Hutchinson's successor a clergyman (hopefully one of their own body) and that Abercorn, 'sporting his guineas', might present the College with an altarpiece for the new chapel.[69] The Knoxes not only strove to acquire influence in College but they aimed for at least one of the university seats. In the early 1790s George Knox was putting himself forward as a candidate and by 1794 he had the backing of a club in the city composed of some of the fellows (and perhaps other electors), and in 1797 he was returned with Arthur Browne. The third candidate was Francis Hodgeson, a *jurist*.

With the reduction in the number of Irish MPs consequential on the Union, Trinity became a one-member constituency. The Act of Union set out that in the new single-member boroughs if one of the two sitting MPs did not withdraw, they should decide by lot which of them should continue to sit. It is probable that Browne withdrew. He was a fellow and was soon to be appointed prime sergeant and obviously would have found it very difficult to attend at Westminster. Knox, who continued to sit for the College, at the general election of 1802 with difficulty held his seat against a very strong candidate, W.C. Plunket, who after a successful undergraduate career, had become an outstanding member of the Irish Bar and during the debates on the Union had shown himself to be a brilliant parliamentary orator. After his defeat in 1802, Plunket (though he was for two short periods a law officer) devoted himself mainly to his practice at the Bar, building up a large fortune. But in 1805 Knox was faced with another strong competitor, John Leslie Foster. Foster was an able young barrister interested in economic and social questions who had the advantage of being backed by his uncle, John Foster, a very powerful politician. On this, his first attempt, Foster received 18 votes to Knox's 33, and Browne, coming out of retirement, secured only a derisory 11. At the next election in November 1806 Foster obtained 32 votes to Knox's 35 and in the following election (May 1807) Knox did not stand, Foster being returned. After he relinquished his Trinity seat, Knox's career petered out and after holding minor offices for about ten years he died in Naples in 1827. It should be said that at the elections of 1802 and 1807 Whitley Stokes, high-minded and intellectually somewhat eccentric – he had been a member of the Dublin Society of United Irishmen and an officer in the College yeomanry corps – called on the candidates to pledge themselves to obey the instructions of their constituents. Plunket took the test; Foster refused it, saying that if he took it Trinity could just as well be represented by a College porter.[70]

In 1812 Plunket again came forward after a ten-year interval. Foster withdrew but at the general election of 1818, Plunket was opposed by John Wilson Croker, a Trinity man, who after practising for some years at the Irish Bar had in 1806 entered parliament, and three years later, having shown himself to be a vigorous partisan and an able debater, had been appointed secretary to the admiralty. A very competent administrator, a man of letters and socially active (he was the leader of the group that founded the Athenaeum), Croker was a man of strong opinions forcibly expressed. His critics (who included MacAulay, Disraeli and Thackeray) portrayed him as overbearing, opinionated, dogmatic and subservient to the great. But he was knowledgeable, diligent, public-spirited and loyal, and regarded by a wide circle with considerable affection. It could be argued he was well fitted to represent a university, and in Trinity it was rumoured that he would be able to obtain the repeal of the celibacy statute – a matter of concern to fellows and potential fellows.[71]

When in 1827 Plunket was appointed chief justice of the common pleas, Croker again came forward. He was opposed by John Henry North, a young barrister, regarded by contemporaries as a brilliant orator and an elegant poet, in politics a Canningite; and by Thomas Lefroy, an erudite lawyer and a stern, unbending Tory. Lefroy had the support of Peel, but according to his friends he started his canvass too late and found three-quarters of the electorate already pledged.[72] Croker was returned with 38 votes against 29 for North and 22 for Lefroy. Two years later Croker (and North, sitting for Milborne Port) voted for Catholic Emancipation so Lefroy must have had a strong incentive to stand again as, according to his adherents, the defender of Protestantism and morality, against Croker 'the obsequious instrument of government'. On a somewhat lower level Lefroy sneered at Croker for wearing a gown, 'a perfect academic in the exterior', and Croker contemptuously referred to Lefroy as parading in a newly washed surplice and being backed by an Orange faction.[73] This time Lefroy was victorious with 33 votes to 20 for Croker and 13 for North. Less than a year later, at the general election of 1831, Lefroy was faced by an avowed Whig, Philip Crampton, a sometime fellow who was solicitor-general in Lord Grey's government. Lefroy emphasized the importance of protecting the Established Church, 'a candlestick from which the light of true religion shines out'; Crampton retorted that by talking about the Church Lefroy avoided the great question of parliamentary reform. In the event Lefroy held his seat by 44 votes to 36. It may be added that Lefroy, Croker and North all voted at Westminster against parliamentary reform.[74] The results of the 1830 and 1831 elections illustrate the strength of Protestant conservatism even in the unreformed Trinity constituency (it was to be much stronger in the reformed). Supporters of the established order were shaken to the core by irresistible demand for parliamentary reform following fast on Catholic Emancipation. Prior, a senior fellow, was convinced the Reform bill would subvert the constitution and 'revolutionize the whole empire into a democracy', and Sir Frederick Shaw (MP for Trinity 1832–48) at the general election of 1835 declared that the conflict was between 'government or confusion, religion or infidelity, the laws administered or trampled on, security for property or a general shamble, the liberty of British freemen, or the licentiousness of an infatuated multitude'.[75]

Understandably, Conservatives were profoundly disturbed because the early nineteenth century marked the beginning of a great age of institutional reform and remodelling by government and parliament. But so far as Trinity was concerned state intervention in its affairs was minimal and benevolent. The recommendations of the two royal commissions into Trinity College and the University of Dublin (1852 and 1906) were, generally speaking, welcomed by College and a third commission in 1920 cheered Trinity by recommending a very large capital grant and a substantial recurrent grant in aid. But alas, owing to a change in regime, these recommendations were not implemented, though after prolonged negotiations Trinity received a capital grant of about £140,000 and a very small annual grant from the state.

The most striking instance of intervention in College affairs during the nineteenth century was Fawcett's Act, which finally reached the statute book in 1873. It abolished religious tests in Trinity (except for teachers in the Divinity School) and the obligation on fellows to take orders. Remarkably, considering Trinity's historically very tight links with the Church of Ireland, the Act was readily accepted by College. Until the late 1860s Trinity had continued to see itself as an essentially Anglican institution, an important part of the Established Church and in 1867 Anthony Lefroy, one of the university MPs, emphasized that Trinity was a Protestant institution, adding that as Catholics could enter and graduate, 'the grievances complained of were imaginary'.[76] But only two years later his colleague, Thomas Ball told the House of Commons that he had been informed by the Board that it did not intend to petition against Fawcett's bill.[77] Ostensibly the reason for this very significant change was Disestablishment which, it could be said, had brought to an end the alliance between Church and College.

More important, however, was the momentous change in opinion which was affecting all the British universities. More and more a university was seen as an institution which 'upheld standards of pure science and disinterested knowledge',[78] and, as Fawcett himself asserted, was a place where 'men of the highest culture, without regard to their religious opinions ought to be able to live together in intellectual communion'.[79] In 1870 David Plunket, one of the Trinity MPs whose hereditary oratorical brilliance made a tremendous impression, could declare that Trinity was 'thoroughly unsectarian, thoroughly national and thoroughly loyal' (his colleague, Ball, rather balked at the epithet 'national' – he wanted Ireland to be considered part of the United Kingdom as much as Devon and Cornwall); and twenty years later two influential fellows, in a memorandum drawn up in the 1890s, referred to Trinity as a national university, which from its foundation had steadily kept up with the march of ideas, citing as evidence of its non-sectarian character that of the First XI, nine were Catholics (it was a sporting era).[80]

Of course secularization, as in the older English universities, was a slow and gentle process. Scepticism and latitudinarianism may have been growing but tolerant goodwill checked the development of violent antagonisms. In Trinity an overwhelming majority of the dons and undergraduates belonged, with varying degrees of commitment, to a Christian denomination; and the Church of Ireland, controlling the Divinity School and the College Chapel, continued, not over-obtrusively, to enjoy a privileged position. The prevalent attitude at the beginning of the twentieth century was summed up by Edward Gwynn, a future provost, when he declared that teaching should be free from partisan spirit or religious bias and that the moral and spiritual welfare of the students should be cared for by the different denominations.[81] Half a century or so later, in the early 1960s, two of Trinity's representatives who appeared before the Universities Commission stated that Trinity could be considered a Christian institution. But one of them, the Provost, granted that it was certainly possible that an anti-Christian position might be taken by some member of the staff, adding, 'I assume the same could be true of most universities.' In a university, he thought, there were bound to be 'clashes of opinion, differences of views'.[82]

The new conception of the university was strongly challenged by the Catholic Church, which held that all knowledge should be interpreted and understood in the light of Christian doctrine, that religion should permeate the life of a university and that if it seemed a conflict had arisen between secular learning and religious faith, the hierarchy, the Catholic bishops, should have the final say. Understandably then, from the mid-nineteenth century the university question loomed large in Irish politics, with successive governments, Conservative and Liberal, striving to find a solution which would meet Irish Catholic claims without jarring on contemporary British opinion (incidentally the more easily satisfied Presbyterian demands in the sphere of higher education had also to be taken into account). For most of the time Trinity, enjoying a private income, was able to stand aloof in splendid isolation from the Irish university controversy. The Trinity MPs did not oppose the foundation of the Queen's colleges, considering that though these new institutions did not offer what was 'properly called a university education', they would provide useful facilities for 'the middling classes',[83] the gentry of all creeds continuing to send their sons to Trinity.

When, half a century later, the creation of a university acceptable to Irish Catholics was being discussed, Lecky, then one of the Trinity MPs, admitted he was 'half-hearted' on the issue. Not wanting Trinity to be 'a dog in the manger', he advised the government to try to meet the Catholics' wishes. But he regretted that Protestants and Catholics should be separated in their undergraduate days and he was firmly opposed to ecclesiastical control over the teaching of secular subjects – it was a system which would turn out 'young laymen either credulous, emasculated, stunted and prejudiced or acidulated and exasperated, inclined to go to all lengths in opposition to that they had been taught'.[84] Carson, Lecky's colleague, took much the same line when in 1908, during the debate on Birrell's bill, he declared that he preferred his Catholic fellow-countrymen to be 'educated and highly educated rather than uneducated', and he ventured to hope that some time in the future University College and Trinity College should join together to form a great national university. But his fellow Trinity MP, James Campbell, condemned

Birrell's bill, being opposed to any scheme which would 'set students up in hostile sectarian camps'.[85]

Twice, in 1873 and 1906, Trinity and its graduates were deeply
perturbed by the suggestion that the Irish university question could
be solved by the formation of a federal university in which Trinity
College would be included. The College's reaction on both occasions can be summed up in the 1906 slogan, 'Hands off Trinity'. It
was strongly felt that if the College lost its independence the Catholic
Church would attain, at least in some areas, a dangerous degree of
influence and that appointments might be to some extent determined
by sectarian considerations. It would be deplorable, Trinity asserted
in 1892 in an address to the Lord Lieutenant, that a competent
teacher should be at a disadvantage 'because he did not belong to
some favoured religion or because his appointment might derange
some prescribed proportion'. Or as Mahaffy bluntly put it, 'once
"redressing the balance amongst religious denominations" becomes
a factor in making appointments, it is all up with a seat of learning'.[86]

Both the federation schemes were defeated and with the Irish
Universities Act of 1908 the idea of a wide federation faded away.
But the fear that Trinity's autonomy might be weakened persisted
and in 1912, when the Home Rule bill was in committee, James
Campbell, one of the Trinity MPs, proposed that Trinity College
and Queen's Belfast should be exempted from the jurisdiction of the
Irish parliament. The Board by a majority of 9 to 3 supported the
proposal but it seems to have been generally felt in Trinity circles
that conferring extra-territorial status on an institution standing
only a few minutes' walk from the Irish Parliament House would
be a continuing provocation to the Irish government. A joint meeting of junior fellows and professors rejected Campbell's proposal
by 22 votes to 13, suggesting that as an alternative no change
should be made by the Irish parliament in the College's constitution
and property rights unless it secured the assent of the Board, fellows, professors and the Senate. The Chief Secretary incorporated
this suggestion into the bill, adding the University Council to the
bodies whose assent would be required.[87] At this time a much-
respected senior fellow, a classicist and philosopher, John Isaac Beare,
in a private letter expressed the feelings of many of his colleagues

(and of a good many academic men before and since). The best for Trinity, he wrote, would be complete autonomy. But if College were to be under the control of an external body, 'better that it should be as it is, 300 miles away and not easily induced to meddle with us than that it should be within 30 paces of our walls and easily accessible to Adullannites'. Finally he optimistically trusted that their fellow countrymen 'will judge us by our scholarship and not by our politics'.[88]

Now we must turn to considering the part, the very distinctive part played by Trinity in United Kingdom politics in the ninety or so years following Catholic Emancipation and the Great Reform bill. In 1832 Trinity again became a two-member constituency, the Irish Reform Act giving the College an additional MP. This decision was vehemently criticized by Richard Lalor Shiel, who asked the Whigs why give a second member to a rich, splendid, lazy 'sacerdotal corporation', which 'had Protestantism and therefore exclusiveness for its principle'. Stanley, replying for the government, explained that in giving Trinity a second member its aim was to give the Protestant establishment its 'just weight', and Philip Crampton, the Solicitor-General, argued that the political influence of both religions in Ireland should be fairly balanced, though indeed he wished to see 'less distinction' between the two parties. There was also some discussion over what should be the university franchise. One suggestion was that ex-scholars should be added to the fellows and scholars, another that all graduates should be enfranchised. In the end it was agreed on Croker's initiative that the franchise should be exercised by the fellows and scholars and all doctors and MAs who paid a fee. Almost ninety years later BAs were enfranchised.[89]

With the enfranchisement of MAs, numerous BAs hastened to take out an MA and the Board placed the windfall in fees in a special building fund – pessimistically Croker, closely in touch with politics, advised the Provost against putting money into building because he would probably be the last holder of his office. The enlargement of the constituency, it was at once realized, was likely to benefit the Conservatives: Prior, a senior fellow and a strong Tory, suggested that a fund should be raised to pay the MA fees of necessitous Conservative supporters. 'Great caution and circumspection', he emphasized, 'should be observed' and 'discreet persons' employed. About the same time, another fellow, Charles Boyton, conspicuous as a robust politician, reminded his fellow Protestants and Conservatives that money was power and that they should use their wealth and prestige effectively in the coming general election (1832). At that election the strength of Conservative feeling in Trinity was manifested: the two Conservative candidates, Thomas Lefroy and Sir Frederick Shaw, received about 1300 votes each and the two Whig candidates, Crampton and George Ponsonby, a member of a great Whig family receiving about 400 each. A contemporary analysis of the poll shows the Conservatives ahead in every category of voter. The clergy were overwhelmingly Conservative, the laity rather less so; the proportion of Conservatives was higher amongst the fellows than the scholars – after all, men tend to become more conservative with age.

This election foreshadowed the history of the constituency during the next ninety years. Between 1832 and 1922 Trinity returned twenty-one members, all Conservative or unionist, with only two exceptions – Frederick Shaw and George Alexander Hamilton, both Oxford men and leading Irish Conservatives – Trinity graduates. The twenty-one comprised seventeen barristers, two country gentlemen (Hamilton and Anthony Lefroy), a man of letters (also a country gentleman, W.H. Lecky) and a medical man (Robert Woods). Of the lawyers, thirteen, having served as law officers, were elevated to the Irish judicial bench, one (Carson) became a law lord and two (Jackson and Thomas Lefroy) went straight from the House of Commons to the bench; Lefroy, later promoted to chief justice of the Queen's Bench, remaining in office until the age of ninety when at last he was able to place his resignation in the hands of a Conservative Prime Minister. Two of seventeen lawyers (Carson and Edward Gibson, Lord Ashbourne) became Cabinet ministers, a third (David Plunket) was a minister outside the Cabinet.

From time to time attempts were made to loosen the Irish Bar's grip on the Trinity seats. Three fellows offered themselves unsuccessfully as candidates: James McCullogh in 1847, Thomas Ebenezer Webb in 1868, and Anthony Traill in 1875. McCullogh stated that a university representative should be a person educated within its walls (a hit at his opponents, Hamilton and Shaw), familiar with its work and having some 'pretensions to represent science and learning'.[90] Webb hoped that the electors would protest against the constituency being treated as a pocket borough and Mahaffy seconded him on the ground that he was a fellow.[91] In 1875 it was reported that there was a general feeling against making the university constituency a means of promotion to the judicial bench, though it was thought there was a general willingness to reserve one seat for a Conservative law officer.[92] Nevertheless, at a by-election in that year, Traill, a very strong Conservative and a future provost, and Alexander Miller, who after a brilliant undergraduate career had gone to the English Bar and was ultimately knighted, were thoroughly trounced by Edward Gibson who, as was probably expected, became a law officer a year or two later. Other unsuccessful candidates who had as a plank opposition to the Irish Bar's quasi-monopoly of the Trinity seats were Richard Clere Parsons, a well-known engineer and a forcible speaker at unionist meetings, and Colonel Lowry Corry, a soldier and country gentleman. Lowry stood against Edward Carson in 1892 – the third candidate being the securely-established David Plunket, who had sat for Trinity since 1870. Arthur Balfour, writing on behalf of Carson, the newly appointed solicitor-general, expressed regret that the constituency had been so long monopolized by the law officers, but he emphasized that Carson's return would be of great service to the unionist cause.[93] Carson was elected, receiving 1609 votes to Corry's 897. It should be added that David Plunket, a barrister and law officer, who, as has just been said, held the Trinity seat for quarter of a century, claimed that he represented the living university 'as distinctly as any professor or Fellow'. He was constantly going in and out of Trinity College and 'so far as sympathy with everything that went on in the university, his heart beat with every throb of university life'.[94]

However, on two occasions, the Irish Bar's grip on the university constituency was broken. In an 1858 by-election there were two candidates – Arthur Gayer, an ecclesiastical lawyer, a pamphleteer and a vigorous upholder of the Established Church, and Anthony Lefroy (son of the Chief Justice), who was a country gentleman 'placed', it was remarked, 'beyond the reach of the place seeking'.

Politically speaking, it was said, there was scarcely 'a partial of dif-
ference' between the two candidates, both being 'conservatives of
the ancient Church and state stamp', and on a very low poll (about
half of the usual number of votes) Lefroy was returned.[95] In 1895,
when David Plunket was created a peer and George Wright QC
(appointed a King's Bench judge in 1901) came forward to succeed
him, a strong non-legal candidate, W.H. Lecky was nominated.
Lecky was backed by a group of influential fellows and a large number of graduates, including many of 'the Upper Clergy'and some
barristers who felt that, though Wright was an able and popular
member of their profession, it was a good opportunity for the Irish
Bar to pay a tribute to literature. Wright could claim that he was
better acquainted with Irish conditions than a resident in Onslow
Square. Also, there were those who suspected that the author of the
History of Rationalism was an agnostic or a materialist, and it was
rumoured that it was doubtful if he would oppose the Deceased
Wife's Sister bill.

Indeed, Lecky's difficulties in dealing with the evangelical clergy
reminded Mahaffy of St Paul fighting with beasts at Ephasus (a
remark which explains why one Lecky supporter wanted Mahaffy
to keep quiet). Lecky's response was to state: 'I was brought up in
the Church of England and have never severed myself from it and I
am quite prepared to support it as an Establishment but I must at
the same time decline to answer any questions about my private
religious belief', and on the hustings he describes himself as a Christian. Having, in Arthur Samuels' opinion, made 'a stern protest
against a religious inquisition ... even in a semi-clerical constituency', Lecky was returned by 1750 votes to 1000 for Wright
and Trinity gained a fitting representative for a learned constituency
whose reputation as a scholar was an asset to the unionist cause.[96]

Lecky always strove to be fair and his opinions on contemporary
issues were delivered dispassionately, with an air of academic
detachment, although he often arrived at conclusions which his
opponents would regard as thoroughly partisan. As John Morley,
commenting on Lecky's contribution to a debate, rather sourly
remarked, 'the cool light of history is really the warm resentment of
an Irish landlord'.[97] Lecky was certainly very critical of recent Irish

land legislation, which, he emphasized, had 'broken down the whole sense of obligations of contract which is the first condition of real, individual property'.[98] He was utterly opposed to Home Rule, believing that all the elements in Irish society whom he respected were convinced it would be a disaster. The Irish nationalists he regarded as enemies of the British empire, which he was convinced was a great and lasting force for good. 'No revolution in the history of affairs', he wrote, 'could ever destroy the future ascendancy of the English language and the English race.'[99] He was contemptuous of the nationalist leadership. When in the House of Commons he generously pleaded for the release of long-serving prisoners convicted of treason felony, he did not fail to point out that they had been driven mad by inflammatory speeches made by men now sitting in the house.[100] Viewing pessimistically the advance of democracy (unlikely, he thought, to be friendly to liberty), he characterized the Irish Local Government Act of 1898 as 'a great and perilous experiment'.[101] On the positive side Lecky strongly supported Balfour's policy of promoting Irish economic development by constructive legislation and, typically, striving to put matters in perspective, he pointed out that neither the government nor the landlords were to blame for distress in the west of Ireland – the culprit was the Atlantic Ocean.[102]

Occasionally the Conservatives', and later the Unionists' hold on the university constituency was unsuccessfully challenged. Three of the challengers were Whigs; Crampton, Ponsonby and Stock. Stock, son of a fellow and later judge of the Admiralty Court, declared on the hustings in 1837 that he would vote for O'Connell in the Dublin City election. He received a derisory 186 votes.[103] Three other challengers were Liberals: Lawson, Webb and Ball. In 1857 Anthony Lawson, a sometime Professor of Political Economy and later a High Court judge, stood as a Palmerstonian Liberal, obtaining about a quarter of the total vote, his resolute defence of the Maynooth grant being, it was said, 'the rock on which he was shipwrecked'. However, 'a super-conservative' who stood at the same election, James Wilson, a country gentleman who suspected Lord Derby of Pusyitism, fared even worse.[104]

In 1865 John Ball, a leading ecclesiastical lawyer, standing as a moderate Liberal, obtained about a quarter of the vote; three years later he was elected, by then being attorney general in a Conservative administration. In 1868 Thomas Ebenezer Webb, a fellow and a versatile scholar besides being anxious to break the legal monopoly of the constituency, declared that he was in favour of Disestablishment and the abolition of religious tests in Trinity – 'Make it unsectarian and free.'[105] He received 216 votes against 1600 for the Conservative candidates and in a few years' time was an ardent opponent of Gladstone's land legislation and Home Rule.

In the tense general election that followed the rejection of the first Home Rule bill, two Home Rulers stood for Trinity: Edward Patrick Sarsfield Counsel, a barrister, and H.H. Johnson, the son of a Welsh clergyman. An Oxford graduate, Johnson had been a civil servant and later became a Professor of English in Constantinople and Cairo.[106] The unionist candidates each received about 1800 votes, Counsel 55 and Johnson 56. At the nomination, the speeches of the Home Rule candidates were drowned by the hearty and repetitive singing of 'God Save the Queen' by the undergraduates.

Nearly thirty years later, in June 1913, Arthur Samuels, a KC and an outstanding Southern unionist who hoped to be elected for Trinity on the expected promotion of James Campbell to the bench, was perturbed to hear that there was a movement in College to invite Sir Horace Plunkett, who by then could be considered to be a Home Ruler, to be a candidate. The movement, Samuels gathered, had been instigated by Mahaffy, and the invitation had been signed by sixteen fellows (fifteen of them junior), 'who are very doubtful unionists or who think in a factious way to make friends of the mammon of unrighteousness'. However, Plunkett was reluctant to stand and when in December 1916 Campbell was appointed lord chief justice, Samuels was elected for Trinity unopposed.[107]

At the general election of 1918 a Home Rule candidate did come forward, Stephen Gwynn. He was in many ways an exceptionally strong candidate – he was a member of a famous Trinity family, a well-known man of letters, had been Nationalist MP for Galway for twelve years and had a good war record (he had joined up though over military age and had served in France). He received 257 votes compared to 1270 for the Unionist candidate who topped the poll.

The staunch adherence of the Trinity MPs to the Conservative cause naturally aroused hostile comment, both from those who thought university representation inconsistent with democratic principles and from resentful Liberals and Home Rulers. In 1868 William Gregory spoke of Trinity being represented by a mouth-piece of the Irish Church, and a Tory law officer and another Liberal, Chichester Fortescue, urged that Queen's University graduates should be permitted to vote in the Trinity constituency. A quarter of a century later John Morley declared that the function of the Trinity constituency was to provide seats for Tory law officers.[108] When the Redistribution bill of 1885 was being debated, an effort was made to abolish the representation of Dublin University. Nationalist MPs, speaking with considerable vehemence, dismissed Trinity as 'an institution with plenty of money, nobody to compete with and nobody to account to'. Trinity, Parnell remarked, was the university of a small section of the population. According to William Redmond it was a foreign institution, or, as T.D. Sullivan expressed it, 'an English fortress for the subjection of the Irish race', 'a prose-lytizing institution'. The Trinity electorate, William O'Brien explained, was 'composed of the sons of land agents and small gentry'. The brighter graduates of the Trinity Divinity School, he asserted, tried to come over to England; Trinity medical and legal graduates now formed a decreasing proportion of the Irish medical and legal professions, owing to 'the working up into the higher social strata … of the National and Democratic movement in Ireland'.[109] Trinity's representation was vigorously defended by David Plunket, who declared that the Trinity MPs represented the great mass of the learned professions who would, he believed, have little weight in the new, large, democratic electorate. They also represented, in so far as it was possible to do so, 'the great republic of letters'.[110] Moreover, they voiced the views of 'the scattered loyalists' outside Ulster.

In the Home Rule bill of 1893 and the Home Rule Act of 1914, Trinity was not included in the constituencies which were to return MPs to Westminster (though in both instances it would have had two seats in the Irish parliament). But the Representation of the People Act 1918, theoretically at least, strengthened Trinity's position by giving the National University of Ireland and Queen's Belfast each an MP. In fact, in the parliament elected at the end of 1918, there were no fewer than fifteen university MPs. Nevertheless in the Home Rule bill of 1920, university MPs were not amongst the forty-two members Ireland was to send to Westminster – though the Irish universities were to be represented in the parliaments of Southern and Northern Ireland. However, when the bill was in committee, Walter Guinness successfully urged that the number of Irish MPs who were to sit at Westminster should be raised to forty-six by the addition of two from Trinity and one each from the National University and Queen's Belfast. The university MPs, he emphasized, would be independent, 'not controlled by secret caucuses', and the Trinity members would represent the Southern unionists.[111] The 1920 Act gave Trinity and the National University each four seats in the parliament of Southern Ireland, and when that body met on 28 June 1921, the Trinity representatives were the only members of the House of Commons to take their seats. They elected one of their number, Gerald Fitzgibbon, as chairman and adjourned. The same four Trinity representatives sat in the third Dáil which enacted the Irish Free State constitution.

Under the Union Trinity had elected a succession of able and articulate unionist MPs. A number of Trinity men, Professor Dowden, Robert Martin of Ross, Thomas Dunbar Ingram, Caesar Litton Falkner, Edward Healy of the *Irish Times* and, in the mid-nineteenth century, the contributors to the *Dublin Magazine*, helped to mobilize unionist opinion, and throughout the country, Trinity graduates, men of light and leading in their localities, inspired and organized their fellow unionists. Nor should the undergraduates be forgotten; their fervent adherence to the unionist faith was from time to time noisily demonstrated and they shared with their seniors the task of shaping the opinions of their own generation. But it would be a mistake to assume that Trinity was politically monolithic. An impressive list can be compiled of prominent Irish nationalists who were Trinity graduates – Thomas Davis, essayist and balladeer; Isaac Butt, the leader of the Home Rule party; the Reverend Joseph Galbraith, a fellow of Trinity, who 'smarting like others ... under a deep sense of wrong to Irish protestants' inflicted by Disestablishment

joined the Home Rule party.[112] Douglas Hyde, the founder of the
Gaelic League, and his biographer, Dermot Coffey, who was
involved in 1914 in smuggling arms for the National Volunteers.
The influence of the Gaelic League was reflected in Trinity by the
foundation in 1909 of the Gaelic Society, which *T.C.D.*, the undergraduate College magazine, welcomed in the hope that the Society
would study the Gaelic past, 'which is neither Orange nor Green'.
Ten years later the Gaelic Society was known not only for the study
of the Irish language but also for its treatment of social and political questions. Its visiting speakers included Douglas Hyde, Lord
Dunsany, Oliver Gogarty and Thomas Johnson, the leader of the
Irish Labour party.[113]

But manifestations of nationalist feeling in Trinity should not be
over-stressed. After all, some degree of dissidence is natural in a university. Moreover, until 1850 Trinity had a monopoly on university
education in Ireland and henceforth for decades its prestige and
pickings attracted men of all creeds and classes. To a nationalist, the
signs that there was national feeling in Trinity is interesting insofar
as it showed how a few blades of grass can grow in a stony place,
but dwelling on these signs without due regard for the prevalent
contemporary tendencies in College is a serious mistake, frequently
committed in the cause of public relations. It falsifies history by giving a misleading impression of Trinity opinion and the College
ethos, and it may nourish institutional complacency, usually a flourishing plant, by implying that Trinity's heart was always in the right
place, or that the College was in the past closely identified with the
tradition that has for the moment triumphed.

From the summer of 1914 the Irish unionists sustained a series
of traumatic shocks. In August 1914 the great European war began,
and in September the Home Rule bill reached the statute book. In
1916, while the struggle for Verdun was raging, there was an insurrection in Dublin, 'a carefully-plotted and planned German movement', Arthur Samuels, one of the Trinity MPs told the House of
Commons.[114] Then came some years of civil strife, the Government
of Ireland Act, 1920, and at the close of 1921, an agreement by
which the South of Ireland acquired dominion status. When this
agreement was being debated at Westminster, Robert Woods, one of

the Trinity MPs who earlier had drawn attention to the plight of the Irish unionists in the areas where the King's writ no longer ran, read a letter from the Board of Trinity, welcoming the agreement on the grounds that 'the true interests of Trinity can only be furthered by Irish peace and the building up of happier conditions'. Woods voted with the majority of 401, which accepted the agreement. His colleague, Henry Jellett, was in the minority of 58 against it. Eighteen months earlier Jellett had exhorted the government to let the people of Ireland know it was determined to put down treason and sedition. Now he felt betrayed. 'If you want in Ireland to be recognised by a British government of modern days,' he bitterly reflected, 'whatever you do, do not be loyal; you will never have a dog's chance if you are loyal.' And he warned the House that the only choice was between the Union and a republic. There was no finality in the government's proposals.[115] It would be easy to dismiss the fight for the Union as a futile attempt to halt the march of history. But it postponed Home Rule for over a generation and enabled Northern Ireland to remain in the United Kingdom, sharing its social services and political and intellectual life. Moreover, during the decisive battle of the Atlantic, one of the three great operational bases was Londonderry.

After 1922, those working in Trinity and the largely Protestant professional and business world in which they moved faced the problems of 'staying on'. Obviously they found the new Ireland vehemently Catholic, striving to return to its Gaelic roots and often stridently antagonistic to England, which in turn it associated with oppression, imperialism, materialism, and uncongenial modern morality. But everyday life in Ireland had its charms, and Trinity, with revenue sufficient for its needs by the somewhat Spartan academic standards of the time, could stand aside from political Ireland, which incidentally did not have university education high on its agenda. 'Bombs may resound in College Green but inside the gates of Trinity there is still peace.' Many of the older generation in Trinity clung to their traditional loyalties, some going into internal exile. One of that generation who was anxious to participate in Irish public life, William Thrift, later provost, expressed himself poignantly in the Dáil. 'Prior to the Treaty', he said, 'I was no politician. I voted unionist, I held unionist views ... but with many, I was sick of strife'. He explained that he had accepted the Treaty because it enshrined an oath of allegiance to the king as the symbol of Commonwealth unity and he had entered the Dáil ready to meet men 'on the level whom previously I had regarded as doing things which my inner conscience once condemned'. But he was disappointed and depressed by the abolition of the oath, the Senate and university representation during the early 1930s.

The younger generation was more ready to accept the *fait accompli* – after all, post-war disillusionment pervaded English intellectual life and in the age of Huxley and E.M. Foster, old-fashioned patriotism was at a discount (the time was to come when Keynes was to remind *New Statesman* and *Nation* readers that the intelligentsia of the Left had abandoned 'the defence of freedom and civilisation to Colonel Blimp and the Old School Tie'). But the progressively-minded Trinity man, while ready to disregard the anachronistic opinions of his seniors, found it hard to identify himself with the new Ireland, fervently Catholic and suspicious of much of modern thought. He did not share the traditions, upbringing, background or principles of his contemporaries in UCD – only half a mile away. Consequently Trinity observed much of what was taking place in Ireland with sceptical and amused detachment. 'Trinity', an editorial in *T.C.D.* declared in 1936, 'is above all an Irish university, but a university whose regard for the cosmopoly of true learning and culture, makes her loath to participate in exaggerated nationalism.' Trinity, the editorial went on to assert, 'views with disquiet the policy of isolation and separation'. Trinity, another editorial pronounced, had not excelled herself in producing 'the fighting patriot', instead, she had produced men who had been good Irishmen and good Europeans.[116]

College naturally had contacts beyond its walls, but these were intermittent and usually lacked the intimacy springing from shared presuppositions and traditions. There was, of course, a sustained interest in the Dublin theatre (though the Gate had few affinities with the Irish people), and there were occasional references in *T.C.D.* to Irish authors – Yeats, critical of many aspects of Irish life, and Sean O'Faolain, according to *T.C.D.* one of the masters of Irish disillusionment.[117]

If after 1922 Trinity was content enough to be an intellectual and social enclave in Dublin, it had to accept with as good a grace as it could that it had far less political influence than in the past. Trinity had four MPs in the parliament of Southern Ireland and under the Free State constitution it had three representatives in Dáil Éireann. University representation in the Dáil was abolished in 1936, but under the constitution of 1937 the National University and Trinity were each given three representatives in the Senate. It may be said that the question of university representation in the Dáil and Senate aroused comparatively little debate, partly because until the 1940s the Trinity deputies and senators were regarded as representing the ex-unionist minority.

Between 1921 and 1991 Trinity was represented in the Dáil and Senate by twenty-three men and women. The first twelve elected comprised five fellows, four professors and three barristers who all became Supreme Court judges. Then in 1954 Owen Sheehy-Skeffington, a lecturer in French, undistinguished academically but keen on politics and a fluent speaker, was elected. Though three of the first group (Fearon, Jessop, Stanford) were returned after 1954 – the last to retire being Jessop in 1973 – Skeffington may be taken as the first of a new sequence of Trinity representatives which, counting Skeffington, numbered eleven. It was less homogeneous than the first group, including a lecturer in mathematics, who was elected to the Senate the year he was elected to fellowship; a lecturer in English, who the year before his election won a case on sexual discrimination in the Court of Human Rights; two Reid Professors of Law; two ex-ministers; a medical doctor; a solicitor; a financial advisor; and a sometime lord mayor of Dublin who was a keen conservationist.

For some time after 1922 the Trinity representatives voiced the views of the ex-unionist minority. They were critical of the majority attitude on divorce, censorship, birth control and the Irish language, arguing that though Irish should be encouraged, it should not be compulsory; and in 1942 two Trinity Senators, Alton and Johnston, vigorously opposed a Schools Attendance bill, which would have empowered the Minister of Education to forbid a parent to send his child to a school outside the state where Irish was not taught –

schools which 'were not in the manufacture of Gaelic Culture'. They valued the Commonwealth connection and favoured the unity of Ireland only if it had the support of a clear majority in Northern Ireland.

When in 1948 the Republic of Ireland bill came before the Senate, one of the Trinity Senators, Joseph Bigger, who saw himself as 'a good Irishman' and who 'believed the best interests of the country demanded close association with Great Britain' (he had served in the RAMC during the war), made 'a lone and fiery speech' against it.[118] He began by stating he had never been a unionist but he had been born a British subject, had served in the British army and remembered how 'Britain stood alone, when France was only a name, when Russia had not made up its mind and when America stood aloof'. He wanted, he declared, a united Ireland, but only by the free will of both parties, unionist and nationalist, North and South. 'We are', he remarked, 'an intolerant people', but the fundamental responsibility for partition rested with the South because it failed to realize it was no use sneering at the sentiment of loyalty to the King, it was real and ought to be respected. His two Trinity colleagues were judicious. Professor Fearon regretted that the Senate had been treated to 'biographical details, political post-mortems and an examination into motives'. He suggested there should be a realignment of parties and a careful consideration of future relations with the Commonwealth. Professor Stanford emphasized the scrupulous fairness with which the government had treated the Protestant minority – fourteen years earlier he had published a pungent little pamphlet detailing the community pressures to which Southern Protestants were subjected – and he was concerned to preserve opportunities for employment in Great Britain and the Commonwealth.

On the whole, the members of the second sequence of Trinity representatives were moderate and pragmatic, but five were socialists, or at least had a bias towards collectivism. All were concerned over civil liberties and 'rights' issues. Critical of many of the conventional Irish social values, contemptuous of the run-of-the-mill Irish politicians and quick to challenge what they regarded as clerical dictation, they in a sense perpetuated the old unionist tradition of dwelling on the faults, failings and fallacious enthusiasms of solid, respectable Irish nationalism and its leaders. This may partly explain why the offspring of the old ex-unionists voted for them. By the close of the twentieth century much of 'the liberal agenda' that the Trinity College Senators championed had been realized and this, with changes in Irish society and in the Trinity College electorate, more integrated with the community, is bound to render the Trinity representation in the Senate less distinctive than in the past.

Now for the influence of the new Ireland on Trinity. In the late 1940s, Trinity was compelled to relinquish its long enjoyment of splendid isolation. With state subsidization on a massive scale becoming an essential factor in university development throughout the British Isles, it was painfully obvious that Trinity could no longer maintain university standards if compelled to rely on its own resources. In 1947 a despairing approach to the government met with a sympathetic response, Trinity receiving a recurrent grant with, it was optimistically said, 'no strings'. Probably Mr de Valera was largely responsible for this. He was an autocratic prime minister; through education he had acquired upward mobility and he enjoyed, as a relief from politics, meeting academic men, who on their part tend to have a deferential respect for men in power. Finally, as leader of a party committed to levering Northern Ireland out of the United Kingdom, he could scarcely allow Trinity, which claimed, with some justification, to be an all-Ireland institution, to collapse. Paradoxically, however, just at the moment that the College started to receive substantial assistance from the Éire government, a steady flow of entrants from outside Ireland (mainly from Great Britain) began, and for over twenty years a buoyant and expanding College was able to combine the enjoyment of a satisfactory (or at least adequate) income with autonomy.

But early in the 1960s there was an intimation of how autonomy could be quietly diminished when a venerable Trinity institution, the Divinity School, was fundamentally changed. In 1963 the government intimated that it was unwilling to subsidize denominational religious instruction through the annual grant to College. As a result the Board froze the salaries of Divinity School professors and lecturers, the Church of Ireland accepting the responsibility of keeping the salaries at prevailing academic levels. The staff of the Divinity School thus became to an increasing extent employees of the Church of Ireland, which soon, logically enough, began to prepare its ordinands in its own college in a Dublin suburb. It wasn't long before the Divinity testimonial was replaced by a Diploma in Theology. The Divinity Chairs, on the retirement of their occupants, were suspended and a Chair of Theology, the holder of which was to treat religion purely as an academic discipline, established – his lectures of course being open to *inter alia* the students attending the Church of Ireland theological college. A number of tendencies may have led to the disappearance of the Divinity School, but state intervention certainly accelerated the process. Perhaps it should be added that at about this time the College further severed itself from its old religious tradition. To a marked degree it ceased to supervise the morals and manners of undergraduates. The last occasion when a College publication was censored was in 1964, when the appearance of an article on sexual behaviour (rather conservative by the standards of a later decade) led to the staff of *T.C.D.* being summoned before the Board.[119]

The replacement of de Valera as Taoiseach at the very end of the 1950s marked the beginning of a new era. The idealism of the early part of the century was not rejected but it received less attention. De Valera's dream of an Ireland which would be 'the home of a people, who were satisfied with frugal comfort and who devoted their leisure to the things of the spirit, a land whose countryside would be bright with cosy homesteads, whose fields and villages would be joyous with the sounds of industry, with the romping of school children, the contests of athletic youth and the laughter of comely maidens' – seemed Arcadian and archaic. Growth, efficiency, and modernization were the keywords of the new era. A small, open economy had to be outward-looking and adaptable and the old certitudes and simplicities were being eroded by, amongst other forces, the Second Vatican Council and TV.

Higher education began to attract more attention. It was believed it would contribute to productivity; it was costing the taxpayer considerably more than in the past and there was an increasing number of parents (and voters) whose children were at or intended going to a university. In the early sixties the government, by appointing a commission to enquire into higher education, showed its concern and provided itself with a reason for postponing immediate action. Painstaking and deliberate, the commission at last in March 1967 produced an intelligent report along conventional lines, backed by a vast quantity of evidence. It fell flat because in the following month Donagh O'Malley, the fertile-minded and eloquent Minister for Education, publicly committed himself to the speedy implementation of a bold scheme; the merger of University College Dublin and Trinity College, in a great University of Dublin. Such a measure, it was argued, would ensure the economic use of resources by avoiding duplication and have a stimulating effect on academic life. But the distribution of activities between the two colleges was left uncertain and the Minister, in deference to institutional loyalties, stressed that each college would retain its 'identity' (a term which became the subject of intensive exegesis – what were 'the notes' of collegiate identity?).

There was a prolonged debate in which the government, the two colleges and groups within each college were involved. Some in Trinity welcomed the proposals either out of deference to the powers that be or because they saw opportunities for improving facilities. In the Senate Professor Jessop professed the hope that a merger would make the provision of clinical teaching easier. On the other hand Dr Sheehy-Skeffington was not convinced that a merger was necessary and he was concerned over the reduction of non-Irish entrants. Professor Stanford, having referred to the merger as 'a confounded nuisance', argued that the government, since it was giving Trinity a large annual grant, was entitled to expect co-operation from the College. But he feared that valuable loyalties, 'emotions', might be at risk. It was these emotions, together with the resistance of vested interests, that nullified O'Malley's initiative, and after his death in 1968 the merger scheme was abandoned.

But not long afterwards a momentous development began, a striking and steady growth in Trinity student numbers. The government was anxious to meet public expectations, and to promote what it conceived to be the national interest, by greatly increasing the number of student places in the universities. The College leadership believed that only by a sustained growth in its financial resources could Trinity remain a viable and developing institution. But of course increased state funding depended on increasing student numbers. At the beginning of the 1960s the carefully considered Trinity opinion had been that if the College maintained its mode of life on its present site it could accommodate only approximately 3000 undergraduates – 3000 it was said was the lower limit for a viable university and upper limit for a College – though Trinity was prepared to contemplate a total of 4000. It was emphasized that to maintain College life it was important to keep the faculties as close together as possible – if the university was too large its faculties would fly apart.[120]

Events were soon to render these views significant only in history. Mid-century the Trinity student population was 2250; by 1969/70 it was 4000; in 1979/80 it was 5400; then between 1980 and the end of the century it jumped to 11,800 – a five-fold increase in half a century. It may be added that while in 1938/39 women were slightly over 23 per cent of the student body, in 1999/2000 they were almost 60 per cent. Moreover, the composition of the student body markedly changed. Throughout its history Trinity had recruited from comparatively small sections of Irish society, and this intake was reinforced from the mid-1940s by a substantial flow from overseas (at the beginning of the sixties about one-third of the entrants were from Great Britain). It was a situation that the government of the Republic could scarcely be expected to regard with satisfaction, and in 1967 the College announced that during the next five years the proportion of non-Irish students would be reduced to 15 per cent – a decision denounced by T.C.D. as chauvinist.[121] The attainment of this objective was facilitated when, in 1970, the Irish Catholic bishops declared they would withdraw the regulations discouraging Catholics from sending their children to Trinity.[122] The bishops probably realized that to discourage young Irish men and women from taking up the places available in Trinity would irritate the government and arouse public resentment, and they may have come to the conclusion that the dangers to undergraduate faith and morals might not be so much greater in Trinity than in University College. By 1980 about 85 per cent of Trinity undergraduates and postgraduate students were from the Republic and the fear was expressed that Trinity was changing from being a colourful, international university into a rather drab provincial institution.

The population explosion substantially affected the Trinity ethos and way of life. The College site was enlarged and planted with new buildings. Departments increased in number and size, becoming naturally more self-contained. Administration, which from the foundation of the College had been for some dons a more or less welcome diversion from strictly academic work, became to a great extent a sphere for experts with managerial skills. Sheer numbers meant that members of the staff knew comparatively few of their colleagues and undergraduates were acquainted with only a very small proportion of the student body.

The state not only greatly influenced Trinity by encouraging growth in numbers but during the later decades of the twentieth century it intervened decisively in a number of ways in the university sphere. In 1969 it was decided to set up the Higher Education Authority, a government-nominated advisory and supervisory body. Under the Higher Education Authority Act of 1971 the Authority was empowered to co-ordinate state investment in higher education, all payments to any institution being subject to whatever conditions the Authority thought fit to impose. The Authority, the Act laid down, was to promote 'the democratisation' of higher education and to 'bear in mind the national aims of restoring the Irish language and developing the national culture'.

Henceforth Trinity was not only the recipient of large sums of public money but of suggestions and directives which clearly had considerable influence on its evolution. Obviously many new developments have to be cleared with HEA staff salaries (which in the 1960s had been equated by the government with those of civil servants in what it regarded as equivalent grades), staff numbers were inevitably fixed by the size of the annual grant, and in 1988 the HEA decided that thirty posts in Trinity should be treated as redundant. In 1974 the government decided that the teaching of veterinary science should be concentrated in University College Dublin, the Trinity teachers of veterinary subjects being transferred to University College. Trinity, conscious that the School, a comparatively large one, was closely connected with the life of the country, remonstrated, demanding that there should be consultations and that the question of veterinary teaching should be considered in the light of a promised White Paper on education. The government replied that its announcement was not a proposal for discussion but an irrevocable and final decision. In a strained interview the Provost said that the government's procedure indicated a marked change in the relationship of the universities and the state. The Minister for Agriculture wearily retorted that his Department did not want to impose a solution but was entitled to withdraw funds. The College, if it pleased, could continue to teach veterinary science so long as it did not claim financial support for the subject.

Then in 1975, eager to conciliate the Minister for Education who favoured a comprehensive system of higher education, Trinity agreed to allow several VEC colleges to become associated institutions. Trinity approved their courses, appointed external examiners for their final examinations and conferred degrees on their students. This meant that a Dublin University degree no longer necessarily implied that the holder had worked and had his academic being within Trinity College – a change of some significance. However, in 1997 the Minister of Education, acting under the Dublin Institute of Technology Act (1992), ordered that from September 1998 the DIT should be the degree-conferring body for the Vocational Education Colleges.[123]

Meanwhile in 1996 the then Minister for Education Niamh Bhreathnach sponsored a measure phasing out student fees, a move which has tended to diminish university autonomy (incidentally, in 1968 O'Malley had remarked that 'academic autonomy really applies in the main to individuals or groups but nowadays there can in practice be very little institutional autonomy').[124] In the same year (1996) the Minister for Education pronounced that with knowledge being the basis of progress to 'a richer culture, greater social justice and harmony and a better quality of life for all', the universities had an essential role to play, both in developing the nation's knowledge and in helping to maintain 'a mature, democratic society'.[125]

This conception of the university was embodied in the Universities Act of 1997, which laid down in some detail what should be the aims of a university in the Republic. It should advance knowledge through research and scientific investigation and promote learning both in its own student body and in society generally. It should foster a capacity for independent thinking and at the same time encourage the official languages of the state and promote Ireland's distinctive cultures. It was to contribute to national economic and social development, facilitate lifelong learning and promote gender balance and equality of opportunity amongst its students and employees. The university was to have the right to regulate its own affairs in accordance with its ethos, but having regard to promoting equality of opportunity and access. It was also enacted that each university, with the exception of Trinity, should have a governing body composed of representatives of the professoriate and other academic grades, the postgraduate students and two groups not involved in research or teaching, the non-academic staff and the Students' Union, together with persons nominated by outside bodies and the Higher Education Authority. For Trinity there was to be special legislation. This was provided a few years later by the Trinity College Dublin (Charters and Letters Patent Amendment) Act, 2000. This Act laid down that the Board should comprise the provost, the four senior officers, six fellows, five non-fellow members of the academic staff, at least three of whom should be of a rank not higher than senior lecturers, two professors, three members of the non-academic staff, four students (of whom at least one shall be a postgraduate student), one 'outside' member chosen by a committee of the Board and one member nominated by the Minister for Education and Science.

Obviously, the ideal of a university was reflected in the Universities Act. An institution closely linked to the community, intellectually, socially and financially, and expected to express and inculcate the cultural and political values in vogue, differs strikingly from the sort of university the late nineteenth century took for granted: an autonomous, self-governing corporation of dons, priding themselves on their independence and detachment, ready to perform what they conceived to be their duties to the country and mankind along lines decided by themselves.

NOTES

1. *SPI 1615–25*, p. 167.
2. *SPI 1601–3*, p. 432.
3. *SPI 1603–6*, p. 59.
4. *SPI 1603–6*, p. 169; *Cal. Carew MSS 1603–24*, p. 134.
5. *Bathurst MSS*, HMC, ii, p. 13; *SPI 1574–85*, p. xxxiii.
6. *Cal. Carew MSS 1575–88*, p. 480.
7. E.P. Shirley, *Original Letters and Papers Illustrative of the History of the Church in Ireland* (1851), pp. 1–14, 126–8, 151–2, 162, 201.
8. *SPI 1509–73*, p. 78. It was to be called Christ Church of the foundation of King Edward.
9. *SPI 1509–73*, p. 428.
10. *SPI 1574–85*, pp. 491, 529, 546, 552.
11. R.B. MacCarthy, *The Trinity College Estates 1800–1923* (1992), especially chapter 4.
12. *SPI 1592–6*, p. 77; *SPI 1603–6*, p. 405.
13. *SPI 1615–25*, p. 277; *The Works of William Laud*, vi (1857), p. 261.
14. For the teaching of Irish in Trinity, see Máirtín Ó Murchú, 'Irish language studies in Trinity College Dublin', in *Hermathena, Quatercentenary Papers* (1991).
15. A. Ford, *The Protestant Reformation in Ireland* (1987), p. 77.
16. Victor Treadwell, 'The Irish Court of Wards under James I', in *IHS*, xii, pp. 1–25.
17. *Works of Laud*, vi (1857), p. 674; vii (1860), p. 246.
18. R. Dunlop, *Ireland under the Commonwealth* (1913), i, pp. 10–11; ii, 491–2.
19. Hely-Hutchinson, 'History of the College' (TCD MS), p. 215.
20. W. King, *The State of the Protestants in Ireland* (1730), pp. 172–3.
21. King to Archbishop of Canterbury, 15 Aug. 1708 (King MS 753/3/229).
22. *House of Commons Jnl Ire.*, iii, p. 616.
23. Sir Richard Cox to E. Southwell, 9 Feb. 1714 (BL, Add. MS 38157); H. Alton, 'Some fragments of College history', in *Hermathena*, lvii, pp. 25–38, 121–65.
24. *Hermathena*, lvii, p. 34; King to M. Coghill, 27 Oct. 1716 (King MS 2534); *The Case of Richard Hartley* (1713).
25. King to the Bishop of Dromore, 6 Oct. 1715 (King MS 2533); King to R. Howard, 27 May, 29 June 1715 (King MS 1489(2) /80); King to Sunderland, 7 July 1715 (King MS 750/5/2).
26. King to Stanhope, 25 Feb. 1715 (King MS 2533).
27. *HMC, 8th report*, p. 586.
28. King to S. Molyneux, 7 April 1719 (King MS 750/5); King to the Bishop of Carlisle, 16 July 1715 (King MS 1533).
29. King to the Bishop of Carlisle, 27 Aug. 1716; to R. Howard, 23 Aug. 1715 (King MS 2533).
30. King to Howard, 3 Nov. 1715 (King MS 2533).
31. *London Gazette*, 17 April 1715.
32. A.A. Luce, *Life of Bishop Berkeley* (1949), pp. 52–5; *Works of George Berkeley*, eds A.A. Luce and T.F. Jessop, vi (1953), pp. 17–46.

33. *House of Commons Jnl Ire.*, iii, 134.

34. King to Molyneux, 9 June 1716 (King MS 2533); King to Captain Pratt, 28 Feb. 1717 (King MS 2354).

35. H.Boulter, *Letters* ... (1770), i, pp. 180, 189.

36. *Heads of a Scheme for Applying the Increased Rents of Erasmus Smith's Lands to the Use of the College or University of Dublin* ... [*c.* 1723].

37. A. Browne, *Thoughts on the Present State of the College* (1782).

38. Cal. Rosse MSS, G8/45.

39. E. Burke, *Correspondence*, vi (1967), p. 192.

40. *IHS*, iii, pp. 49–52.

41. *DEP*, 7, 9 April 1795.

42. *To the Scholars and Students of Trinity College* (1796); F. Higgins to — 19 Nov. 1796 (NAI, Rebellion Papers 620/36/226).

43. Prior, Diary, 20 Nov. 1796 (TCD MS 4956).

44. A. Browne, *Some Brief Principles of Tactics* (1797).

45. W. Magee, *Works* (1843), ii, pp. 359, 366.

46. Preface to Elrington's edition of Locke's *Essay*; T. Elrington to G. Knox, 1 Feb. 1805 (BL, Add. MS 35756).

47. *Gentleman's Magazine*, lxviii, pp. 180–1.

48. Prior, Diary, 19 May 1797 (TCD MS 4957 (3)).

49. E. Lambert to E. Cooke, 15 Feb. 1798 (NAI, Rebellion Papers 620/35/141); Prior, Diary, 31 May 1798 [reports of Visitors] (TCD MSS 1203, 3373); *Dublin Journal*, 6 May 1798.

50. Elrington, Diary, 14 April 1798 (TCD MS 4958).

51. Sir John Stewart, 7 Aug. 1798 (NAI, Rebellion Papers 620/39/156).

52. There are verbatim reports of the visitation in TCD MSS 1203 and 3373.

53. Elrington, Board diary, 22 Jan. 1800 (TCD MS 4959).

54. *Some Documents Relative to the Late Parliamentary Conduct of Dr Browne* (1800); TCD MUN P1/1232.

55. *Memoirs of Viscount Castlereagh*, ed. Marquess of Londonderry, ii (1849), pp. 229–30.

56. *Parl. Reg. Ire.*, xv, p. 217.

57. Elrington to Sir Robert Peel, 8 Dec. 1812 (BL, Add. MS 40223).

58. Prior, Diary, 30 Feb. 1819 (TCD MS 3367).

59. *Proceedings of the Irish Parliament, 1793*, ii, pp. 159, 236; *Parl. Reg. Ire.*, xv, p. 377; *Hansard*, 2nd series, xx, pp. 1056–61; *The Croker Papers*, ed. L.J. Jennings (1884), i, p. 135.

60. E. & A. Porritt, *The Unreformed House of Commons* (1903), ii, p. 210; L. Parsons, *A Proof ... that Minors have a Right to Vote* (1791), p. 8.

61. *Swift Correspondence*, ed. H.W. Williams, v (1965), pp. 56, 72, 141–5, 150, 158; A. MacAulay, *Septennial Parliaments Vindicated* (1766).

62. For French's candidature see MS note in volume containing printed reports of the House of Commons' committees on the TCD elections of 1776 and 1790 in TCD Library.

63. TCD MS 3364.

64. *The Conclave Dissected* (*c.* 1726).

65. *Freeman's Jnl*, 26 Nov. 1771; *Hibernian Jnl*, 22 Nov., 4, 11 Dec. 1771; 15 May 1776.

66. *EHR*, xxxiv, pp. 491–504.

67. *Belfast Newsletter*, 20 Dec. 1775, 20 Feb., 2 June 1776.

68. 1791 report, p. 8.

69. PRONI, T/2541/1/K15/1; 2541/1/B/9/5; 2541/1/B1/2/8, 18; 2511/1/B/1/5.

70. TCD MS 3363.

71. TCD MS 3364.

72. *Gentleman's Magazine*, NS xxiv, pp. 466–7; *DEP*, 15 May 1827.

73. *DEP*, 4, 6 Aug. 1830.

74. *Ibid.* 9 May 1831.

75. Prior, Diary, 20 April 1831; *The Times*, 12 Jan. 1835.

76. *Hansard*, 3rd series, clxxx, pp. 63–4.

77. *Ibid.* cxcviii, 1202.

78. *The Times*, 10 June 1892.

79. *Hansard*, 3rd series, clxxxviii, p. 57.

80. *Ibid.* cc, 1102; ccxv, 756; TCD MUN/P1/2461.

81. E. Gwynn, in TCD MS 2661/38(1).

82. *Higher Education Commission*, TCD MS 7185 (answers 3805, 3800, 3816).

83. *Hansard*, 3rd series, lxxx, pp. 392, 1256–7.

84. *Ibid.* 4th series, xlv, 313–19.

85. *Ibid.* 4th series, clxxxviii, 803–11, 847.

86. TCD Address to the Lord Lieutenant, TCD MUN/P1/2451; *Nineteenth Century*, xxxii, p. 35.

87. *The Times*, 28 Oct., 12 Nov. 1912; TCD MUN/P1/2834.

88. Beare to —, 28 Oct. 1912 (TCD MUN/P1/2822).

89. *Hansard*, 3rd series, ix, p. 624; xiii, pp. 606, 599; xiv, pp. 124, 191–4, 599–600, 627, 788.

90. B.K.P. Scaife, 'James McCullagh', in *Proc. RIA*, sect. C, no 3.

91. *The Times*, 6, 10, 19 Nov. 1868.

92. *Ibid.* 25 Jan. 1875.

93. *Ibid.* 1 July 1892.

94. *Hansard*, 3rd series, ccxcv, pp. 376–8.

95. *The Times*, 27 March 1858.

96. For this lecture see Lecky Papers (TCD MS), especially letters numbered 876, 699, 930, 931, 965, 1003, 1054, 1080, 1083. Also see *The Times*, 14 Nov. 1895.

97. *Hansard*, 3rd series, xlviii, p. 212.

98. *Ibid.* 3rd series, lxxxi, 104.

99. W.H. Lecky, *Historical and Political Essays* (1910), pp. 79–80; Lecky, *The Empire* (1893), p. 47.

100. *Hansard*, 4th series, xxxvii, pp. 494–5.

101. *Ibid.* lv, 456.

102. *Ibid.* lxvi, 1495.

103. *Dublin Evening Mail*, 31 July 1886.

104. *The Times*, 20 March, 7 April 1857.

105. *Ibid.* 6 Nov. 1868.

106. *Malvern College Register*; *The Times*, 7 July 1886.

107. A. Samuels to E. Carson, 27, 28 June 1915 (Carson Papers, PRONI D/1507/A/12/40, 41); T. West, *Horace Plunkett: Cooperation and Irish Politics* (1986), p. 59.

108. *Hansard*, 3rd series, cxcii, pp. 1772, 1776; 4th series, xiii, p. 1364.

109. *Ibid.* 3rd series, 645–1714.

110. *Ibid.* cxcv, 377–81.

111. *Ibid.* 5th series, cxxx, 2067.

112. *The Times,* 22 Oct. 1890.

113. *T.C.D.,* 19 Feb. 1910, 19 Feb. 1920.

114. *Hansard,* 5th series, xci, p. 528.

115. *Ibid.* cxxviii, 1300–08; cxxix, 188–9; cxxxiv, 1459; cxlix, 216; cl, 1351–8.

116. *T.C.D.,* 6 Feb. 1935, 8 Nov. 1946.

117. *Ibid.* 15 Nov. 1934.

118. *Trinity,* no. 3, p. 30.

119. *Ibid.* 3 Jan. 1964.

120. *Higher Education Commission* (TCD MS 7183) [answers 3488, 3495–7]; MS 7185 [answers 7151, 3769, 2210–13].

121. Provost's letter in *Higher Education Commission, evidence* (TCD MS 7183); *T.C.D.,* Nov. 1967.

122. *The Irish Times,* 26 June 1970.

123. Statutory instruments, no. 224 of 1997.

124. *Ibid.* 24 Jan. 1968.

125. *Dáil Éireann, Official Report,* cccclxx, 1393.

III The Dublin Society of United Irishmen, 1791–4

The eighteenth century was a very clubbable age and throughout the British Isles clubs – political or social or both combined – proliferated, some meeting in taverns, a few in impressive club houses. By joining a political club a man could enjoy congenial and, at times, convivial company and have a gratifying awareness that he was participating in the political process – after all, it could be said that in Great Britain economical reform, and in Ireland 'the constitution of 1782', were to a great extent obtained by associations or clubs (many Irish volunteer corps transforming themselves on occasion into political clubs).

In August 1789, following the regency crisis, an event that was regarded at the time as being of portentous significance, the Irish Whig Club was founded. Its object was to maintain the constitution of 1688 as re-established in Ireland in 1782, and to press for a number of anti-corruption measures. Its membership included a duke, an archbishop, a dozen other peers and fifty MPs. It held dinners with 'beef, claret and conversation': Charlemont, the Nestor of the Irish Whiggery, wrote, being 'no bad incentives to patriotism'.[1] To William Drennan, a fervid Ulster radical, the Whig club was merely 'an eating, drinking, aristocratical society without any fellow feeling with the commonalty'. He must have been pleased when in 1791 it was supplemented by the Whigs of the Capital, composed according to Drennan of 'good, honest men ... not so genteel as to gain admission' to the Whig club.[2] Charlemont pronounced that the members of the new club were 'wealthy and respectable citizens' and dined with them. But soon he must have been perturbed to hear that the club was planning to disseminate Paine's *Rights of Man*.[3]

At the close of 1789 Charlemont had been anxious that an Ulster Whig club should be established in Belfast, 'our political metropolis', and early in 1790 the Northern Whig Club was founded, its programme being similar to that of the Whig Club of Ireland, with the addition of parliamentary reform. Since its membership largely consisted of 'country gentlemen of superior rank and fortune', it was thought that 'very many good Whigs' in Belfast, feeling they would be socially over-shadowed, would decline to join it. So it was considered desirable that there should be a Belfast Whig club, but for some time nothing came of this suggestion. However, over a year later, in June 1791, it was rumoured that some Belfast Whigs were forming a society 'in imitation of the Whigs of the Capital'.[4] In fact what emerged was a definitely left-wing club. In the autumn of 1791 the secret committee of radically minded business men, 'not known nor suspected of co-operation', which directed 'the movements of Belfast', decided to form a political club, devoted to promoting parliamentary reform and Catholic Emancipation.[5] They must have been stimulated by the course of events in France, and they may have been influenced by a rhetorical paper circulated by Drennan, in which he urged the formation of a club, with 'something of the ceremonial of freemasonry', and with its objectives 'the rights of man, the greatest happiness of the greatest number' and the real independence of Ireland. They were certainly impressed by Theobald Wolfe Tone's recently published powerful pamphlet, 'An Argument on Behalf of the Catholics of Ireland'. Tone was convinced that English influence in Ireland could only be successfully opposed by a radically reformed parliament, and, 'a pioneer in political log-rolling',[6] he urged Protestants intent on reform and Catholics striving for Emancipation to unite to promote both causes.

Tone, and his friend Thomas Russell, who had been stationed in Belfast when serving as an army officer, were both present at the first meeting of the Belfast Society of United Irishmen held on 18 October. About thirty members were in attendance and they agreed on a declaration and resolutions, embodying the Society's principles and aims.[7] Ten days after this meeting Tone returned to Dublin, accompanied by Russell. They met James Napper Tandy, a strong radical and astute municipal politician. Tandy took up with alacrity the idea of a Dublin society on the Belfast model and on 9 November he assembled a group of eighteen composed of Protestants and Catholics with the Honourable Simon Butler, the brother of Lord Mountgarret, in the chair. The meeting balloted for one another and elected to membership another eighteen who were not present. It named itself the United Irishmen of Dublin and adopted the Belfast Society's declaration. According to Drennan, Tandy's 'object was a citizen's club – hence his dislike of lawyers, orators and critics'.[8]

But if Tandy hoped to dominate the new Society he was soon disappointed, a number of lawyers and other professional men being elected to membership. At the second meeting of the Society, Drennan proposed that every newly elected member should, on being admitted, publicly pledge himself to forward the Society's objectives. Tone, Russell and Stokes, a fellow of Trinity, opposed the proposed test as being too rhetorical and likely to discourage some potential members. Tandy robustly retorted that the Society would be better off without them. Drennan's proposal was accepted but by April 1792, according to Thomas Collins, 'it was in contemplation to abolish the test' as it prevented a number of warm friends of reform from joining. Two months earlier Drennan himself had privately pronounced that the test had advantages and disadvantages. 'It has', he wrote, 'kept out many able men here [in Dublin], chiefly lawyers and the society is not as genteel as it might be without it, chiefly composed of catholics.' However, the test was not abolished and the discussion about it reveals there could be two conceptions of the Society – a body of dedicated activists or a broadly based pressure group. It also shows a proclivity to dwell at length on forms and procedure.

It is probably safe to say that no contemporary radical club in the British Isles is better documented than the Dublin Society of United Irishmen. It published a number of manifestos. It was referred to in the House of Commons, and two of its members, William Drennan and Thomas Collins, wrote in some detail about its proceedings. Drennan, a romantic poet, a radical publicist and a surgeon, was, in his own words, 'a democrat without being popular … social in his mind yet repulsive in his manners';[9] he was diffident, high-minded and courageous. A very loyal and somewhat acerbic member of the Society, he frequently, and at times rather sharply, commented on its proceedings in his correspondence with his sister and brother-in-law in Belfast. Thomas Collins, an unsuccessful businessman (linen draper) joined the Society shortly after its foundation, and from December 1791 was supplying John Giffard, a senior revenue official and a leader of the government interest in the city, with information about its proceedings which seems to have been passed on to Edward Cooke, an under-secretary. French events had reminded men in power that discontent could develop into sedition, so it was advisable to keep a watch on radicals and reformers. Collins' regular reports were models of their kind – crisp, clear and well-arranged. They are spiced with malice (Collins clearly wished to preserve a sense of superiority to his political associates) and naturally, to enhance his value, he stressed what he saw as revolutionary symptoms in the Society's proceedings. Also, he was very critical of the Catholics in the Society, an attitude he shared with Drennan. To preserve his self-respect he occasionally offered political advice to his employers – making interesting suggestions for fiscal changes while he was dodging his creditors.[10]

The Society, which flourished for two and a half years, met at 8 p.m. on Fridays, at first in the Music Hall, Fishamble Street, and then from 23 November 1792 in the Tailors Hall in Back Lane. The Society had a president, a secretary and a treasurer, each elected for a three-month term. Members were elected by ballot. Candidates were proposed and seconded and from February 1792 a candidate, before being balloted for, had to deposit his admission fee of one guinea with the Society. If he was resident in Dublin and failed to take the test within a fortnight of election, he would not be considered a member. The Society's proceedings were conducted on formal lines with great attention to procedure and its rules (revised in October 1792). It had a number of committees, on finance, publications, penal laws, and the expediency of the war (1793).[11] It is clear that a fair amount of time was absorbed in the management of the Society, its 'private business' and, as shall be seen, in disputes with the authorities. However, it was primarily an opinion-forming Society. Its members were committed radicals, clarifying their views in debate and discussing manifestos, setting out radical principles and vigorously criticizing those in power. Sometimes there was a warm debate. For instance when, in December 1792, the Society was asked to resolve that it would resist the parliamentary proceedings against Tandy, a few alarmed lawyers stressed that it should be made quite clear that only legal resistance was contemplated. Then in January 1793, when an address of thanks to the King for making concessions to the Catholics was moved, Drennan, who was presiding, said he would leave the chair rather than agree to the adoption of the address, unless a phrase implying that the Society was attached to 'the existing constitution' was omitted. This, he remarked, 'produced observation in plenty', but in the end he prevailed. In the following February, when a member used the term 'citizen president', Thomas Emmet 'at great length completely showed the impropriety of adopting such new appellations as inconsistent with our professed creed'. A year later there was another debate on terminology – whether, in an address to Hamilton Rowan, the abbreviation 'Esq.' should be appended to his name. It was.[12]

Naturally, the Society produced its own plan of parliamentary reform. In January 1793 it appointed a committee of twenty-one to draft a scheme. This committee, impressed by Emmet's 'great eloquence', decided by eleven to nine that there should not be a property qualification, a decision which Drennan thought 'premature, impolitic and impracticable'. When in January 1794 the Society debated the plan, an amendment substituting the ballot for *viva voce* voting was rejected. A number of members believed that it would 'only corrupt the morals of the people by holding out a mode of deception'. The Society had already considered publishing a collection of its manifestos and a 'small, neat volume' appeared in March 1794, containing the Society's addresses and resolutions, along with its plan for parliamentary reform and the proceedings in the suit of *Tandy v. Lord Westmorland* (of interest at least to lawyers) appeared in March 1794 – without a publisher's name.[13]

The Society corresponded with a number of like-minded bodies: the four United Irishmen's societies in Belfast, United Irishmen's societies in about eight other provincial Irish centres, the Scottish convention (meeting in Edinburgh), the Norwich Revolution Society, the Derby Political Society, the Friends of the People in London, which offered 'a sort of honorary seating there to any of our members when in London'. The Society displayed its solidity with British radicalism by electing Thomas Paine to honorary membership and by expressing its sympathy with Joseph Priestly and Thomas Muir in their travails.[14] The Society also reacted vigorously when an English political organization, The Association for Preserving Liberty and Property against Republicans and Levellers, called for the suppression of seditious publications, denouncing 'speculative men who have conceived ideas of perfection which never yet were known in the world' and who infused into ignorant men causes of discontent, some of which were 'wholly imaginary', others inseparably belonging to civil society. The Dublin Society of United Irishmen responded by asking their members to write to their country correspondents cautioning them against 'the artifices of a corrupt administration'.[15]

Nearer home, in December 1792 the Society sent a deputation of five members to the Catholic Convention to assure that it could 'rely on our zealous co-operation'. Hamilton Rowan, the leader of the deputation, hoped to be invited to address the Convention, but the Catholics who were preparing for negotiations with the government tended, Drennan irritably exclaimed, to regard the United Irishmen as 'republicans and sinners', and the deputation, though politely received, did not get further than an antechamber.[16] The Society was happier in its dealings with an important section of the Dublin working class. In March 1793 Dr Burke proposed that as Irish trade was likely to suffer owing to the war, 'to give bread to thousands of our famishing artizans', the Society should pledge itself to 'the consumption of Irish manufactures *only*'. His proposal seems to have been accepted by the Society in spite of some opposition from members who were importers of English goods, and a few days later the Liberty broadcloth weavers addressed the Society, thanking it for its non-consumption resolution. An answer to the weavers' address was prepared but 'it was withdrawn', it being contended, according to Collins, that if it were published the Society's enemies would say it was reduced to addressing a mob.[17]

From early 1792 the Society became involved in a series of confutations with parliament and with the administration. The Society, or at least its more pugnacious members, threw itself into these conflicts *con amore*. Battling against authority was exhilarating, attracted desirable publicity and offered opportunities for demonstrating that the defenders of the established order were capable of violating the constitution. In February 1792 Toler, the Solicitor-General, a tough, hard-hitting lawyer, referred in the House of Commons to 'political quacks' who had the 'countenance' (approval) of Napper Tandy. Later in the debate Toler explained that he was referring to that 'blasted society', the United Irishmen.

The reference to Tandy did not require an explanation, his features were distinctive: Drennan once wrote of him as 'grinning most ghastly smiles'.[18] Tandy at once sent 'a friend' to Toler to demand an explanation, which Toler most pointedly refused to give. However, Tandy then refrained from challenging him, ostensibly on the grounds that if he did so he might be charged with a breach of parliamentary privilege. The matter was taken up by the House of Commons and Tandy was summoned to the Bar. He escaped from the messenger sent by the Sergeant at Arms to arrest him by scrambling through a window, and evaded arrest until the last day of the session, was brought to the Bar, committed to Newgate and almost immediately released on the prorogation of parliament. Eighteenth-century gentlemen were very ready to dwell with pleasurable solemnity on the issues arising from an affair of honour and Tandy's conduct seems to have been severely criticized even in radical circles. 'Poor Tandy', Drennan reflected, 'after eighteen years' struggle against his own interest in the public cause has nearly lost his reputation as a gentleman in a quarter of an hour'.[19] The Society, feeling that it must not display timidity, took up Tandy's cause. It passed motions challenging parliamentary privilege and questioning the legality of Tandy's arrest. A committee was appointed to manage the question.[20] and when Tandy sued the Lord Lieutenant, Lord Westmorland, in the Court of Common Pleas for issuing the proclamation for his apprehension he was represented by four barristers, all members of the Dublin Society of United Irishmen (Emmet, Butler, McNally and G.J. Browne). They argued that Westmorland was not Lord Lieutenant because he had been appointed under the English great seal. This argument would have had such far-reaching consequences that it is scarcely surprising that the judges held that they had judicial knowledge that Lord Westmorland was Lord Lieutenant. It was also argued by Tandy's council that the Lord Lieutenant could be sued for an 'act of state'. The court held that this was not so; any act of state would be countersigned by a responsible minister.

At the end of February 1793 the Society published an address attacking the House of Lords committee appointed to inquire into the disturbances in several counties. Butler and Oliver Bond, who signed the address as president and secretary, were summoned before the House and sentenced to six months' imprisonment in Newgate and fined £500 each. The Society agreed to pay the fines and meet Butler and Bond's expenses in Newgate. This turned out to be an onerous commitment. Butler and Bond entertained generously, each in turn giving in his room a dinner for eight persons. They seem to have ordered quantities of good food, 'all the rarities of the season', and their wine bill was large. Great efforts had to be made to obtain payments or promises of subscriptions to the Butler-Bond fund and the Society appointed collectors and for a short time met twice weekly until the full sum was raised. Indeed it was even rumoured that the debt had discouraged persons from joining the Society.[21] On their release from prison Butler and Bond were entertained by the Society at 'an uncommonly splendid dinner' with a long list of political toasts in the Druid's Head tavern. One member characteristically did not attend: William Drennan. On the evening of the dinner he went to see *The Grecian Daughter* at the theatre, 'where I admired and wept for two shillings what would have cost me three crowns to get drunk at the other'.[22] A few weeks after Butler and Bond were sent to Newgate, another member of the Society, Dr James Reynolds, on refusing to give evidence to the House of Lords committee was sent to Kilmainham, where he had a very large room and liberty to walk in the garden, until the end of the session. A deputation from the Society presented him with a consolatory address and it was planned that a group of members in turn should give a daily dinner to Reynolds.[23] In February 1794 Hamilton Rowan was at last brought to trial for distributing in December 1792 the Society's address to the volunteers. The Society voted an address of condolence and sent a deputation to wait on him in Newgate.[24]

[1] Entry of George IV into Dublin, August 1821. (Kildare Street and University Club)

[2] Entry of Queen Victoria into Dublin, April 1900. (Board of TCD)

[3] King Edward VII and Queen Alexandra in procession, with members of the household carrying white staves, July 1903. (Board of TCD)

[4] The Viceroy and Lady Aberdeen with staff at Dublin Castle, *c.* 1905. (*We Twa: Reminiscences of Lord and Lady Aberdeen*, vol. ii [1925], p. 176.)

[5] Arthur Browne
(1756–1805) by Hugh
Douglas Hamilton.
(Board of TCD)

[6] William Lecky
(1838–1903) facing the
Atlantic Ocean, March
1899. (Board of TCD)

[7] Napper Tandy (1740–1803), October 1784. (Board of TCD)

[8] Tailors Hall, Dublin. (Copyright Alice Lacy)

[9] James Butler, 2nd Duke of
Ormonde, Lord Lieutenant
1703–7, 1710–13. (From the
studio of Sir Godfrey Kneller)

[10] John Hely-Hutchinson (1724–94), by Joseph Peacock. (Board of TCD)

[11] Edward Carson (1854–1935). (*Vanity Fair*)

[12] New Square, which shows the back of the Rubrics (or Rue Bricks) and the window of no. 25 at which Edward Forde was killed. (Board of TCD)

[13] John Barrett (1754?–1821), by G.F. Joseph. (Board of TCD)

Another member of the Society involved in legal proceedings over the address to the volunteers was William Paulet Carey, the editor of the *National Evening Star*. Carey, a Catholic, was a poet, an artist and a political journalist. An enthusiastic radical, he was consequential, sensitive and, certainly in print and probably in conversation, excessively fluent. Already threatened with a prosecution for publishing an extract from the *Northern Star* early in 1792, he was charged with publishing the Society's address to the volunteers a year later. In November 1792 the Society, on the recommendation of a committee, agreed to support him, and at the end of March 1793, drawing attention to the prosecution being carried on against him, he asked for pecuniary help. His case was referred to a committee which seems to have been sympathetic but ineffective (the Society's resources having been sorely taxed by the Butler-Bond episode). Carey asked the Society to agree to reimburse his bailsmen so that he could flee the country. The matter was adjourned; anonymous letters referring to the matter appeared in the *Morning Post*. Carey was summoned to the next meeting of the Society and called on to state if he was the author. He replied that he would not incriminate himself but that he heartily approved of the letters. Having compared the Society to a House of Lords committee, he was immediately expelled. 'If Councellor Sheares adheres to his *Parisian* system of *equality*', Collins wrote, 'he must fight the dirty printer as the lie passed between them,' and the latter threatened a challenge.[25] Instead of issuing a challenge, Carey published a bulky pamphlet, passionately attacking the Society. He had, he contended, been the victim of snobbery. The professional men who dominated the Society looked down on the men from behind their counters. He warned the Society against men who were professionally engaged in making truth appear as falsehood, and he stated that he hoped to establish a newspaper which would appeal to 'the unbiased part of the community'. Six months later Carey was the principal Crown witness when Drennan was put on trial for being responsible for the publication of the Society's address to the volunteers. After Carey was pulverized in cross-examination by Curran, Drennan was acquitted and Carey soon left for England. There, full of 'simplicity and earnestness', he became well-known and respected in the art world.[26]

At the end of its first year in November 1792 the Dublin Society of United Irishmen was in a flourishing condition. Membership was growing, attendance was good and Irish radicals could eye the political future with cheerful confidence. The Catholic agitation was gathering strength and a Catholic Convention met in Dublin in December 1792. In Ulster, the heartland of Irish radicalism, a provincial reform convention was being organized, the forerunner, it was expected, of a national reform convention. In Ulster and in Dublin the volunteers were aggressively active. But within a few months the scene had significantly changed. The Irish administration, by a combination of concessions and firmness, had conciliated some of its critics and crippled its more extreme opponents; and with the outbreak of war against revolutionary France, large sections of the community rallied round the government in defence of King and country.

From March 1793 attendance at meetings of the Dublin Society of United Irishmen fell off and in August (with some Catholic members expressing the opinion that the Society was 'imprudent'), the possibility of its dissolution was in the air.[27] Some members may have felt that the reform agitation should be suspended for the duration of the war. Others, at a time when ardent Conservatives tended to see radicalism as akin to treason, may have become worried about their career prospects. Almost certainly, the Society was menaced by apathy, insidious enemy of all voluntary associations. In the instance of the Dublin Society, apathy was generated by boredom. Busy men must have grown tired of listening to fine-spun argument over procedural questions and the wording of manifestos. As early as August 1792 a very keen member, Simon Butler, declared that they 'ought to do something more than meeting constantly for the purpose of balloting for members'. His remedies, however, were to create a committee to revise the constitution of the Society and to issue addresses to the people.[28] It is then easy to understand why a number of members, after a hard day's work, sought relaxation elsewhere rather than attend a meeting in the Tailors Hall.

From the close of 1793 efforts were being made to revive the energies of the Society by tightening up its organization. At the end of November it was resolved that members who did not pay their arrears within a month should be reported as defaulters. At the beginning of February 1794 a Belfast member, Samuel Neilson, told the Society that there were traitors in its ranks who were sending information to the Castle. He suggested that a committee should be appointed that would be empowered to transact the Society's business and it was also suggested that there should be a committee to purge the Society of suspected members. To all this, Simon Butler responded that he wished their meetings were open to the public because there was nothing unconstitutional in their debates.[29]

Nevertheless, three weeks later John Sheares said that he intended to propose a new ballot for the whole Society. But at the next meeting he withdrew this proposal. In March he suggested the appointment of a committee empowered to convene the Society at a moment's notice because he had heard that it was the government's intention 'to put down the Society'. Again he seems to have dropped his proposal.[30] Six weeks later, on 9 May, Surgeon Wright said that he intended to propose that the Society should appoint a committee to scrutinize 'the character and conduct of its members and of all other persons in the city who profess patriotism'.[31] But the night his motion was due for discussion, the meeting was forcibly interrupted. On 28 April the Rev. William Jackson, a French agent who had discussed Irish conditions with two prominent members of the Society, Rowan (still in Newgate), and Tone were arrested. Rowan immediately escaped from Newgate and fled the country, and Tone had to admit that he had discussed Irish political trends with Jackson.

The government now had grounds for taking the offensive and on Friday, 23 May, the Tailors Hall was raided by the Chief Commissioner of the Dublin Police, accompanied by the high sheriffs for the city and a party of police officers. The Society was dissolved, presumably as an illegal assembly, and its books and papers seized.[32] Some members wanted to challenge the authorities by adjourning the meeting to a tavern but nothing seems to have been done until August when a committee of twenty-one, named on 'the night of the dispersion', started to revise the membership list. This committee reballoted the whole Society, rejecting one in five, 'twice as bad as a decimation'.

In October about fifty members gathered at Henry Jackson's

house in Church Street, where two courses of action were suggested. John Sheares proposed that the Society should be organized in groups of fifteen, each group sending a delegate to a central committee, a scheme which would have protected the Society against informers and government interference. Simon Butler's approach was different. He 'highly reprobated skulking in holes and corners'. He wanted the Society to meet at its usual meeting-place and, if the government tried to suppress it, to fight the issue in the courts. Butler carried his proposal by a large majority but the Society, as hitherto conducted, faded out.[33] Some of the more extreme members continued to meet in private and numerous radical, indeed revolutionary societies – United Irish societies, Defender societies – were springing up. These societies were popular associations. They were secret, with revolutionary objectives, and they were prepared to contemplate direct action.[34] Irish political conditions in the late 1790s were not propitious for an earnest, middle-class debating society led by men with intellectual leanings, eager to expound in polished prose how radical ideals and ideas could be applied in contemporary Ireland.

Not only are the aims and activities of the Dublin Society of United Irishmen well documented but there is a remarkable amount of material available relating to its membership. As regards the membership of the Society, Collins is an invaluable source. He, of course, mentions the names of those who took a prominent part in its proceedings, or whose presence attracted his attention. He often gives the names of those who took the test. Furthermore, he frequently encloses in his reports his own summons to the meeting. This summons, which was sent by the secretary to every member, was a printed slip of paper containing not only the date, time, and place of the next meeting, but also the names of the candidates for membership and those of their proposers. Collins nearly always annotated these papers, indicating whether the candidate had been admitted, rejected, or withdrawn. Usually a larger bracket, and the word 'admitted' sufficed. There are thirty-five of these summonses in the Rebellion Papers,[35] and interestingly enough there is one in the Home Office Papers, in the English Public Record Office, enclosed in a letter to Nepean.[36] Now Collins, as Cooke remarked, was a very capable man, and from time to time he sent the government a list of the members of the Society, compiled from memory. There are five of these lists in the Rebellion Papers. The shortest contains sixty-five names, the longest a hundred.[37]

From what can be described as the 'Collins sources', we get over 360 names of persons who were at least admitted into the Society. And this collection helps us to understand what appears to be another source. In the Rebellion Papers there is a large document consisting of eight pages of tough paper, containing 300 names in alphabetical order, with addresses and notes as to sums promised and paid. On the back is the date 20 June 1793, and the names of a dozen collectors, all keen members of the Dublin Society of United Irishmen. Unfortunately, the part of the document where one might expect to find a title or endorsement has been torn or burned away. But nine-tenths of the names, arranged in alphabetical order, are those of persons whom we know to have been members of the Society, and it seems almost certain that the list is a list of members drawn up in connection with the Society's expensive efforts to assist Butler and Bond in 1793.[38]

These sources taken together give between 400 and 425 names.[39] Can this be regarded as approximately the total membership of the Society? Here again we have to rely on Collins. He tells us that in December 1791, fifty-six members had signed the roll, and by August 1792, 146 had done so. By the end of 1792 the Society had a membership of 240, and in March 1793 he wrote that he had learned from a roll-call of the Society 'that there are about 350 names on the Books but several of them have not signed the Rolls'. This last remark is significant, for as early as February 1792, the Society had resolved that any gentleman who had been elected, and had not signed the roll and taken the test within a fortnight of that date would, unless he had a good excuse, cease to be a member. So already we must presume that some of those who had been elected had not bothered to go further. Thus there are several uncertain factors to be taken into account. Assuming that a man's name should have been entered in the books immediately after his election, we cannot discover from Collins how many people were admitted into the Society, for the latest figure he gives is the one just quoted for March 1793, and we know the names of about twelve persons admitted between that date and the dissolution of the Society by the police in May 1794.[40] Others were possibly admitted between those two dates, and, on the other hand, some of those whom we know to have been admitted before March 1793 may for some reason not have been entered on the books. Thus it cannot be claimed that the 400-odd names which have been mentioned constitute a definitive list of the Society. But they probably include the names of the great majority of those who sought, or were considered by their friends to be worthy of, membership. Besides, by taking the names on the five lists compiled by Collins, and adding to them the names of proposers and others who took part in the Society's business, we can compile a list of what might be called the active members of the Society. This list, after overlapping has been eliminated, comprises 200 names. It probably includes everybody who at any time regularly attended the meetings. It appears from Collins's figures that the average attendance at a meeting up to the end of November 1792 was only fifty-six, and though, while the Catholic Convention was sitting, it rose to nearly ninety, from the end of April 1793 it was only about forty.

The great majority of the Society's members lived in Dublin, but nearly fifty came from other parts of Ireland. Some of these were active in local politics. Others were members of the Catholic Convention. Also, the election of Thomas Paine and Thomas Muir to membership reminds us that the Society was the local manifestation of a widespread radical movement.

As to religion, it can be ascertained that 120 of the members were Protestants and 115 were Catholics. Of the active members, eighty can be identified as Protestants and seventy-three as Catholics. If we have here a fair sample, it seems that the Society was almost equally divided between the two denominations.

Two things that stand out from the following table are the number of professional men in the Society, and the number of members connected with the manufacture and sale of cloth. If the legal and medical elements are taken, along with the booksellers and a few miscellaneous individuals, it appears that the 'intellectuals' in the Society numbered ninety-nine (of the active members, sixty-three). In addition, many of the presidents and secretaries of the Society were drawn from their ranks, and they controlled the various committees.

Occupations of the Majority of the Members

Apothecaries	6	Land-surveyor	1
Attorneys	30	Leather-sellers	2
Barristers	28	Music-seller	1
Biscuit-baker	1	Merchants	32
Booksellers and printers	14	Paper-maker	1
Builders	4	Perfume-seller	1
Butchers	2	Medical men	19
Captain of a merchantman	1	Pin-maker	1
Chandlers	7	Pump-borer	1
Cloth merchants	67	Saddler	1
Cooper	1	Salesmasters	2
Distillers and brewers	12	Schoolmaster	1
Fellow of TCD	1	Shoemakers	4
Flour-factors	3	Ship-broker	1
Glovers	2	Slater	1
Grocers	15	Soldiers	6
Haberdasher	1	Tanners	11
Hatters	3	Tavern-keeper	1
Hosier	1	Textile-manufacturers	31
Ironfounder	1	Timber-merchant	1
Ironmongers	6	Tailors	4
Jewellers	6	Wine-merchants	4

As to the number of members connected with the clothing trade, it can be seen that ninety-nine members at least were cloth merchants or manufacturers (of the active members, fifty-four). An explanation of this is, of course, that the manufacture and sale of cloth was an important Irish industry, and one would expect to find a number of persons connected with it in any large group of Irish businessmen. But there was probably another reason. From the time when Ireland obtained legislative independence there had been a persistent and at times vociferous agitation in favour of protection for Irish industries. And the clothing industry, which was peculiarly exposed to English competition, was particularly insistent in its demands. It might be said that the cloth merchant would have no particular interest in reform, for presumably it would not matter to him whose cloth he sold. But it is worth noting that the distinction between the merchant and the manufacturer does not seem to have been a rigid one. Many of the merchants were probably more closely connected, by both practical and sentimental ties, with Irish rather than English manufacturers. It need scarcely be said that other industrialists in the Society would also have benefited if English competition had been hindered by legislative action. But *a priori* argument is apt to be deceptive as well as attractive, and fortunately we have some concrete evidence as to the attitude of some of the members to the tariff question.

Napper Tandy, one of the founders of the Society, was a leader of the great outburst of protectionist agitation, which had begun in 1783.[41] In 1784 the master tailors of Dublin passed resolutions emphasizing the necessity of promoting the use of Irish manufactures; four of the signatories later became members of the Dublin Society of United Irishmen. Eleven silk mercers swore that they would not deal in English or foreign silk for four years unless protection was granted; four of them were later members of the Society.[42] The names of six other future members can be seen appended to a similar resolution of the woollen drapers.[43] And Nicholas Butler, a jeweller who was to be a prominent member, produced, in 1784, an emblematic button to be worn with Irish cloth. More evidence of the same kind can be adduced, but probably enough has been said to show that, to some Irish radicals, a reformed parliament would have connoted amongst other things a parliament of tariff reformers.

After classifying the members according to their occupations, the next task is clearly to try to determine their social and economic status. To begin with, it is unlikely that any of the members belonged to the working classes. All the non-professional men whose occupations we know seem to have had shops or establishments of their own. Of the remainder, about thirty were country gentlemen, and nearly forty were given an 'Esq.', which, in spite of Gibbons' complaint, was still a prerogative of well-established members of the middle class. Collins indeed talks once or twice of obscure persons being admitted to membership, but he is probably only being snobbish about small businessmen. Twice only he refers to an employee being a member of the Society, and in each case the member in question was a clerk.[44] If working men had been admitted, Collins would scarcely have failed to dwell on the fact. In this connection it is perhaps worth noticing that one of the leading members, Abraham Creighton, was involved publicly in a violent dispute with his journeymen. It may be added that the bourgeois character of the Society is reflected in its patronizingly friendly addresses to the people, and is also shown by the fact that the adoption of the principle of universal suffrage (which was only accepted by the committee on reform by a narrow majority) seems to have caused a considerable withdrawal of members.[45] Moreover, a fair number of the members appear to have been comfortably off. Several were enterprising and successful businessmen, a few were landed gentlemen of some standing, and some of the Dublin tradesmen possessed landed or housing property. Thus, even though about forty-five of the members went bankrupt during the period 1788–1803, it would be a mistake to regard the Society as composed of failures and misfits.

In conclusion, it is perhaps worth looking for a moment at the later political careers of those members about whom information is available. Five certainly, and possibly seven, gave information to the government. We know of thirteen who diverged completely from the radical line. Three of these resigned formally from the Society; several others served in the Crown forces during the '98 Rebellion. It is likely that a number of others supported the government, for McNally, who was well informed, declared during the Rebellion that many who 'were of the first Society of United Irishmen of Dublin' were thoroughly opposed to the idea of securing parliamentary reform and Catholic Emancipation by force, and, being Protestants, were terrified at the thought of 'a banditti of Roman Catholics' entering the city.[46] On the other hand, we know from different sources that at least seventy of the members were concerned or sympathized with the activities of the extreme radicals during this period. Admittedly, some of the evidence should be scrutinized carefully, for panic-stricken Conservatives and mercenary or malicious informers were apt to accuse anyone of known radical proclivities of sedition. Nevertheless it is safe to say that over fifty members seem to have come to the conclusion that their objectives could only be gained by direct action, and to have taken part in organizing the country for what became an armed rising. Others wrote or published radical propaganda or gave legal or financial assistance to political prisoners.

NOTES

1. *Charlemont MSS*, HMC, ii, p. 105.
2. *The Drennan-McTier Letters*, ed. J. Agnew, i (1998), p. 357. The Agnew edition of the Drennan-McTier letters will henceforth be referred to as '*Drennan Letters*'.
3. *Charlemont MSS*, HMC, ii, pp. 133, 136.
4. *Charlemont MSS*, HMC, ii, pp. 110, 117, 140.
5. *The Writings of T.W. Tone*, eds T.W. Moody, R.B. McDowell and C. Woods, i (1998), pp. 131.
6. C.L. Falkiner, *Studies in History and Biography* (1902), p. 37.
7. *The Writings of T.W. Tone*, i, pp. 131–48.
8. *Drennan Letters*, i, p. 370
9. *Ibid*. i, p. 537.
10. Collins' reports and letters are printed in 'Proceedings of the Dublin Society of United Irishmen', ed. R.B. McDowell, *Analecta Hibernica*, xvii. Henceforth referred to as 'Collins' Reports'.
11. Collins' Reports, pp. 7, 34, 63, 73, 87, 114.
12. *Ibid*. pp. 52–3, 59, 112; *Drennan Letters*, pp. 465–6, 495.
13. *Drennan Letters*, p. 471; Collins' Reports, pp. 87, 99, 105, 121.
14. Collins' Reports, pp. 8, 19, 23, 26, 30, 47, 51, 58, 69; *Drennan Letters*, p. 502.
15. *Annual Register, 1792*, pp. 92–4; Collins' Reports, p. 47.
16. *Drennan Letters*, p. 444–5.
17. *Ibid*. p. 508; Collins' Reports, p. 70.
18. *Drennan Letters*, p. 349.
19. *Ibid*. i, p. 398.
20. Collins' Reports, p. 20.
21. *Ibid*. pp. 74, 81, 85; *Drennan Letters*, i, pp. 512, 536.
22. *Ibid*. pp. 97–8; *Ibid*. i, p. 583.
23. *Ibid*. p. 71; *Ibid*. i, pp. 505–8.
24. *Ibid*. pp. 110–11.
25. *Ibid*. p. 93.
26. W.P. Carey, *An Appeal to the People of Ireland* (Dublin, 1794); Collins' Reports, pp. 41, 71–3, 87, 91; *Gentleman's Magazine*, NS, xvii, p. 139.
27. *Drennan Letters*, p. 558.
28. Collins' Reports, p. 30.
29. *Ibid*. p. 108.
30. *Ibid*. pp. 111–12, 119.
31. *Ibid*. pp. 127–8.

32. *Ibid.* p. 128.

33. *Drennan Letters*, ii, pp. 85, 90–3, 107. Sheares' scheme for organizing the Society in groups seems to have been modelled on the plans adopted by the London Corresponding Society with its members grouped in divisions, each of which sent a delegate to the general committee (*First Report of the Committee of Secrecy*, H.C. 1794, p. 6).

34. See N.J. Curtin, 'The Transformation of the Society of the United Irishmen into a Mass-Based Revolutionary Organization', in *IHS*, xxiv, pp. 463–92.

35. In the National Archives of Ireland. They are the most important collections of archive material relating to the radical movement from 1790 to 1803, and include all the known communications from Collins to the government.

36. Lauzun to Nepean, 3 Dec. 1793 (PRO, HO/100/34).

37. NAI Rebellion Papers, 620/54/12, 13, 18, 20.

38. Dr Drennan's subscription as given in the list is the same sum as he stated to his sister that he had given to the fund for Butler and Bond (*Drennan Letters*, p. 142). From notes on the side it is possible that the list was later used in connection with a contemplated purge of the Society.

39. Cooke to Nepean, 26 May 1794 (PRO, HO/100/52).

40. *Ibid.*

41. *Volunteer Journal* (Dublin), 12 April 1784.

42. *Ibid.* 7 July 1784.

43. *Ibid.* 19 July 1784.

44. NAI Rebellion Papers, 620/20/49, and notes on Samuel Otway and James O'Bryan in the appendix.

45. Drennan Letters, p. 122, and note on James Tandy in the appendix.

46. J.W. [i.e. Leonard McNally] to —, undated, probably June 1798 (NAI, Rebellion Papers, 620/10).

IV Ireland and England

A lmost 800 years ago a small force of men-at-arms and bowmen, led by a group of Welsh marcher lords, intervened vigorously in Irish politics, and began the process of forging innumerable links between Great Britain and Ireland. Since then, the two islands have been in close, continuous and significant contact. But while the influence of England on Ireland has been immense, the impact of Ireland on England has been sporadic and limited. To discuss the former would be to drive a wide corridor through Irish history: dealing with the latter is a question of following up a number of threads, not always easily discernible in the general pattern of British history.

Some features, of course, stand out boldly. For instance, British expansion overseas first began in Ireland. It was there that English and Scottish settlers acquired land and learned the technique of settlement, and their successful endeavours stimulated the colonizing impulse in their fellow countrymen. Again, the first large expeditionary force maintained by England in modern times was the Elizabethan army in Ireland – almost four times as large, by the way, as the force sent at about the same time to assist the Dutch. And Irish armies of course played an important part in seventeenth-century English history. One of the most potent forces in seventeenth-century English politics was the fear of popery. This fear was intensified by the belief that the Crown might secure the support of a Catholic army from Ireland. Indeed, in James II's reign, Irish Catholic regiments were encamped on Hounslow Heath and their presence was of considerable propaganda value to the Whigs. A night long-remembered in London history was 'Irish night', 12–14

December O.S. 1688, when frightening rumour spread throughout the city that the Irish regiments were running amuck.

By the close of the seventeenth century, however, the danger of a Catholic Ireland interfering in British politics had been eliminated. The Protestant ascendancy was firmly established in Ireland, and Ireland was, in the words of Blackstone, 'a dependent, subordinate kingdom', 'conquered, planted and governed' by England.¹ Ireland, of course, possessed a parliament of medieval origin, with two houses and a procedure closely resembling that of Westminster. But nevertheless this parliament had little more than the status of a colonial assembly. The Declaratory Act of 1720 enunciated that the British parliament was competent to legislate for Ireland and that the British House of Lords was the final court of appeal for Irish litigants. Poynings' Act (an Act passed by the Irish parliament in 1494) provided that legislation had to be initiated by the Irish Privy Council, and approved and possibly reshaped by the English Privy Council, before being placed before the Irish parliament. Moreover, the Irish executive, which controlled the patronage of the Crown in Ireland, was appointed by the British government. During the American War of Independence – that great colonial rebellion that broke up the first British empire – the Irish parliament protested against the legislative restraints to which it was subject. Since it moved considerably more slowly than either Irish public opinion or the Continental Congress, by the time its demands were formulated and pressed, Great Britain, fighting with mixed success on two fronts, was in a conciliatory mood. In 1782 the Declaratory Act was repealed, Poynings' Act was drastically amended, and theoretically Ireland became an independent country, sharing a common Crown with Great Britain. Co-ordination of policy between the two countries was, in practice, assured by the fact that the Irish executive continued to be appointed by the British government of the day, and by using the patronage it possessed, it managed to maintain control of the Irish parliament. But 'influence' was scarcely a reliable instrument for harmonizing British and Irish action in imperial concerns. It might be weakened by administrative or parliamentary reform, and even the unreformed Irish House of Commons, on three important occasions between 1782 and 1800 threw off ministerial control.

Pitt, from the time he became Prime Minister, was anxious to put Anglo-Irish relations on a safe and satisfactory footing. In 1785 he made a bold effort to create a community of mutual economic self-interest between the two countries by forming a common market. He was defeated by national suspicions and economic jealousies on both sides of the Irish Sea, and in the following decade Ireland became one of Great Britain's major problems. Catholic discontent, agrarian disturbances and radical agitation made Ireland during the war with revolutionary France one of the most vulnerable areas in the British Isles. In 1796 Wolfe Tone, the celebrated Irish radical, pressed the French government to send an expeditionary force to Ireland. In a couple of powerful memoranda, he argued that if an Irish republic were established as a result of French aid, Great Britain would be deprived of supplies and recruits. 'It is', Tone wrote, 'with the poor and hardy natives of Ireland that she mans her fleet and fills the ranks of army.'[2] Tone was indulging in pardonable exaggeration; nevertheless the population of Ireland was one-third of the total for the British Isles, and Ireland was also 'one of the great victualling centres of Europe'.[3] Moreover, though Tone did not trouble to make this point, if an Irish republic was established France would obtain a number of bases from which British commerce could be attacked and the west coast of Britain menaced. Carnot, possibly influenced to some extent by Tone, planned a descent on Ireland and in December 1796 a force of 14,000 under the command of Hoche sailed from Brest. The expedition was defeated by wind and weather, and in the following year a Dutch fleet, which might have escorted a force bound for Ireland, was defeated off the Texel by the blockading squadron. And from then on the French, when contemplating an invasion of the British Isles, concentrated on plans for throwing a force across the English Channel. But until the close of the Napoleonic wars the British government was very conscious of the danger that the French would launch an expedition against Ireland.

The threat of invasion and rebellion convinced Pitt that Ireland demanded immediate attention. His policy was a parliamentary union, which would both symbolically proclaim the indissoluble unity of the two islands, and to some extent, in practice, facilitate administrative co-operation. In addition, a union would tend to remove the deeper causes of discontent by opening the way for Catholic Emancipation and encouraging British capital investment in Ireland. It is important to remember that the Union was born of strategic necessity and was enacted in a time of crisis. So the Trojan horse, stocked with future problems and difficulties, slid remarkably easily into British political life. During the debates on the Union at Westminster, nationalism, the new force which was to dominate European history for the coming century, was ignored. British members of parliament quite appreciated that the Irish political community might possess strong institutional loyalties. But they showed no sign of realizing the power of a passionate belief in common historical and cultural ties. The classic expositions of nationalism were still to be penned. In any event, English nationalism, if intense, has always been to a great degree unconscious and implicit. But the advocates of Irish parliamentary independence were already trying to express what nationality meant, and in the 1840s the Young Irelanders were to expound in essays, speeches and ballads the full nationalist creed and spiritual experience – that all the activities of a community should be animated by the national spirit and should be directed to sustain in all its fullness the national being.

What was appreciated at the beginning of the nineteenth century was that Ireland differed strikingly from England in two respects – religious and economic. England and Scotland were overwhelmingly Protestant countries, and Protestantism was to be one of the fundamental components of the Victorian outlook. In Ireland about three-quarters of the population was Catholic, and their Catholicism had been tested and strengthened by generations of endurance. But there was a substantial Protestant minority, Protestants predominating in the landed world and in the industrial and prosperous north-east. Again, the industrial revolution affected the two islands very differently. During the nineteenth century England grew in economic power, importance and prosperity. Ireland, an agricultural country lacking coal and iron, saw much of its industry decline in the face of British competition: its ill-adjusted agrarian system was severely strained, and throughout the nineteenth century large parts of Ireland formed distressed areas. Economically backward and adjusting itself with difficulty to the new century, Ireland irritated and disturbed English opinion.

A decade after the Union one of the most sensitive of English thinkers, Samuel Coleridge, conversationally summed up his views on Ireland as follows: 'He represented the Irish as owing all they possessed to us. Their language, laws, all are English. The clothes which stick to their bloody back are ours. The serious point of this statement is simply this, that a people that are highly civilized ought to conquer and govern semi-barbarians for the common good, but then he confessed they should civilize their subjects.'[4] Thirty years later Carlyle, reminding his contemporaries with savage indignation of the daunting problems which confronted them, declared that the wretched Irish could not continue in a perennial ultra-savage form in the midst of civilization, but he added that justice to Ireland is 'a deep matter, an abysmal one, which no plummet of ours will sound'. And in a burst of testiness he wrote of the Irish as brawling, unreasonable people, whose industry was beggary.[5] Thackeray was moved to contemptuous pity by Ireland's pathetic mixture of poverty and pretentiousness. Cobden hoped that the English middle classes would profit by the lessons of history when dealing with the Irish, whom he compared to the Poles in the Russian empire or the negroes in the United States. 'The spectacle of Ireland', he wrote, 'operating like a cancer in the side of England, of Poland paralysing one arm of the giant that oppresses her – of the two millions of negroes in the United States', all reminded mankind that 'no deed of oppression could be perpetrated with impunity'.[6]

Forty years later Matthew Arnold dwelt on the failure of the philistine English middle classes – narrow, self-satisfied and insensitive – to handle the Irish question satisfactorily.[7] Tennyson, about the same time, wished that Ireland was in the middle of the Atlantic, a thousand miles from England, adding, 'I like the Irish – I admit the charm of their manners – but they are a frightful nuisance.' And he referred with brusque indignation to the Irishman's over-awareness of history. 'The Normans came over here', Tennyson remarked, 'and seized the country and in a hundred years the English had forgotten all about it. The same Normans went to Ireland and the Irish with their damnable unreasonableness are raging and foaming to this hour.'⁸ Ireland, in short, was a standing challenge to Victorian complacency, or rather to what was a much more marked quality of the Victorian mind – concern.

The force of this challenge was scarcely apparent when, a few months after the Union was enacted, the first MPs and peers from Ireland arrived at Westminster. In background and training they were remarkably similar to the other members of both Houses and they fitted in easily. Soon Grattan and Plunket were being acclaimed as outstanding debaters; within a few years another member of the old Irish House of Commons, George Ponsonby, became the leader of the Whig opposition. Castlereagh became Foreign Secretary, and Wellington, who as a young man had been a member of the Irish House of Commons, became Prime Minister. Until the 1870s the Irish landlords exercised considerable influence in parliamentary elections, though after Catholic Emancipation they had, in many constituencies, to share power with the Catholic priesthood. The result was that the Irish MPs were, on the whole, men who could be easily absorbed by the British party system. For instance Croker, the secretary of the Admiralty, sat for Downpatrick; Taylor, for seventeen years the Conservative chief whip, sat for County Dublin; Spring-Rice, who was to be Chancellor of the Exchequer, sat for Limerick; Fortescue, the president of the Board of Trade, sat for County Louth; and Phineas Finn, the hero of Trollope's great study of mid-Victorian politics, was an Irish MP.

O'Connell, who forced his way into the House of Commons in 1829 as the leader of a great protest movement, was significantly an exception. He and his small following ('his tail'), for a time, held aloof from the great English parties, and his political position was always a highly unconventional one. It might be claimed that O'Connell was the first great popular politician in the British Isles – the first parliamentarian to pay continuous attention to an outside public and to devote much thought and energy to building up a widespread organization. He kept in touch with his followers by forming associations and by undertaking annual speaking tours; he planned immense demonstrations, inspiring or intimidating, which were meant to display in a concrete form the weight of public opinion behind him; and he seems to have discovered the simple fact that making people pay a regular subscription greatly increases their loyalty to an organization – besides providing funds. And when his opponents depicted him as a brutal, blarneying beggar man, dependent on the support of a stunted peasantry, they were paying an involuntary tribute to the power that a demagogue and caucus manager could wield, once democracy was triumphant.

But O'Connell was working within a system still well removed from democracy, and he found it politic to ally himself for years with the Whigs. An independent, numerically strong, cohesive and influential Irish party in the House of Commons did not emerge until the political power of the Irish landlords had been undermined by the Ballot Act of 1872 and the Reform Act of 1884, which extended the franchise to the labourer in the counties. Conservatives recognized that both these Acts would have profound effects on Ireland, and their gloomy prophecies were soon fulfilled. In 1874 a group of determined 'Home Rulers' took their seats. In 1880 the Home Rule party numbered about sixty, and after the general election of 1885 Parnell led a tightly organized party of eighty-five. Cold, self-contained, clear-headed and commanding, Parnell used the instrument he had forged with ruthless skill, and by the mid-eighties he had made Home Rule the major issue of British politics.

The effect of Home Rule on British political life was far-reaching. It led to the great schism in the Liberal party. A split in that party had been expected for some time. Sooner or later it was assumed that the Whigs would break away from the more advanced Liberals, and as Chamberlain's power in the party waxed, the crisis was coming nearer. But in fact the schism that occurred in the spring of 1886 over Home Rule was along a jagged line. Some Whigs were converted to Home Rule. Some radicals were determined upholders of the parliamentary unity of the British Isles. The Liberal party, which seemed to be on the point of becoming a social reform party, found itself committed to an Irish policy which was not very popular in the constituencies, and aroused little enthusiasm amongst Liberal imperialists, nonconformists or social reformers. In the general election of 1906 the Liberals put Home Rule into cold storage and their overwhelming majority made it impossible for the Irish party to force them to introduce a Home Rule bill. But the battle for the budget left the Liberals dependent on the Irish parliamentary party in the House of Commons and the party's energies during its last years of office had to be devoted to pushing a Home Rule bill through parliament.

The Conservatives gained from their opponents' misfortunes. Chamberlain, forced by his position on the Irish question into an alliance with the Conservatives, successfully pressed them to adopt Liberal measures. This probably increased their hold on the widened electorate, and the Conservatives themselves, when resisting Home Rule and upholding strong government (combined with kindness) in Ireland, had a policy that expressed the party's instinctive loyalties. In an age of self-conscious imperialism the conception of a great unified empire, treating its more backward subjects with paternal care, could be expressed in domestic politics.

The great Home Rule debate was a fascinating one. Moral as well as political issues were involved. Emotions were deeply stirred. And, unlike subjects such as bimetallism and tariff reform, which called for a grasp of statistics and economic subtleties, Home Rule was an issue in which the facts were comparatively simple, and on which the discussion largely concerned political fundamentals. For instance, what was a nationality? (Balfour, in an ingenious essay, tried to prove that Irish nationality did not exist.[9]) Or what degree of national consciousness entitled a community to self-government? What rights had a minority to be considered? And the minority question raised more than one problem – the position of Ireland in the United Kingdom, the position of Northern unionists in Ireland, and that of Catholic nationalists in Ulster. Another question: to what extent should a great power allow the claims of a section of its people autonomy, if this would imperil its own strategic safety? It was often pointed out that Ireland was too near to Great Britain to be granted independence: any form of self-government, unionists believed, would lead to separation. Should parochialism or a wider patriotism be allowed to prevail? Salmon, the Provost of Trinity College Dublin, attacking Home Rule, said that there were 'a number of small men who would like small parliaments in which they might gain a celebrity which they could never gain in a wider competition'.[10] Matthew Arnold put the same argument more politely.

He said that 'the proper public field for an Irishman of signal ability is the imperial parliament'. 'He would', Arnold explained, be able 'to find scope for his facilities in an Irish parliament only by making it what it was not meant to be, and what it cannot be without danger. It will be a sensation Parliament – a Parliament of shocks and surprises.'[11]

Then there was the question: to what extent should qualitative as well as quantitative values be taken into account in politics? Unionists had to admit that a majority of the inhabitants of Ireland wanted Home Rule. But they pointed out repeatedly that the great bulk of the propertied and educated classes supported the Union. And this division seemed to extend across St George's Channel. Gladstone himself 'sorrowfully' had to admit that against Home Rule 'in profuse abundance were station, title, wealth, the professions ... in a word, the spirit and power of class'. And Goschen, a strong Conservative, summed up Gladstone's attitude on Home Rule in a couple of sentences: 'There are some old rafters holding the framework of British society together. But fling them into the fire.'[12] During the debates on the first Home Rule bill, British railway shareholders equated their own impending fate with that of the Irish landlords.[13] English socialists of the eighties sympathized with the Irish tenants in their struggle against their landlords (it need scarcely be said that the Irish tenant farmers were far from being socialists). The great Trafalgar Square riot in 1887, a striking demonstration of proletarian strength, was ostensibly a protest against William O'Brien's imprisonment: a Fabian coldly deplored the English out-of-work, whose coat was in pawn, rioting in Trafalgar Square in defence of Mr O'Brien's claim to dress like a gentleman when in gaol.[14]

Another very painful subject, the place of force in politics, was brought into prominence by the debates on the Irish question. One of the great British achievements in the years following the Glorious Revolution had been the elimination of violence from political life. In the eighteenth century it was established that an unsuccessful politician, instead of being forced to mount the scaffold, was given a peerage. It was accepted that all who were engaged in public life agreed on some fundamentals, and that problems should be solved by debate and compromise. But many Irishmen could not share these feelings. It was one of the Young Irelanders who in 1846 – the age of Peel – declaimed: 'Be it for the defence or be it for the assertion of a nation's liberty, I look upon the sword as a sacred weapon. And if it has sometimes reddened the shroud of the oppressor, like the anointed rod of the high priest, it has also at other times blossomed into flowers to deck the freeman's brow.'[15] And the Church of Ireland Bishop of Derry, addressing a unionist meeting in the Albert Hall in 1893, declared that many words had been spent upon metaphysical questions with regard to the lawfulness of resistance, but, 'The matter comes pretty much to this – that after all there are things which a strong race will hardly submit to, unless they are compelled.'[16] When Home Rule was impending, the unionists of Ulster showed their determination to offer well-organized resistance to an act of parliament they abhorred. And in the high Victorian age the Fenians tried to conduct a war in England, an incident at Chester in 1867 illustrating rather well the contrast between two attitudes to politics. The Fenians plotted to capture the Castle and seize the arms stored there for use in Ireland. When it was clear danger was impending, the local volunteer corps was called out. But there was considerable doubt whether they could legally be used. On the advice of the Home Office they were sworn in as special constables.[17]

Fortunately the Irish example has not spread to England. But in so far as there is British political thinking of the more passionate kind – a belief in 'direct action' – it must owe something to Ireland. And the repercussions of the Irish national struggle have had world-wide consequences for Great Britain. In 1886 Lecky warned Englishmen that a policy of surrender in Ireland would influence Indian opinion. 'Some of the most distinguished men who are or who have lately been connected with the government of India', he asserted, 'are watching with keen anxiety the triumphal progress of Irish dissatisfaction on account of the influence it is likely to have on that country.'[18] The Indian National Congress was formed in the same year as the Irish Home Rulers won their great electoral victory. Later Gandhi met Redmond in London. Nehru, as a young man visiting Dublin, was interested in the newly formed Sinn Féin movement, but respected his father's injunction not to go up to the North

to see the Belfast riots.[19] Throughout, the Indian nationalist movement was greatly encouraged by the happenings in Ireland.

In the United States a large Irish-American community, which
because of religious and social reasons preserved its identity beyond
the first generation, was traditionally anti-English. An Irish-American rarely attained Cabinet rank or sat in the Senate, but the Irish-
American played a big part in the political machines which mustered votes. The Irishman in America, according to Kipling, pre-
eminently knew how to work a saloon parliament '... he has no sort
of conscience and only one strong conviction – that of deep-rooted
hatred towards England'.[20] The Irish-Americans undoubtedly contributed to the Anglophobia, which, as a factor in American politics,
could never be ignored. And in Australia the Irish immigrants built
up the Catholic Church and formed an important section of the
Labour party, to whose tradition of isolationism they contributed –
it is significant that in the great Australian conscription controversy
of 1917 the opposition to conscription was led by an Irishman,
Archbishop Mannix.

There were other spheres in which Englishmen, during the nineteenth century, were compelled to relinquish accepted opinions
because of Ireland. *Laissez-faire* was in many ways an economic
policy well-suited to an advancing country. But in Ireland, neither
capital (the Irish landlords) nor labour were able to display the
qualities which contemporaries expected to be inherent in the economic man. In the decades following the Union, when the state was
supposed to be retiring from economic life, it was compelled to
encourage public works in Ireland on an extensive scale. The Great
Famine is often pointed to as a tragedy accentuated by an insensitive doctrinaire adherence to *laissez-faire*. But it also led to state
intervention in the economic sphere on a scale unprecedented in
British history. At one time the government was theoretically
employing 700,000 men.

Then, in 1869, the greatest measure of nationalization in British
history between the abolition of the monasteries and the nationalization of the railways and the coal industry was accomplished with
the Disestablishment and disendowment of the Irish branch of the
Established Church. Twelve years later the introduction of judicial

rents was a drastic interference with property rights. In the next decade the Conservatives, by setting up the Congested Districts Board, began an experiment in state assistance to a distressed area. In Ireland Peel studied problems about fifteen years before he set up the Metropolitan police (the first two chief commissioners of that force were in fact Irishmen), and it was in Ireland that the British state first subsidized universities and set up a nation-wide system of primary education.

So far I have been dealing with the effect of Ireland on British politics. Now let me turn to Irishmen in British life. From early in the eighteenth century there was a considerable amount of working-class emigration from Ireland to England. Some of it was seasonal – Irishmen came over for the harvest – and in 1753 mobs in the London area attacked the Irish haymakers. But there were also permanent settlements, there being in London a large enough Irish community to provoke hostility. In 1736 mobs attacked Irish weavers and labourers for working 'at under rate', and the Gordon Riots of 1780 threatened the Irish, who in Wapping gathered together to defend their chapel. Statistics are hard to obtain for the eighteenth century; but from the beginning of the nineteenth century Ireland was one of the great emigration zones of Europe. By 1841 there were 419,000 Irish-born people in Great Britain, about 2.25 per cent of the total population. The Great Famine sent masses of hungry and fever-stricken Irish across the channel and by 1871 there were 773,000 Irish-born people in Great Britain. Then there was a fall, and by 1911 the Irish-born population had declined to 549,000. To these figures, of course, might be added children born in England to Irish-born parents. On the other hand, the Irish community is continually melting away. Irishmen were easily absorbed, since 'They were invisible because they were white.'[21]

Arriving poverty-stricken and starting at the bottom of the occupational ladder, the Irish immigrants created grim patches in the slums of the industrial centres – London, Liverpool, Manchester, Glasgow – where they congregated. Their critics accused them of being drunken, dirty and disorderly. Even in eighteenth-century London the Irish incurred censure for three practices – keeping pigs in their homes, overcrowding their dwellings and holding wakes. At the beginning of the nineteenth century it was implied that the most pertinacious, dishonest and ingenious beggars in London were Irish. And towards the end of the century the Scottish census commissioners rather priggishly declared that 'the very high proportion of the Irish race in Scotland has undoubtedly ... produced deleterious results, lowered greatly the moral tone of the lower classes, and greatly increased the necessity for sanitary and police precautions wherever they have settled in numbers'.[22] On the other hand, the Irish seem to have been generous to their fellows, and often very hard-working, and they made an important contribution to Britain's economic development by helping to supply the muscle-power needed to supplement the machine. They were dockers, navvies, bricklayers, miners, gas-workers, scavengers and general labourers.

The Irish immigrant also played a very important part in building Catholicism in Great Britain. Admittedly, men of Irish birth were not conspicuous in the administrative or intellectual life of the Church. Of the ninety-one Roman Catholic bishops appointed to English sees between 1850 and 1950, only ten were born in Ireland.[23] And the English Catholic intellectuals – Ward, Newman, Allies, Acton, Von Hügel, Chesterton, Belloc, Knox, Waugh – were all English (or French or German). Only Maturin and Tyrrell, that stormy theological petrel, were Irishmen. And they were born and brought up as Dublin Protestants. What the Irish contributed to the growth of English Catholicism was numbers and their traditionally strong and simple piety.

Catholicism was one of the forces that held many of the Irish immigrants together and enabled them as a group to play some part in English politics. Until the late sixties few working-class Irishmen would have possessed a vote, and even after the Reform Act of 1867, according to an experienced observer, the Irish frequently moved house and were careless about registering.[24] Nevertheless, in a number of urban constituencies the Irish vote could not be disregarded. For instance, at the general election of 1868, a large number of Irish voters were expected to support the Liberal candidates in Liverpool. 'This very fact', it was said, 'tended to increase the zealous adherence of English artisans to the Conservative, or what they considered the Protestant cause', and the Conservatives won two out of three seats.[25]

In 1873 the Home Rule Confederation was formed with local branches, which meant that the Irish vote was organized, and at the election of 1885 the Irish vote played an important, perhaps a decisive, part. During the election Catholics were advised by their bishops, concerned over education questions, to vote Conservative. Irishmen were advised by Parnell to vote against the Liberals who had supported a policy of coercion in Ireland. It is impossible to say which directive exercised the greater influence on the Irish Catholic vote, but they both in practice meant the same thing, and the Irish Catholic vote was transferred to the Conservatives. This cost the Liberals a number of seats – Parnell claimed ninety-seven and the Liberals themselves acknowledged the loss of between thirty and forty. Before the next general election the Liberals had adopted Home Rule. From then onwards the Irish Nationalist party tried to ensure that the Irish vote in Britain should go to the Liberals, even though in 1906 the Liberals' education policy had earned the disapproval of the English Catholic bishops.

This Liberal-Irish electoral alliance was one factor – a small one admittedly – which retarded the growth of an English Labour party, keeping in the Liberal ranks voters who might, for social reasons, be expected to vote Labour. Hyndman attributed his defeat at Burnley in 1906 partly to the Irish vote,[26] and Wheatley, a young Waterford man who was to be one of the most successful men in the first Labour Cabinet, began his career in Glasgow by trying to show that Catholicism and Socialism were reconcilable. Partly as a result of his work, the Irish vote in the Gorbals division of Glasgow went Labour, and William Barnes defeated Bonar Law, the future prime minister, who was the son of an Irish Presbyterian minister.[27]

The Irish working-class immigrants formed a large, homogeneous body with easily discernible and describable features, and their contribution to British life can be comparatively easily assessed. But many Irishmen who were not working-class lived and worked in Great Britain or in the British possessions overseas, and their contribution is not so easily discerned and characterized. Dr Johnson, referring to Irishmen in the social circles in which he moved, remarked:

The Irish mix better with the English than the Scotch do; their language is nearer to English; as a proof of which they succeed very
well as players, which Scotchmen do not. Then, Sir, they have not
that extreme nationality which is found in the Scotch. [Boswell was]
almost the only instance of a Scotchman that I have known, who
did not at every other sentence bring in some other Scotchman.[28]

It might be argued that Scotsmen, coming from a society which was
growing more happily integrated, would have more fellow-feeling
for one another than Irishmen, members of a sorely divided community. In any event a considerable degree of conformity is usually
a prerequisite for a successful political or professional career. Moreover, it is often difficult to determine what, if any, elements in a
man's character are derived from the place of his birth and upbringing. In what follows I do not want to be guilty of overplaying that
worn historical card, national character. On the other hand it is
probably true to say that Irish conditions did accentuate certain
traits, and at any rate an Irishman who made his career in England,
even if he reacted strongly against his 'domicile of origin', was to be
influenced by the fact that he was in Great Britain perhaps to some
extent an 'outsider'.

During the eighteenth century a number of Irishmen played a
part on the higher levels of English life. There were men of families
with political connections in both countries who opted for a career
on the wider stage: men such as Shelburne, a distrusted intellectual
who for a very short time was prime minister; Hillsborough, Secretary of State in the 1770s; Luttrell, of Luttrellstown near Dublin,
who was Wilkes's opponent in the stormy Middlesex election; and
Mornington, Wellington's elder brother, who hesitated between a
career in the Irish House of Lords or the British House of Commons. Then there were those MPs whom John Brooke calls 'Irish
adventurers' – a term, he adds, which does not imply anything
'unworthy or reprehensible'.[29]

Of these, of course, the most outstanding were Sheridan and
Burke. Let me dwell for a moment on Burke because, combining as
he did a philosophical approach, vast stores of knowledge and an
intimate experience of affairs, he made a large and lasting contribution to English political thought, and furthermore his intellectual

make-up was undoubtedly influenced by his Irish background. In Ireland history was on the surface and Burke, brought up in cultural borderlands between Catholic and Protestant, Irish and English, early became aware of the enduring strength and integrating force of a historic tradition – national, religious or social. This shows itself in what would later be termed his romantic appreciation of the texture of society, and also in his language. He had a far richer and more flexible vocabulary, and a far greater command of metaphor and simile, than any of his parliamentary contemporaries. If his oratory was formed on classical models, it was influenced by the Celtic bardic tradition. Again, Ireland was a good vantage-point from which to survey British imperial problems – near the centre, yet retaining a degree of independence. And it was there that Burke laid the foundations of the generous and just imperialism of which he was to be the first great advocate. Finally, when visiting his Munster relations, who were Catholics, he must have realized that a group or section of society might have great cultural values, proud traditions and an acute sense of honour, and yet be subject to ruthless oppression. The passionate sympathy Burke was to display for plundered Indian princes, and the dispossessed clergy and *noblesse* of France, was first aroused amongst the Catholic gentry of north County Cork.

Burke was only one of a number of Irishmen of letters who, during the eighteenth century, came to England seeking the intellectual stimulus of a greater reading public. They ranged from rich amateurs such as Holroyd, the economist and editor of Gibbon, or Malone, the great pioneer in Shakespearian studies, through pamphleteers such as Swift to literary hacks such as Toland, the deist, or Goldsmith. Early in the century Swift, then an Irish country clergyman, arrived in England at a time when public opinion was being recognized by politicians as a most important force, and at a moment when the Tory party desperately needed a publicist. Swift soon became an outstanding political pamphleteer, and was the first journalist to be admitted to the counsels of a great party. Augustine Birrell, in one of his brilliant essays, said that to call Swift an Irishman 'is sheer folly'.[30] But it is probable that his hard-hitting, unsparing partisanship was partly derived from his frontier background.

Goldsmith, after years of easy-going avoidance of a fixed occupation in Ireland and some years of drifting round the Continent, settled in London and started to keep alive by doing ephemeral or routine literary work. He finally became one of the most enthralling and delightful playwrights, one of a succession of Irish dramatists with an Anglo-Irish background – including Farquhar, Congreve, Murphy, Sheridan, Wilde, Shaw, Synge and Beckett. This list is too striking to be explained by mere chance. To begin with, the Irish or Anglo-Irishman, balanced between two countries, was able to develop a detachment of value to the dramatist. Also, Ireland was a country which enjoyed conversation. Gaelic civilization bred a delight in words, a sheer enjoyment in verbal fireworks. And as fashion can spread upwards, the Anglo-Irish landed world, eager to enjoy the elegant idleness characteristic of a gentleman, seems to have prided itself on its conversational powers. So an Irish-born dramatist absorbed good dialogue in his daily life. Irish society, too, abounded in incongruities – and incongruity is a staple of the theatre. Finally there was an 'organizational factor'. In the eighteenth century, Dublin was second only to London as a theatrical centre.

Irishmen seem to have comparatively rarely attempted a professional career in eighteenth-century England. After all, in such a career local connections, family and university were important. If an Irishman was a Protestant he would have better opportunities at home; if he was a Catholic and wanted a wider field than Ireland, he would emigrate to a European Catholic country. No Irishman was placed on the English judicial bench during the eighteenth century; and the only two Irishmen who mounted the English episcopal bench, Wilson and Crigan, only obtained the very meagre see of Sodor and Man. On the other hand a fair number of Irish-born medical men seem to have practised with a fair measure of success in the eighteenth century, blazing a trail which many Irish doctors have since followed. About 5 per cent of the fellows and licentiates of the College of Physicians were Irishmen who practised in England. They included Babington, the outstanding London physician at the opening of the nineteenth century, and Tierney, the Prince Regent's medical attendant (though Tierney's appointment may have been due to the fact that the Prince's secretary, Bloomfield, was also an Irishman).

There was one profession, indeed, in which Irishmen distinguished themselves during the eighteenth century and after – the army. The Irish government at this time had a considerable amount of military patronage at its own disposal; the sports of the Irish countryside were a good apprenticeship to military life; and the sons of the Irish squirearchy, when mixing with a quick-witted tenantry, learned the arts of leadership – how to command and when to persuade. Statistics are hard to come by, but it is certain that in the 1870s between 17 and 20 per cent of the officers of the British army were Irish-born. As for the list of names, it is Homeric – Wellington, Pack, the Napiers, Beresford, Lowry Cole, Gough, Wolseley, Roberts, Kitchener, French, Henry Wilson, Dill, Brooke, Montgomery, Alexander. Again, it is not easy to say what proportion of the rank and file at any time were Irish. Kipling implies a very high proportion (but then only an Irish soldier could be represented as talking in the style a Kipling story needed); on the other hand, the recruiting statistics suggest an intake from Ireland relative to the size of the population. But many Irishmen probably enlisted in England. In the 1870s the Irish-born were over 20 per cent of the rank and file;[31] and in 1914, of the reservists recalled to the colours, over 13 per cent came from Ireland.

With the opening of the nineteenth century the number of Irishmen seeking careers in Great Britain steadily increased. To begin with, though Dublin remained an important administrative centre, London had the magnetic pull of a capital. What was more important was that the opportunity gap between careers in Ireland and across the Irish Sea widened as Great Britain grew in economic strength and prosperity; and as Irish higher educational facilities expanded during the century, the country's absorption power did not increase quickly enough. By the close of the century the attraction of the English Bar for Irishmen was evinced by the fact that ten Irishmen attained places on the English bench. Of these, the most outstanding were Lord Russell of Killowen and MacNaghten, whose style (characterized by a harsh critic as 'refulgent rhetoric') won him a place in *The Oxford Book of English Prose*. Two Irishmen were placed on the episcopal bench and by 1820 the flow of Irish-educated clergy into the Anglican Church was sufficiently noticeable to inspire Blomfield, Bishop of Chester, to announce that one of the reform measures he intended to take was not to accept Irish-educated candidates for ordination.[32] However, between 1873 and 1913 over 3 per cent of the clergy ordained for dioceses in England were educated in Ireland – a figure which may seem small until it is taken into account that the Irish Anglicans were a small community, only half a million strong.

The growth of the civil service, accompanied as it was by a growing reliance on competitive examination as a method of recruitment, offered opportunities of which Irishmen took advantage. Indeed, early in the twentieth century it was asserted that even 'in the most remote parts of Ireland candidates are preparing in primary schools with a view to subsequently passing a Civil Service examination'.[33] Statistics are not easily obtained, but we do know that towards the close of the nineteenth century the Irish intake into the executive and clerical classes of the civil service was about 9 per cent.[34] The Irish intake into the administrative class was, on average, 5 per cent: the successful Scottish candidates far outnumbered the Irish. For almost twenty years, from the mid-nineteenth century, Ireland supplied over 20 per cent of the entry into the Indian civil service;[35] later the intake fell to about 5 per cent, although a somewhat higher percentage of Irishmen were recruited for the colonial services. These figures are not very striking on a population basis – but if the proportionate size of the Irish middle class is taken into account they are more impressive.

Irishmen were not only prominent in these; they were also to be found in every walk of British life. And if a great civilization benefits from the enlivening variety provided by a minority group – the members of which are themselves stimulated by the need to establish themselves in their new environment – then Ireland, which has given Great Britain for over two centuries a large minority (or two minorities), has made a substantial contribution to British life.

NOTES

1. W. Blackstone, *Commentaries on the Laws of England*, i (Oxford 1765), p. 98.

2. *Life of Theobald Wolfe Tone*, ed. W.T. Wolfe Tone, ii (Washington 1826), p. 182.

3. Hon. J.W. Fortescue, *The British Army 1783-1802* (London 1905), p. 19.

4. *Henry Crabb Robinson on Books and their Writers*, ed. E.J. Morley, i (London 1938), p. 19.

5. T. Carlyle, *Critical and Miscellaneous Essays*, iv (London 1899), pp. 136-40.

6. *The Political Writings of Richard Cobden*, i (London 1867), pp. 95-6.

7. M. Arnold, *Works*, xi (London 1904), pp. 57-78.

8. *William Allingham: A Diary*, eds H. Allingham and D. Radford (London 1908), pp. 293, 297.

9. A.J. Balfour, *Aspects of Home Rule* (London 1912), pp. 13-20.

10. *Church of Ireland Gazette*, 1891, p. 315.

11. *Nineteenth Century*, xix, p. 655.

12. *Annual Register, 1886*, pp. 165, 207.

13. W.H.G. Armytage, *A.J. Mundella* (London 1951), p. 247.

14. H. Bland, *Fabian Essays* (London 1889), p. 211.

15. *The Nation*, 1 August 1846.

16. *The Times*, 24 April 1893.

17. *Annual Register, 1867*, p. 25.

18. *Nineteenth Century*, xix, p. 639.

19. D. Norman, *Nehru: the First Sixty Years*, i (London 1965), p. 12.

20. R. Kipling, *From Sea to Sea*, ii (London 1900), pp. 208-9.

21. *The Times*, 1 August 1969.

22. Census of Scotland, 1871, Report, p. xxxiv, H.C. (1873), [C 841], lxx-ii.

23. G.A. Beck, *The English Catholics 1850-1950* (London 1950), p. 187.

24. *Fortnightly Review*, new series, xl, p. 244.

25. J.A. Picton, *Memorials of Liverpool*, i (London 1873), p. 629.

26. H.M. Hyndman, *Further Reminiscences* (London 1912), pp. 66-74.

27. R.K. Middlemas, *The Clydesiders* (London 1965), pp. 35-41.

28. *Boswell's Life of Johnson*, eds G.H. Hill and L.F. Powell, ii (Oxford 1934), p. 242.

29. Sir L. Namier and J. Brooke, *The House of Commons 1754-1790*, i (London 1964), p. 164.

30. A. Birrell, *Collected Essays and Addresses*, i (London 1922), p. 92.

31. Army (number of English, Scotch and Irish officers), and Army (number of English Scotch), H.C. (1872), (315), (171), xxxii.

32. G. Biber, *Bishop Blomfield and His Times* (London 1857), pp. 43-4.

33. *Royal Commission on Civil Service: First Appendix to Fourth Report, Minutes of Evidence*, p. 222, H.C. (1914) [7338], xvi.

34. *Civil Service Candidates, Return*, H.C. (1898), (287), lxxii.

35. *Civil Service of India: Selection and Training of Candidates*, p. 35, H.C. (1876) [C 1446], xiv.

In a recent work, seven archbishops were used as pegs on which to hang an oddly balanced exposition of Anglicanism from the Middle Ages to the present day. It need scarcely be said that this is an unfruitful approach to ecclesiastical history. A prominent churchman in any epoch may be unrepresentative, or even reticent. The method, however, has this to be said for it – that if the leading group in any organization be taken as a whole, it will reflect tendencies governing that organization's development. And if one wishes to study any community it is vital to discover on what grounds its leaders are selected and what types of men are placed in posts of high responsibility.

The promotions to the episcopate made in the half-century before 1830 reflect strikingly the eighteenth-century political compromise. The great landed families who kept in their hands the mainsprings of political power were ready to respect and employ ability from without their ranks. Control but not monopoly was their guiding principle. This did not, of course, imply an undue degree of renunciation. Of the sixty-three bishops placed on the bench during this period, eleven were the sons of peers, one (Bathurst of Norwich) was the nephew of a peer and three were the grandsons of peers. In addition, Cornewall of Worcester was a cousin of the Speaker who aided him at the outset of his career, Madan was the son of an MP, Moss was the son of a bishop and brother of a chief justice, and Thurlow was a brother of the most overbearing political lawyer of the day.

It is easy to understand why Bathursts, Bagots, Norths and Ryders, members of families that supplied Cabinet timber for a century, were elevated to the bench. The promotion of men not born in the governing class is often less easily explained. In each case probably several factors played a part. To attribute a particular bishop's elevation to one of them alone would tend to give a false picture. However, it may be noticed that, of the remaining forty-three bishops, five had helped to educate members of the royal family (and it may be added that Jackson of Oxford received the mitre declined by his brother, the preceptor of George IV), and that eight others had been tutors in noble households – thus justifying the belief that educating the great was a pathway to preferment. Moreover, Pretyman, Randolf and Lloyd (as college tutors) and Huntingford (as assistant master at Winchester) had respectively as grateful pupils, Pitt, Grenville, Peel and Addington. Goodenough of Carlisle had conducted a fashionable school, and Buckner of Chichester, as private chaplain to the Duke of Richmond, had officiated with the regiment that his grace commanded at the siege of Havannah. Carey of Exeter had been a popular and successful headmaster of Westminster. Sumner of Winchester and Carr of Worcester directly owed their promotion to even more august patronage. They had both attracted the attention of George IV – the one by his manners, the other by his preaching – and he had pressed their names on his ministers. Three bishops before their promotion to the bench had attracted attention as pamphleteers: Butler of Hereford by defending Lord North's American policy; Marsh of Peterborough, an erudite and pioneering scholar, by providing (at considerable risk to himself) Pitt's government with war propaganda for home and foreign consumption; and Phillpots of Exeter by proving himself to be an indefatigable and undaunted Tory controversialist.

Distinction of scholarship might also lead to the bench. Indeed Fox, during one of his brief periods of power, declared that he would never make a man a bishop who was not eminent in some branch of learning.[1] More successful politicians who enjoyed more substantial terms of office honoured Fox's ideal at least intermittently. Hurd, Kaye, Monk and Blomfield were distinguished members of the learned circle that centred around Parr and Porson (thus illustrating the truth of Dean Gaisford's remark on the advantages of a classical education). Horsley was well known for his work in astronomy, mathematics, theology and classical philology. Porteus, Gray, Bethell and Van Mildert were the authors of theological works which commanded contemporary respect.

It would be trite to emphasize that pressure exerted by the great political families played an important part in determining the composition of the episcopate in the pre-reform era. Indeed, Butler, the famous headmaster of Shrewsbury, having surveyed the bench with the penetrating severity of a disappointed man, declared that one could not find a man on it who did not owe his promotion to 'private tuition or family connection'.[2] But it should not be overlooked that only about one-third of the bishops appointed between 1781 and 1830 (twenty out of sixty-three) were connected with the ruling families; and even this figure of twenty is arrived at by counting such men as Thurlow, Moss and Cornewall. Only about a quarter of the total of sixty-three were closely connected with the peerage. But though two-thirds of the episcopate were not drawn from the ruling classes, it is true, as Butler says, that many of them had been associated with a great family at some stage of their careers. And though in a few rare cases an outstanding reputation in scholarship might attract the attention of a minister, normally a patron was the means through which a clergyman was brought to the notice of the appointing powers. Again, it must not be forgotten that several of the early nineteenth-century prime ministers, for instance Perceval, Addington, and Liverpool, were keen churchmen. Their critics might say that they identified the Church too closely with the Tory party. If this is true, it at least increased their zeal for its welfare.

After 1830 English politicians had to work in a new and changing environment. An era of efficiency had begun. Public opinion was powerful, alert, critical and well-informed. Within the Church of England, tendencies which had existed for centuries became embodied in ecclesiastical parties equipped with the usual persuasive apparatus of the period – societies, periodicals and public meetings. These factors naturally influenced episcopal appointments. Admittedly, some little time passed before their effect was apparent. Grey, the first post-reform Prime Minister, filled only two sees during his term of office. To one of them he appointed his brother Edward, to the other, Malby, a distinguished classical scholar who had once been tutor in a great Whig household. But when Melbourne was asked to make Arnold a bishop, he refused, not wanting to give High Churchmen a handle against his government.[3] Peel and Russell agreed in disliking and distrusting the tractarians.[4] Aberdeen, probably influenced by the fact that several of his political associates sympathized with the Oxford Movement, was willing to place on the bench a man belonging to any church party, provided he was distinguished by true 'moderation of character and opinions'.[5]

Palmerston, Aberdeen's successor, was in his episcopal appointments actuated by a convenient mixture of prejudice or conviction and blatant opportunism. Having in the course of his career left the Tories and quarrelled with the Whigs, he was largely dependent on his popularity in the country – and this he knew could be affected by his ecclesiastical appointments. Being ignorant of Church matters, not knowing 'in theology Moses from Sydney Smith', he relied almost entirely on the advice of his relation, the high-minded and hard-working evangelical leader, Lord Shaftesbury. Shaftesbury was a thorough-going partisan and aimed at packing the bench with evangelicals of his own school. Of Palmerston's first five bishops, four (appointed in succession) were distinguished in the words of *The Times* 'less for intellectual culture than for their practical piety, their success as parochial ministers and their sympathy with Protestant dissenters'. The Queen remonstrated, arguing that Lord Palmerston should not 'confine the selection to respectable parish priests', for the bench would be seriously weakened if 'in controversies on points of doctrine agitating the Church no value were attached to the opinions at least of some of those who govern her'. Shaftesbury, ruefully reflecting that the 'knowledge of mankind and parochial experience are not acquired in musty libraries or armchairs', was compelled to modify his policy in deference to public opinion. And though the nine bishops appointed by Palmerston between 1860 and his death were, with one or two exceptions, low churchmen, they all had respectable academic records.

In one respect, however, the early episcopal appointments were a success. According to Shaftesbury, they 'influenced elections,

turned votes in the House of Commons, and raised him [Palmer-
ston] a strong party in the country'. Shaftesbury of course is scarcely
an unbiased witness, but Aberdeen, a critical opponent, agreed with
him. Palmerston, he complained, could do anything with impunity,
for 'should the public disappropriation become more and more
manifest the early appointment of one or two low church bishops
will set it all right'.[6] Disraeli, too, appreciated the strength of Protestant feeling in England, and at a critical stage of his career, when the
election of 1868 was approaching, he was anxious to conciliate this
feeling – and thus capture a substantial block of voters – by the
appointment of an indubitable low churchman to the bench. Unfortunately (from the electioneering point of view) he was handicapped
by the refusal of any of the existing bishops to die, and was compelled to display his Protestant principles by presenting a vociferous
low churchman to a deanery.[7]

The general principle, however, which Disraeli wished to follow
in making ecclesiastical appointments was to select men from 'the
legitimate High Church and evangelical parties, discountenancing to
the utmost Romanism [i.e. ritualism] and not patronizing neology
[i.e. the extreme broad Church outlook]'. Indeed, when a certain
amount of ingenious if eccentric theorizing is discounted, it is clear
that Disraeli, like the other Victorian prime ministers, simply
aimed at placing moderate men on the bench. At the beginning of
the Victorian era Russell had laid down that a bishop should 'avoid
quarrels and crochets and live quietly with all men'. And near the
era's close, Salisbury declared that 'combative men', 'mere gladiators',
were a curse to the Church. Most prime ministers in the century
following the Great Reform bill admittedly had their predilections
when it came to making ecclesiastical appointments – for instance,
Gladstone was very ready to promote the new species of High
Churchman; Campbell-Bannerman tended to appoint liberal and
low churchmen (because he believed that the High Church party
had been unduly favoured in the recent past); and naturally
enough, while Asquith was interested in a potential bishop's academic record, Lloyd George set a high value on oratorical ability.[8]
Nevertheless, all the prime ministers of the period would have
agreed with Halifax that 'nice disputes [on religious topics] are

never of equal moment with the public peace'. And it may be added that Archbishop Davidson, who as the friend and adviser of successive sovereigns and ministers enjoyed an impressive and unprecedented position, thoroughly sympathized with the instinctive eagerness of English politicians to keep a mean between the two extremes. As a result, at a time when the Church of England was rent by conflicts and distressed by novelties, the bench of bishops remained a comparatively homogeneous body, intent, in spite of urgent and often contradictory exhortations to decided action, on maintaining the greatest possible degree of unity.

After the 1830s the ministers who managed the ecclesiastical patronage of the Crown could not ignore the problems arising from the vehement party divisions within the Church, yet in another respect their task was lightened. The new standards of public behaviour that rapidly gained ground during the nineteenth century inhibited or at least checked the more direct methods of importuning for promotion. Partly as a result of this, political factors played a remarkably small part in determining who was to be placed on the bench. Of course, during the long era of Tory ascendancy which ended in 1830, a tincture of Whiggery in a clergyman's outlook would have been a bar or at least a hindrance to his promotion. And naturally enough, when the Whigs came to power they showed a tendency to redress the balance. Consequently, with one or two exceptions, the bishops appointed in the decade after 1830 were Whig or Liberal in politics. Melbourne indeed expected 'a general disposition to support the measures of his government in the bishops he appointed'.[9]

But a decade later Palmerston, writing privately to a friend, declared that he never considered ecclesiastical appointments 'as patronage to be given away for ... personal or political objects'.[10] And this dictum, slightly qualified, sums up the accepted practice from then onwards. Admittedly in a few cases, a bishop's political views may have been an important factor in securing his elevation to the bench. For instance, Jacobson of Chester acted as chairman of Gladstone's committee at Oxford in the election of 1859, and shortly afterwards Gladstone pressed his claims for a mitre on Palmerston. It is unlikely, too, that Mackarness of Oxford, who lost his seat in convocation over his attitude to Irish Disestablishment, or Stubbs of Truro, who strongly sympathized with the agricultural labourer, or Percival of Hereford, whose general outlook led him on most issues 'to claim moral sanction for the liberal solution of the question', would have mounted the bench if the Liberals had not been in office. But since many *episcopabili* had not pronounced political views; the appointing politicians, who were after all genuinely concerned for the Church's welfare, seldom if ever considered using their ecclesiastical patronage for the purpose of increasing their political influence. In this connection it may be observed that Gladstone's comment that 'the attendance of bishops in the House of Lords, except upon church and semi-church questions, has immensely fallen off, and the political function is upon the whole sacrificed to diocesan duty',[11] is confirmed by a study of the Lords' division lists. Rarely in the last hundred years have more than a dozen bishops voted, even on an important issue (though interestingly enough in 1893 almost the whole bench attended to vote against the Home Rule bill), and frequently in a comparatively full house, no episcopal votes have been cast.

In another way the links between the episcopal bench and the lay peerage have been weakened. In the half-century preceding 1830 there were eleven peers' sons placed on the bench. In the century following that date there were only nine, and eight of these were consecrated before 1900. On the other hand, Sydney's assertion that 'the great emoluments of the Church are flung open to the lowest ranks of the community. Butchers, bakers, publicans and schoolmasters perpetually see their children elevated to the mitre,' has become even less true in the last hundred years than when he made it. It is difficult to arrive at a generally accepted system of social stratification; but even allowing for the somewhat supercilious standards that Sydney Smith may have imbibed in Whig society, he greatly exaggerates. Of those who were elevated to the bench in his lifetime, only two or three could reasonably be regarded as coming from the lower ranks of the community. Parsons, who was the son of a butler (though indeed a college butler), and Butler of Hereford, who 'began life in an obscure situation from which his first marriage did not elevate him'[12] (his second, combined with vigorous pamphleteering, fortunately did), had perhaps the humblest origins. The pugnacious Phillpots was indeed the son of a publican, but his father was also a manufacturer and land agent. Moore of Canterbury was said to be the son of a butcher, but (as in the case of a more famous ecclesiastic) the report was based on the fact that his father was a well-off grazier. An archbishop (Markham of York) and a bishop (Blomfield of London) were admittedly the sons of schoolmasters. Hurd's father was a substantial farmer, and several bishops were the sons of more or less prosperous tradesmen.

As the instances we have just given include all the bishops who began life in comparatively humble circumstances, it is scarcely necessary to say that on the whole the episcopal bench was recruited from what on any sensible analysis would be called the middle and upper classes, coming from a diversity of parental occupational backgrounds – for instance, Longley was son of a police magistrate, Hampden of a militia officer, Westcott, Lightfoot, Stubbs and Creighton were the sons of a science lecturer, an accountant, a solicitor and a timber merchant respectively. And it is possible to argue that since 1830 there has been a tendency for bishops to come from the upper rather than the lower sections of that vague entity, the middle class. The following table, showing the percentage of those appointed during different periods educated at a public school, certainly suggests that conclusion.

Period	Percentage of Public-School Men Placed on the Bench
1831–1880	42
1881–1905	50
1906–1930	79
1931–1945	76

Of course these figures may merely show the rapid evolution of the public-school habit among those classes which approved of the institution and could afford to pay the fees demanded.

There is one striking feature about the parental origins of bishops which is shown in the following table – the residual importance of family association with the Church.

Period	Percentage of those Appointed Bishops who were Sons of Clergy
1781–1830	32
1831–1880	20
1881–1905	44
1906–1930	55
1931–1945	44

But though the members of the bench may have come from widely differing types of home and school, some degree of uniformity in tone and outlook has been imparted to them at the university. For nearly all the English diocesan bishops appointed between 1781 and 1945 have been educated at either Oxford or Cambridge. In fact there have only been eight exceptions – Magee (an episcopal Sydney Smith) and Bardsley, both graduates of Dublin; Wakefield, Partridge and Simpson, educated at Bonn, London and Durham respectively; Butler of Hereford and Cash who did not attend university; and Watts-Ditchfield, who began as a Methodist and whose promotion aroused considerable comment since he had not enjoyed the usual education of an Anglican clergyman.

Some time about the end of the third quarter of the nineteenth century a change occurred in the academic standing of those placed on the bench. Of the bishops appointed between 1830 and 1880 about four-fifths had had distinguished academic careers, but of those appointed after the latter date, only half could be said to have distinguished themselves at university. For the purpose of comparison, election to fellowship shortly after graduation or the possession of a first-class degree has been taken as indicating academic distinction. Admittedly these criteria are open to criticism: men of decided and original ability have failed to win the approval of the governing body of their college, and dull and commonplace men have secured high places in the class list.

Still, allowing for the unsatisfactory nature of the standards selected, the following table may be of some interest.[13]

Period	Percentage of those Appointed Bishops who were Academically Distinguished
1830–1880	80 (incl. six heads of colleges)
1881–1905	49 (incl. three heads of colleges)
1906–1930	46 (incl. four heads of colleges)
1931–1945	41 (incl. one head of college)

These figures reflect both changes in the realm of scholarship and the emergence of a new type of bishop. At the beginning of the nineteenth century mathematics, classics and philosophy practically monopolized the prestige pertaining to learning. Thus a sound theologian ought to have had an easy command over most of the subjects on which other scholars laboured and with which all cultivated men wished to be acquainted. In addition, the great majority of academic posts were reserved for persons in holy orders. But the rapid increase of cultural activities, the widening scope of scientific investigation and the growth of specialization weakened the prestige of theology as an academic subject. After the middle of the nineteenth century most academic posts were open to laymen. Thus a keen and competent theologian had less opportunity of winning academic distinction and office.

Simultaneously, there was a growing tendency to emphasize the value of pastoral and administrative ability. In the pre-reform era a few bishops, such as Charles Sumner at Highclerc and Blomfield at St Botolph's, Bishopsgate, had been capable and devoted parish ministers before their promotion. Still, a reputation for parochial work would by itself have scarcely proved sufficient to ensure elevation to the bench. But a number of the bishops chosen after 1830 were men who had striven by teaching, preaching and building to Christianize the new industrial centres. For instance, in the half-century after 1860 no fewer than five vicars of Leeds were appointed bishops.

It was not only in the parochial sphere that a clergyman could display administrative capacity. The heads of houses at Oxford and Cambridge were from time to time placed on the bench. Then, from the thirties onwards, the public school – a comparatively malleable institution whose head was practically an autocrat – offered a sphere in which organizing ability could have full scope; and between 1830 and 1945 about eighteen public-school headmasters were placed on the bench. Six, indeed, became archbishops – the two Temples, Tait, Benson, Fisher and Longley – though the last named's sufferings at Harrow scarcely foreshadowed his success as a vigorous diocesan.

To try and estimate the part played by the episcopate in English life during the last two centuries would be a bold, probably impossible and certainly impertinent task. Only one or two generalizations will be attempted. On the whole, the status of the individual bishop has declined. If he is a scholar, his subject is one which, at the moment, does not command the attention of the public. And in any case his administrative duties leave him little leisure for learned pursuits. Again, the fact that England is no longer a hierarchical society dominated by a landed aristocracy has helped to diminish the bishop's state. Harcourt, with his public days on which any gentleman might dine at his table, or Hurd, a modest scholar, going to Bath with twelve attendants (not, as his biographer is careful to point out, 'from ostentation'), were naturally more outstanding figures than their less picturesque and more utilitarian successors.[14] That unbending Tory, the Duke of Cumberland, unconsciously imitating Carlyle, dated the decline of the bishop's status from the surrender of the episcopal wig. Writing in the forties, he bitterly compared the bishops of the past, arrayed in purple coats, short cassocks, silk stockings and cocked hats, with Blomfield of London, whom he had 'seen in a black Wellington coat, top boots and hat like a butcher or a coal merchant'.[15]

But though the modern bishop may in his secular aspects resemble a higher civil servant or business executive rather than a great nobleman, the episcopate can continue to make a useful contribution to English life. With greater independence than any elected persons and possessing a far older and more generous tradition than any bureaucrat can lay claim to, the English bishops can still fulfil their twofold function of guiding the Church and supporting the state with wise counsel and candid criticism.

[1947]

Addendum

As a pendant to the above, it may be interesting to survey briefly the bench at the opening of the twenty-first century. Until the later 1970s British prime ministers continued to fill vacant sees by submitting a name to the monarch. Often the Archbishop of Canterbury and occasionally the Archbishop of York were consulted, and an important go-between, the prime minister's patronage secretary, could exercise considerable influence. Prime ministerial interest in ecclesiastical matters varied considerably. But even Eden, who 'was never keen on clerics', and Harold Wilson, who was a nonconformist, took their duties regarding 'the national church' seriously, and Macmillan was sufficiently concerned over theological issues to be annoyed, when he wished to discuss religion with Fisher of Canterbury, that the archbishop 'reverted all the time to politics'. A later Conservative Prime Minister, Mrs Thatcher, regretted that there was 'not a decent training school' for bishops – she was probably exasperated by the tendency of a section of the Church of England to identify Christian social teaching with collectivism or socialism.[16]

Shortly before Mrs Thatcher became Prime Minister, a new procedure for filling vacancies on the bench was agreed upon in February 1977. A Crown Appointments Commission was established – with each vacancy, it involved the two archbishops, three clerical and three lay members elected by the General Synod, together with four representatives of the diocese. This body then sent two names to the prime minister. He or she was expected to choose one of these but could ask for further names. By 2001 all the members of the bench, with one exception, had been appointed by this method.

Of the forty-three diocesans (two archbishops and forty-one bishops) in 2001, three were the sons of clergymen. All but one were married. Seventeen had gone to an independent school (i.e. a Headmasters and Headmistresses Conference school), including Westminster (2), Wellington, Manchester Grammar and Edinburgh Academy (it may be added that Eton, Harrow and Winchester were not represented on the bench). The other twenty-six had attended a variety of secondary schools – for the most part grammar schools;

the Archbishop of Canterbury had been at a secondary modern
school. Nine had taken their primary degree at Oxford, sixteen at
Cambridge. The others had taken a primary degree at a variety of
universities, ranging geographically from Queen's Belfast and Edinburgh to Exeter and Karachi. Three were sometime fellows of an
Oxford or Cambridge college, another had been Dean of King's
College, London. Three had been head of a theological college and
about ten had been university, college or school chaplains. All had
had some parochial experience, and all had played an active role in
ecclesiastical administration – either traditionally (for instance, as
an archdeacon or rural dean), or in a more modern way (one bishop
had been an industrial chaplain and later a diocesan communications officer). Twenty-one could list publications.

Four members of the bench had taught overseas – in Pakistan,
Nigeria, Uganda and Zambia. One had worked for a short time east
of the Iron Curtain as a chaplain in Bucharest. Two had had military service, and one had been a naval chaplain. Three had been
schoolmasters before ordination; one had been a civil servant;
another had worked in a bank; a third had been employed by
BOAC. A fair number had rather idiosyncratic recreations – bee-
keeping, brass bands, vintage cars, table tennis, brick-laying, writing unpublished novels. More conventionally, fifteen belonged to
London clubs (six to Athenaeum, one to the Garrick, and one to the
National Liberal of which he was president).[17]

Composed of a number of talented men with many varieties of
experience, the bench of bishops at the beginning of the twenty-first
century was less homogeneous, less conspicuous and less influential
than in the past. Its members were expected to devote a considerable amount of effort to keeping an ecclesiastical organization,
which in the previous century had grown greatly in size and com-
plexity, functioning efficiently; and they were working in an England where tradition was at a discount, where there was widespread
uncertainly over social, political and moral values, and where established institutions were being continually subjected to corrosive criticism. It was an environment chilling and challenging to the leaders
of the Church of England.

[2003]

NOTES

1. J. Russell, *Memorials ... of C.J. Fox* (London 1858), iv, pp. 141–2.

2. S. Butler, *Life and Letters of Dr Samuel Butler* (1896), ii, pp. 95–6.

3. Torrens, *Memoirs of Viscount Melbourne* (1878), ii, p. 181.

4. C.S. Parker, *Sir Robert Peel* (1899), iii, pp. 416–22.

5. F. Balfour, *Life of 4th Earl of Aberdeen* (1922), ii, pp. 199–200.

6. Hodder, *Life of 7th Earl of Shaftesbury* (1886), ii, p. 505; iii, pp. 183–202; Balfour, *Life of Aberdeen*, ii, p. 315; *Letters of Queen Victoria*, iii, p. 529.

7. Buckle, *Life of Disraeli* (1920), v, chapter 2; *Letters of Queen Victoria*, 2nd series, i, pp.548–51.

8. G. Cecil, *Life of Robert Marquis of Salisbury*, iv, p. 215; J.A. Spender, *Life of Rt. Hon. Sir Henry Campbell-Bannerman* (1924), ii; G.K.A. Bell, *Randall Davidson* (1935), chapter 78; *Letters of Queen Victoria*, ii, p. 159.

9. Butler, *Life and Letters of Samuel Butler*, ii, p. 148.

10. E. Ashley, *Life of Viscount Palmerston* (1876), ii, p. 226.

11. *Gladstone's Correspondence on Church and Religion* (1910), ii, p. 181.

12. *Gentleman's Magazine*, xxii, pt. 2, p. 1070; *A Second Letter to Archdeacon Singleton* (1838), p. 10.

13. *Annual Register*, 1923, p. 140.

14. Kilvert, *Memoirs of Rt. Rev. Richard Hurd* (1860), p. 127; *The Harcourt Papers*, ed. E.W. Harcourt, xii, p. 263.

15. *Letters of the King of Hanover to Viscount Strangford* (1925), pp. 70–2.

16. D. Thorpe, *Eden* (London 2003), pp. 378, 446; P. Ziegler, *Harold Wilson* (London 1993), p. 417; H. Macmillan, *Riding the Storm* (London 1971), p. 344; M. Thatcher, *The Downing Street Years* (London 1993), p. 31; E. Carpenter, *Archbishop Fisher* (London 1991), pp. 215–36; H.H. Henson, *Retrospect of an Unimportant Life* (London 1943), ii, p. 101.

17. For details on members of the bench in 2001, see *Church of England Yearbook*; *Dodd's Parliamentary Companion*; and *Who's Who*.

VI Swift as a Political Thinker

Swift's political outlook evolved during a momentous era in English political history. Between the Restoration and the flight of James II it was not improbable that England might have become an absolute monarchy on the fashionable continental model. But at the revolution of 1688 other trends triumphed and English constitutionalism soon had as its outstanding features a severely limited monarchy, a powerful parliament and a strongly emphasized respect for civil and religious liberty. Swift was only twenty-one at the time of the Glorious Revolution. If already a High Churchman, he must have had to make a painful readjustment of some of his political first principles. But many of his contemporaries accomplished this operation with smooth dexterity, and by the early eighteenth century, when Swift expounded his political creed, he enunciates what had become within less than a generation the accepted orthodoxies of English political thinking; for instance, that the supreme legislative power was vested in the king, lords and commons, that parliament could settle the succession to the Crown, that executive power was lodged in the Crown but had to be exercised in accordance with the laws, and that 'the ministers of the Crown were liable to prosecution and impeachment'.[1]

But though these opinions would have commanded a very wide degree of general acceptance there were, of course, issues over which men who agreed on constitutional fundamentals could vehemently differ, and Swift during one of the most critical periods of British political history was a strong and outspoken partisan. By conviction and professional bias he was a stern High Churchman. Denominationalism may have been already a declining force in

British politics, but since for another couple of centuries Church and chapel were to remain focal points of political loyalties, Swift may be forgiven for not realizing that theological issues were, relatively speaking, losing or at least about to lose, their earlier significance. In fact to him, as to many keen churchmen, politics largely derived their importance from the effect that changes in the political balance of power might have on the fortunes of the Church of England. Educated in an Anglican university and coming to intellectual maturity in the golden age of Anglicanism, Swift was absolutely convinced of the essential importance to a community of a national church, and of the pre-eminent claims of the Protestant Churches of England and Ireland to be taken into a partnership with the state, which would confer inestimable benefits on the community. At the close of the seventeenth and beginning of the eighteenth centuries, Anglican divines, often men of wide erudition and powerful intellect, were confident that their Church provided a most desirable *via media* between the extravagances and absurdities of Geneva and Rome. Level-headed, rational moderation was their ideal, an ideal which Swift shared.

Anglicans were devoted to their Church with its respect for doctrinal truth combined with an aversion for over-defining, its reverence for tradition and awareness of modern thought, its dignified but restrained ceremonial and its deference to lawful authority. But intellectual self-assurance was not accompanied by complete political confidence. Their intense sense of the tremendous value of their Church made Anglican churchmen tremulously sensitive to every threat to its well being. And when contemplating the dangers to which their Church was exposed, Anglicans had not to rely wholly on their imagination. The reign of James II and the civil wars of the seventeenth century had left a legacy of fears – fears not only for the Church but for the established order. Swift himself sketched vividly the horrible consequences of the Puritan revolution; an Irish rebellion, the murder of the king, the abolition of the House of Lords, constitutional change and confusion, the rise and progress of atheism, the corruption of 'the old virtue and loyalty and generous spirit of the English nation'.[2]

The apprehension that the Whigs might try to weaken the

Church's position by repealing the Irish Test Act was a potent factor in determining Swift's political course in 1710, when he abandoned his Whig friends for the Tories. It was an opportune if honest change of allegiance. The Tories, at last in control of the government, were about to carry through a bold reversal of foreign policy; they were acutely conscious of that growing force, public opinion, which could play with such effect on parliament and they were desperately in need of an effective publicist. Swift, with his great literary powers and well-controlled pugnacity and partisanship, was a superb exponent of Tory policy. His party realized the value of his political journalism at a critical time. Fortunately, too, the Tory leaders enjoyed literature, wit and conviviality, and for three years Swift shared the conversation and confidences of statesmen and was a well-established figure in political, literary and even fashionable London.

It should perhaps be emphasized that he was a well-informed observer rather than a participant. He was not in the Cabinet or the Commons, the places where policy was shaped and debated. Thus his political writings are those of a publicist, a moralist and a historian, and lack that intimate awareness of political forces, that sureness of touch of a Burke, a Disraeli, a Churchill or a Lloyd George. Debarred by his profession from the House of Commons, the only substantial rewards Swift could win were bound to be in the form of ecclesiastical preferment and he made an effort (hard for a proud man) to secure an English deanery. He was, in the event, given as a consolation prize the best Irish deanery, Saint Patrick's, a piece of preferment which he accepted as a *pis alier*.

Ireland, which it seemed at first might be his Elba, soon, in the summer of 1714 turned into a Saint Helena for him. His appointment to Saint Patrick's was followed by a series of catastrophes – the breach between Oxford and Bolingbroke, the death of the Queen and the rout of the Tory party. As he himself summed it up, 'The queen was dead, the ministry changed and I was only the poor dean of Saint Patrick's.' Swift, isolated in Ireland, realized that for him, the conspicuous adherent of disgraced ministers and a discredited cause, the avenues of promotion were blocked. England, where, as he said, 'I made my friendships and there left my desires,' was closed to him.[3] He was condemned to spend his life in what he clearly considered a second-class environment and even a visit to England was 'attended with an ugly circumstance of returning to Ireland'.[4]

Swift, however, though he had a harsh view of human nature took a continuous and lively interest in human activities. He knew the Irish countryside well, and living in the centre of a small, compact and talkative capital he could scarcely avoid being in touch with Irish politics. Moreover, his sense of frustration and disappointment brought him into sympathetic accord with important currents in Irish public life. Ireland at the beginning of the eighteenth century was undoubtedly an unhappy country. During the previous century it had been twice ravaged by civil war and the victors' determination to entrench themselves securely for the future was embodied in the penal laws, which were having crippling effects on Irish social life. In an age when mercantilism dominated economic thinking, Ireland was compelled by restrictive legislation to conform to the pattern of imperial economic development laid down by the Westminster parliament. Finally, Ireland, in spite of possessing a parliamentary constitution rooted in the Middle Ages, had to accept the legislative and judicial supremacy of the imperial parliament and saw its executive nominated by the British ministry of the day and many of the best public appointments in the country going to Englishmen.

Some years before he became dean of Saint Patrick's, and probably while pent-up in Ireland, Swift summed up what he thought to be Ireland's grievances in a small, unpublished tract, 'The Story of the Injured Lady': the assertion of supremacy by the imperial parliament, absenteeism, the granting of major posts in Ireland to Englishmen, and, above all, the commercial restrictions. After he took up permanent residence in Ireland, it was the commercial restrictions, the legislation that 'made wool a drug to us and a monopoly to them' and rendered Ireland's ports and harbours 'to be of no more use to us than a beautiful prospect to a man shut up in a dungeon',[5] which aroused his anger. This legislation was to Swift both unjust and stupid, a vivid demonstration of what he considered to be an outstanding element in human nature, more conspicuous perhaps than even original sin – inherent stupidity.

Restrictive economic policies, whatever may be their ultimate justification, always offer an easy target to the satirist, and as they are certain to curb the activities of some sections, they are likely to be vigorously denounced. Theoretically, British commercial policy was meant to benefit the whole empire; in practice, since it was dictated by the parliament of Westminster, it was bound to be biased in favour of British interests. To what extent it was biased and to what extent completely mistaken in conception are debatable issues. Swift, however, does not discuss how imperial commercial policy should be shaped. He does not balance free trade and protectionist arguments, though he does support the policy still in vogue of encouraging national self-sufficiency to the greatest possible extent, his support being strengthened by his bias in favour of 'an austere economy'. Luxury exports, he argues, should be banned – incidentally, wine, which he consumed, was a permissible import, 'all we have to comfort us', while feminine frippery was to be discouraged.[6] But what infuses terrific force into Swift's writings on the commercial restrictions is not his ideas on international trade, but the vehement indignation with which he protests against external interference with Ireland's trade and calls for retaliation. And since the Irish parliament would not impose protective or retaliatory duties, he exhorts the Irish public to voluntary action.

From attacking the trade restrictions Swift moved boldly on to attacking the authority that imposed them. To him, the subordination of Ireland to Great Britain was slavery, and he bitterly resented finding himself a member of a servile community. In 1724 he had a good opportunity of stating his views and of proving to the Irish public that it was indeed in a humiliating situation. The terms of Woods' patent were such as to intensify the suspicions that a currency issue with its inherent complexities is liable to arouse. In 1723 the Irish House of Commons had passed a series of strong resolutions against Woods' patent – a committee of the Privy Council had reported on it, influential members of the Irish Privy Council were against it. So Swift, when he drew up his scarifying denunciations of Woods, had plenty of material to draw on and was sure of a receptive audience. Having prepared the ground and won his readers' attention by demonstrating that the currency project was both damaging to Ireland's economic interests and a scandalous job, he went on to emphasize what he, and 'the best whigs in England', regarded as a fundamental political truth, 'that all government without the consent of the governed is the very definition of slavery' and that Irishmen 'by the laws of God, of nature, of nations and of your own country ... are and ought to be as free a people as your brethren in England'. Swift's ringing outspokenness invested his arguments with dramatic force. And the fact that The Drapier was known to be an ecclesiastical dignitary – in every sense of the word a member of the establishment – lent a piquancy to his protest which delighted the public.

But if Swift was a superb political pamphleteer, Walpole was an intelligent and adroit politician who knew well when to retreat. The patent was withdrawn, Irish indignation died down, and Swift later bitterly reflected that while in the British parliament a 'patriot' opposition was to be found, Irish MPs could be comprehended under two categories – young dunces and atheists, or old villains and monsters.[7]

The fourth, and most powerful, of *The Drapier Letters* was addressed to 'The whole people of Ireland' and in it Swift addresses his 'dear countrymen'. But it is often difficult, when studying writings which are the immediate product of a particular political crisis, to distinguish between rhetoric and hard, basic conviction. This problem definitely arises when an attempt is made to discover the nature of Swift's conception of the Irish people. To begin with, he identifies complete citizenship with membership of the Established Church. In any country, he laid down, there should be one established faith, and 'consequently only the priests of that particular form are maintained at the public charge and all civil employments are bestowed amongst those who comply (at least outwardly) with the same establishment'.[8] Two large sections of the Irish population of Ireland were obviously therefore excluded from full citizenship. Swift was strongly anti-Catholic: 'popery ... which for a thousand years passed has been introducing and multiplying corruptions both in doctrine and discipline', he regarded as 'the most absurd system of Christianity professed by any nation'. He seems to have had little contact with Irish Catholics and he never dwells on the penal laws as a cause of Ireland's economic retardation. By the early thirties he seems to have thought it possible to consider relaxing the penal laws simply because the Catholics were a defeated and declining community. Their estates were few and 'crumbling into small parcels', 'their common people sunk in poverty and ignorance'.[9] Further, in controversy they could be usefully contrasted with the aggressive Presbyterians.

Swift's hostility to the Presbyterians, which was a strong and consistent element in his thinking, was strengthened by their success in building up their ecclesiastical organization in the North of Ireland. And his almost hysterical dislike of Presbyterianism (in 'The Story of the Injured Lady' the Scots are said to 'have no reputation for virtue, honesty, truth or manners') blinded him to the economic virtues of the Ulster Scot, which were already making their mark on the province. When the question of relaxing the Presbyterians' disabilities was raised, Swift vehemently tried to prove that during the civil wars the Presbyterians were more disloyal and destructive than the Catholics. If penal laws against dissent were going to be relaxed, he argued, the Catholics had a good or a better claim to consideration. It hardly need be stressed that if an Irish MP accepted this contention, it would merely stiffen his determination to retain the disabilities on Catholics and Presbyterians alike.

It was not only on theological grounds that Swift excluded the bulk of the inhabitants of Ireland from complete citizenship. He believed that historical developments in Ireland had created an elite of which he was proud to be a member. He belonged to the section that had conquered Ireland and deserved to be on as good a footing as any subjects of Britain.[10] Thus, both on religious and historical grounds, Swift's conception of the Irish people was a narrow one, which placed him in a position of unchallenged supremacy. Moreover, when he addressed the inhabitants of Ireland he rebuked them with prophetic severity and thoroughness. Every section he refers to, with one exception, is sharply criticized. Landlords are blamed for letting large tracts to greedy graziers and for not trying to improve the value of their estates by insisting on improvement clauses. Yet improving landlords, of whom he admits there were a few, are sneered at because 'through covetousness or want of skill' they generally leave things worse than they were. Farmers are

denounced because through 'poverty', laziness or ignorance they
have failed to treat the soil properly. The majority of the Irish rural
masses were sunk in 'an idle, savage, beastly thievish manner of life'.
Those reduced to beggary were the most 'undeserving, vicious race
of human kind'.[11] As for Irish businessmen, the Northern weavers
were dishonest and the Dublin weavers slack and unreliable.[12]

There was one group in Ireland, however, about whom Swift
wrote with sympathy and whom he was quick to defend – the clergy
of the Established Church. Admittedly, Swift was often highly critical of one section of the clergy – the bishops. But after all many English High Churchmen, while venerating episcopacy, were quick to
detect the frailties of latitudinarian prelates placed on the bench by
the Whigs. So Swift was by no means unusual in combining a strong
belief in episcopacy with a poor opinion of many bishops. And any
threat to the privileges of the Church of Ireland roused him to
action. It has already been mentioned how strongly he defended the
tests that excluded the Protestant nonconformists from office. Tithe
was another ecclesiastical issue on which he felt strongly. Tithes, he
held, were 'the patrimony of the church; and if not of divine origin,
yet at least of great antiquity', and to deprive the clergy of tithe, or
any portion of it, would be 'the great violation of common justice'.
And, he asserted, 'any income in the hands of the clergy is at least
as useful to the public, as the same income in the hands of the laity'.
To those who complained that tithe was a heavy burden on the tiller
of the soil, Swift retorted indignantly, 'I defy the wickedest and most
powerful clergyman in the kingdom to oppress the meanest farmer
in the parish'.[13] Understandably, then, he was very hostile to a
scheme for encouraging the linen industry by providing that a
modus should be substituted for a tithe on flax and his opposition
was apparently largely responsible for the bill being dropped.

Swift was not, it should be said, merely a negative critic of his
fellow countrymen. He interspersed his criticism with advice. In one
respect he was very much a man of his age. Western European man
was rapidly coming to appreciate technological achievement. Intelligent men prided themselves on producing practical solutions for
economic and social problems. Swift, with his wide range of interests and avidity (at times rivalling Defoe) for matter-of-fact detail,

perceived plenty of opportunities for making improvements in Ireland. Ireland, he thought, should have a mint. Fields should be
drained, trees should be planted and roads should be made or
repaired by introducing a turn-pike system on the English model.[14]
Another English institution that Swift was anxious to see established
in Ireland was the law of settlement, which obliged each parish to
support its own paupers. As an inhabitant of Dublin to which the
beggars of Ireland tended to be drawn, and as a clergyman, an obvious if not in fact a very vulnerable target for importunity, Swift was
deeply conscious of this lacuna in Irish life (which was not to be
filled until a century after his death). And he strongly urged as an
immediate step in the direction the 'badging' of Dublin-born beggars, which of course would discourage country beggars from ply-
ing their trade in the capital. Also he thought 'it would be a noble
achievement to abolish the Irish language, at least so far as, to oblige
all the natives to speak only English on every occasion of business
... in shops, markets, fairs and other places of dealing'. This would
promote both civilization and Protestantism in Ireland.

Above all, he wanted tillage to be encouraged – because it would
increase the number of people, 'without which any country however
blessed by nature must continue poor'.[15] And he viewed with disapproval emigration to North America, already becoming a feature of
Irish life. Here, in Swift's thinking, there seems to be the makings of
an inconsistency. On the one hand, he clearly favoured a large population growth, on the other hand, sharing the apprehensions with
another country clergyman expressed half a century after his death,
was haunted by the spectre of a population pressing steadily on the
means of subsistence. And his fears are crystallized in the most sick-
ening satire in English literature, 'A modest proposal for preventing
the children of poor people from being a burthen to their parents or
country and/or making them beneficial to the public'. Swift could,
of course, say that the waste of life which he brings home with such
horrifying force was the consequence of the distortion of Irish economic life by the commercial restrictions. But it would surely be
optimistic to suggest that the pressure of population on subsistence
would be removed merely by an increase in subsistence – and Swift
is not in his general approach an optimist.

It was indeed his sombre pessimism which made him such a forcible and acceptable spokesman for Ireland during the first half of the eighteenth century and later. Swift's pessimism, his indignation when he contemplated the results of human mismanagement, may have been a compound of bitter personal experience and profound awareness of the fundamental conditions governing man in society. To his Irish contemporaries his severe and righteous indignation well reflected present discontents. And, as John Redmond pointed out eighty years ago, Swift played a strange role in Irish history. A fervent Anglican and a Hanoverian Tory, his nationalism was a narrow one. 'Yet he did as much', Redmond declared, 'as any man in history to lift Ireland into the position of a nation.'[16] It is ironic that Swift should have come to be regarded as one of the prophets of the movement of which Redmond was a leader. Would the great master of irony have done justice to his own position in Irish history?

NOTES

1. *The Examiner*, ed. H.Davis (1940), pp. 163–4.
2. *Irish Tracts 1720–1723 and Sermons*, ed. H. Davis (1948), p. 224.
3. *The Correspondence of Jonathan Swift*, ed. H. Williams, ii, p. 133.
4. *Ibid.* ii, p. 441.
5. *Ibid.* iii, p. 189.
6. *Irish Tracts 1720–1723 and Sermons*, p. 15; *Irish Tracts, 1728–1733*, ed. H. Davis (1955), p. 8.
7. *Ibid.* pp. 124–6.
8. *Correspondence of Swift*, iv, p. 477.
9. *Irish Tracts 1728–1733*, p. 243.
10. *Ibid.* pp. 272–3.
11. *Correspondence of Swift*, iii, p. 132; iv, p. 229; *Irish Tracts 1728–1733*, p. 177.
12. *Irish Tracts 1728–1733*, pp. 8, 17, 89; *Directions to Servants and Miscellaneous Pieces 1733–1742*, p. 35.
13. *Irish Tracts 1728–1733*, pp. 69–70.
14. *Directions to Servants ...*, pp. 106–7; *Irish Tracts 1728–1733*, p. 78.
15. *Ibid.* pp. 9, 57, 86–9.
16. *Ibid.* p. 89.

VII Edmund Burke and the Law[*]

Edmund Burke, born in Dublin in 1729, grew up in a very practical legal environment. His father, Richard Burke, was an attorney in the Court of Exchequer. Richard had been born a Catholic but had conformed, otherwise he would have been debarred from the legal profession. However, as it seems that much of the law business in Dublin was handled by 'new converts',[1] Richard Burke would not have been unpleasantly conspicuous for his change of denomination. Indeed his Catholic connections may have been useful when it came to building up a practice. In any event, according to Edmund Burke, his father was 'for many years not only in the first rank but the very first man of his profession in point of practice and credit' and, after maintaining for years a high standard of living and 'some heavy losses by the banks', he was able to leave a substantial sum to his family.[2] Richard's eldest son, Garrett, enrolled as an attorney, working with his father. The second son was Edmund. The third, Richard, after an adventurous but unprofitable career, was called to the English Bar when he was forty and through his brother Edmund's influence was elected recorder of Bristol. To go back in the seventeenth century, Edmund Burke was remotely connected through his mother, Mary Nagle, with James Nagle, Attorney General of Ireland under James II, and to go forward to the later eighteenth century, Edmund's son Richard was called to the Bar in 1780.

Edmund Burke entered Trinity College Dublin in 1744, was elected a scholar in 1746 and graduated in 1748. In his senior

---

[*] The text of an address delivered in The Queen's University, Belfast on 24 October 1998.

sophister year he was introduced to jurisprudence, Pufendorf being one of the prescribed authors. Pufendorf (1632–94) was praised by Mackintosh – with significant qualifications: 'Without the genius of Grotius', Mackintosh wrote, 'and with very inferior learning', Pufendorf treated natural law 'with sound sense, with clear method, with extensive and accurate knowledge and with a copiousness of detail, sometimes indeed tedious, but always instructive and satis-factory'.[3] Pufendorf taught that the Creator, besides giving to mankind divine law, had implanted in men an awareness of the rules that should govern them in their relations to one another – rules which taken together comprised natural law, an essential ele-ment in all legal systems. The conviction that law fundamentally was of divine origin must have awakened a ready response in a reli-giously-minded youth such as Burke.

For two years after graduating Burke stayed on in Dublin, enjoy-ing the entitlements of his scholarship, dabbling in journalism and reading widely. He could have attended the lectures of the Regius professor of laws and of the professor of oratory and history, assuming they were delivered. But the holders of those chairs at the end of the 1740s were undistinguished senior fellows. In 1750 Burke left Dublin to read for the Bar. He had already been entered as a law student in the Middle Temple in 1747, when still an under-graduate. This step suggests that his father, a successful attorney presumably concerned with upward mobility, was keen that his bright son should join the senior branch of the profession and, a masterful man, he was ready to subsidize his son generously as a law student. How far Burke himself was eager to embark on a career at the Bar is hard to say. He had already a number of other intellectual interests and aspirations. But reading for the Bar pro-vided him with an immediate objective and left him fairly free to have a stimulating life in London. It is also impossible to say which Bar, the English or the Irish, he intended to practice at, since as a prelude to admission to the Irish Bar a law student had to spend 'eight terms commons' in an English inn of court.[4] So the fact that Burke entered the Middle Temple leaves the matter open. Of course, if he had been called to the Irish Bar, his father, controlling a supply of briefs, could have given him a good start.

In the Middle Temple it was required that every person should keep commons in hall for twelve terms before being called to the Bar – the only requirement except, of course, the prescribed fees.[5] It is easy to sneer at the system of eating one's way to a professional qualification. But a barrister's clients were hard-headed attorneys, and a law student who hoped to earn his living as a barrister, in addition to dining, read systematically and attended the courts, taking notes and even perhaps worked in an attorney's office to gain some knowledge of procedure. Burke certainly made an effort to prepare himself for the Bar. After rather more than a year in London, referring to his legal studies, he wrote: 'I read as much as I can (which is however but a little), and I am just beginning to know something of what I am about, which till very lately I did not; this study carries no difficulty to those who already understand it and to those who will never understand it, and for all between those extremes (God knows) they have a hard task of it.'[6] Burke writes modestly, but he was possessed by a driving determination to master intellectually any subject he was engaged with, and in his efforts to comprehend the law he must have been encouraged by the admiring and cheerful companionship of his cousin, William Burke, also a student at the Middle Temple, who was called to the Bar in 1755.

Burke was soon distracted from his legal work by other interests; poetry, history, philosophy, general literature – 'the fatal itch that makes me scribble still', travel and London life. So, after some years he came to the conclusion that the law 'has been confined and drawn up into a narrow and inglorious study ... insomuch that the study of our jurisprudence presented to liberal, well-educated minds, even in the best authors, hardly anything but barbarous terms, ill explained; a coarse but not plain expression; an indigested method, and a species of reasoning the very refuse of the schools'. 'Young men', he added, 'were sent away with an incurable and, if we regard the manner of handling rather than the substance, a well-founded disgust.'[7] One young man was ready to broaden the English legal mind. At the age of about twenty-eight, Burke, who seemed to have already lost interest in a career at the Bar, decided to embark on a history of the English law, a work of which only a few introductory paragraphs survive. English lawyers, he wrote, laboured under two misapprehensions – that the English law had remained very much 'in the same state from antiquity' and that it was entirely English in origin, 'in every respect peculiar to this island'.⁸ He intended to show that the English law had evolved through the centuries, drawing from a variety of sources, Anglo-Saxon custom, Norman law, canon law and civil law.

That Burke had been greatly stimulated by his legal studies emerges in a work he wrote at the outset of his political career. When, at the beginning of the 1760s, he was private secretary to William Gerard Hamilton, the Irish Chief Secretary, Burke drafted a sweeping attack on the penal laws against the Irish Catholics which, in addition to citing some of the standard arguments for the modification or complete abolition of the laws – that they hindered Irish economic development, introduced discord into family life, reflected an anachronistic intolerance and discriminated against a loyal section of the community – he endeavoured to show in a few paragraphs, studded with quotations from Cicero, Philo, Suarez and the Digest, that they were against 'the acknowledged principles of jurisprudence'. They challenged, Burke contended, the two great principles on which law was based – equity, which 'grows out of the great rule of equality which is grounded upon our common nature', and utility, 'that is to say general and public utility'. The consent of the people, actual or implied, he wrote, was absolutely essential to the validity of a law. Admittedly, the people were presumed to consent to whatever the legislature ordained for their benefit and should 'acquiesce in it … as an act of homage and just deference to a reason which the necessity of government has made superior to their own'. But the exclusion of a great body of men from the common advantages of society could not be intended for their good, and could not be ratified even by an implied consent. Indeed, he stated, if the people, or presumably, a majority, consented to a law prejudicial to the whole community, it would be against 'the principle of a superior law … I mean the will of Him who gave us our nature and impressed an invariable law upon it'. Finally, 'it would be hard to point out any error more truly subversive of all the order and beauty, of all the peace and happiness of human society, than the position that any body of men have a right to make what laws they please'.⁹

This is a suitable point to stress to what an extent Burke's reverence for law was closely connected with his religious beliefs. An evangelically minded youth, attending a Quaker school at an impressionable age, a loyal and devoted member of the Church of England, he was tolerant of other Christian denominations and had a measure of respect for other great religions, 'the synagogue, the mosque, the pagoda'.[10] Throughout his political career he frequently referred to Providence, apparently not as a synonym for inevitable or vague destiny, but as denoting a merciful and just Creator, keeping a concerned watch over humankind. Law, 'beneficence acting by a rule',[11] was God's gift to man, and we were all born in subjection 'to one great immutable, pre-existent law, prior to all our devices, prior to all our contrivances, paramount to our very being itself, by which we are knit and connected in the eternal frame of the universe, out of which we cannot stir'.[12] Law, rightly conceived, representing the Creator's intentions, was, along with other institutions and customs, prejudices and traditions, an important element in binding society together. Broadening down from precedent to precedent, it vividly illustrated how the rules governing human behaviour in society evolved. Indeed, when Burke wanted to illustrate how greatly Englishmen were indebted to past generations, he employed a legal metaphor: we 'derive all we possess as an inheritance from our forefathers' – 'an entailed inheritance'.[13] Moreover one very significant legal principle, prescription, part of the law of nature, was of essential social value because it protected private property, inherited and acquired, the great guarantee of independence and happiness.[14] So anxious was Burke to preserve property rights that he went so far as to imply that parliamentary interference with those rights could be quashed by the courts: 'We entertain', he wrote, 'a high opinion of legislative authority, but we never dreamt that parliament had any right whatever to overrule prescription or force a currency of their own fiction in the place of that which is real and recognised by the law of nations.'[15]

Law was not only a cohesive element in British society. It was, Burke declared, 'a similitude … of religion, laws and manners',[16] which bound the nations of Europe together. Europe, Burke considered, was a Commonwealth, 'virtually one great state', based on the general law derived from German customary law and feudal law, all 'improved and digested into a system' by Roman law.[17] Going much farther afield in 1788, during Hastings' impeachment, he emphasized that in Asia, as in Europe, the same law of nations prevailed: 'the same principles are continually resorted to, the same maxims sacredly held'.[18] All civilization, in short, was underpinned by the same legal fundamentals. This was well-illustrated, Burke pointed out, during the American War of Independence by the respect 'civilised states' paid to the rules of war, established not 'in black letter by statute and record' but by reason, 'by the convention of parties', and by the authority of writers, who took the laws and maxims not from their own invention and ideas but from the consent and sense of ages and from precedent. One of the rules was that the private property of individuals in a conquered territory was immune from seizure. After all, every monarch, even a conqueror, was bound to respect property rights – 'a principle inspired by the Divine Author of all good'.[19]

In the 1790s French developments forced Burke to face an important question in international law. In what circumstances was it justifiable for a foreign power or powers, 'the potentates of Europe', to interfere in the domestic affairs of another country? Burke had to admit that the rules relating to this question were uncertain. But fortunately, from his point of view, it seemed that jurists were agreed that when 'a country was divided [between warring factions] other powers were free to take which side they pleased' – a position upheld by 'a very republican writer', Vattell. Burke also justified the allied invasion of France by citing Roman civil law, pointing out that 'the law of neighbourhood', an important head of praetorian law, would not permit a man to carry out operations on his own property detrimental to his neighbour.[20] It should be added that, when optimistically looking forward to the restoration of the *ancien régime* in France, Burke revealed his ingrained respect for law. Though, he stated, 'bloody and merciless offenders' must be called to account, no man should be punished until after a trial 'carried on with all that caution and deliberation which has been used in the best times and precedents ... of the French jurisprudence'. In addition, anything that could be brought

forward in mitigation of an offence was to be taken into consideration: 'Mercy is not a thing opposed to justice.'[21]

In dealing with domestic questions, Burke displayed the same
reverence for law he showed in the international sphere. Shortly
after he entered the House of Commons, Burke pronounced that
'whatever the sacred seal of judicature impressed upon it, let it rest
inviolate for ever'.[22] How concerned he was to protect the sanctity
of the law was illustrated a few years later by his attitude to the
Juries bill of 1771. As an opposition Whig he supported the demand
that in a trial for libel the jury should be entitled to give a general
verdict on the whole issue, and he wished the question to be settled
by an act empowering the jury to give such a general verdict. But he
was definitely against a declaratory act enunciating that the judges
had been wrong in restricting juries to finding only on the fact of
publication: a declaratory act, 'a measure which tended to blacken
the character of the judges', was, he wrote, 'utterly impracticable'.[23]

On crime and punishment Burke's views were enlightened and
humane, but not excessively sentimental. As a schoolboy, discussing
the situation of an acquaintance facing the possibility of a murder
charge, Burke wrote that 'human sufferings call for human compassion'; thirty-five years later, as an influential MP, he emphasized
that justice should be tempered with mercy.[24] But he also stressed
that it was wrong to yield to the compassion that was rooted in 'a
flimsy, prevaricating, petty, peevish morality, incompatible with the
dignity of public justice'. There is nothing, he remarked, 'so
immoral as perverted morality'.[25] This insistence on the importance
of controlling compassion was, it is scarcely surprising, a reaction
to what Burke regarded as misguided sympathy for Warren Hastings in his impeachment ordeal.

Admitting that punishment was 'a melancholy necessity'[26] and
was usually greater than the offence merited, Burke emphasized that
the penalty should be proportionate to the offence and should oper-
ate as a deterrent rather than as a torment. Considering in 1789 that
'the whole system of the penal laws in this country is radically defec-
tive' and requiring revision, he was strongly against the multiplica-
tion of offences. The existing laws would often meet the case if the
magistrates were less negligent in enforcing them. He also suggested

that, where possible, instead of creating a criminal offence a civil
remedy should be provided – the damage could be assessed by a jury
and the injured party receive compensation.[27] Naturally, he was
highly critical of conventional reliance on capital punishment. Experience had shown, he declared, that capital punishment was not
more certain to prevent crimes than inferior penalties, and with the
excessive use of the death penalty 'the laws lose their terror in the
eyes of the wicked and their reverence in the eyes of the virtuous'.[28]

A capital sentence was often commuted to transportation, which
to Burke was an acceptable penalty – 'an unpleasant remedy, but
still a remedy in a desperate disease'.[29] But he considered it should
not be inflicted for trivial offences and that the convicts should not
be transported to an unhealthy zone, such as Gambia, 'the capital
seat of plague, pestilence and famine'. Burke saw transportation as
a desirable substitute 'for the butchery which we call justice', and as
a means for keeping the wicked from being let loose on the world
and for rendering those of mischievous disposition useful.[30] Referring to a well-known confidence trickster about to be transported,
Burke painted transportation in glowing colours:

> He goes to a place [Botany Bay] where he is not oppressed by the
> judgment he has suffered and where none but honest ways of life are
> open to him. The climate is good, the soil is not unfavourable. There
> is even some choice in the society. God knows that they who have
> suffered, and even deservedly suffered, by the sentence of the law,
> are very far from the worst or most disagreeable men in the world.
> I assure you that if I were to fall into a misfortune of this sort, and
> have youth and vigour of body and mind, I should think this change
> of place a thing to be desired, and not shunned.[31]

A substantial category of the prison population who were not
criminals but debtors, detained by their creditors, aroused the sympathy of many peers and MPs, including Burke, who on one occasion wrote to an undistinguished poet imprisoned for debt that
'some mistakes in conduct are natural or almost inevitable to men
of lively imaginations and narrow circumstances, particularly during
the warmth and openness of youth'. It was inhuman, Burke argued,
to keep thousands in a state of slavery, detained not by the judgment
of a court but at 'the arbitrary discretion of a private, nay interested

and irritated, individual'. Moreover, in addition to those debtors in prison, there was a multitude of insolvents hiding in terror, 'a dead-weight on the community'. A modification of the law, Burke argued, would protect credit by making lenders more cautious.[32]

Burke's belief that punishment should be tempered by well-measured leniency is illustrated by his attitude during the aftermath of the Gordon Riots (riots in which he was in considerable personal danger). He urged the government, while discouraging violence, 'to avoid an injudicious severity'. 'The appetite of justice', he declared, 'is easily satisfied and is best nourished with the least possible blood.'[33] He strongly deplored 'long strings of executions'.[34] Instead, after carefully examining all the cases of convicted rioters, the government should select a small number, at the utmost six, 'sufficient to mark and discountenance the general spirit of tumult', to be executed in the most solemn manner that could be devised. All the other malefactors were to be sent to the hulks or enlisted in the navy. Incidentally, he was inclined to be more lenient to the 'common plunderers' than to those rioters who had been led into crime 'by a false or pretended principle of religion'. Naturally enough, as a zealous advocate for the repeal of penal laws against the Catholics, Burke blamed anti-Catholic propaganda for the riots, and as a member of the parliamentary opposition, he asserted that the government's failure to take firm measures had encouraged the rioters.[35]

Though Burke gave serious attention to crime and punishment, and occasionally expressed his opinion on issues relating to the subject, he never participated in a major campaign to reform the criminal law. In fact, it might be said that his efforts in that direction were few and ineffective. In 1776 he introduced a bill to prevent the plundering of shipwrecks, 'a barbarous practice'. But his plan for levying compensation from the area in which the crime was committed, 'a remedy' which, he remarked, 'may be justified by the violence of the disease', aroused considerable opposition. Also, it was asserted that, given the legislation already in force, the bill was unnecessary. Understandably, then, it never reached the statute book.[36] Burke was eager to abolish the pillory. After an outburst of mob violence had resulted in two pilloried criminals being killed, the pillory had, he declared, been transformed from 'a punishment of shame' into 'an instrument of death', 'a death of torment'.[37] He initiated a discussion in the House of Commons, but does not seem to have taken the question further and the pillory was not abolished until 1837. In 1785 Burke informed the House that he intended to propose a series of resolutions on the treatment of convicts awaiting transportation;[38] but he does not seem to have persevered, possibly because from 1787 convicts were steadily being transported to Australia. Finally, near the end of his parliamentary career, in 1791, he expressed regret that he never had an opportunity of bringing forward the question of imprisonment for debt, and offered his services to those 'who might bring it up'.[39]

In one sphere, the law of marriage (or 'family law'), he enunciated firm views, reflecting profound convictions. In 1781 he opposed Fox's attempt to remove the bar on minors marrying without parental consent. Matrimony, Burke emphatically declared, was instituted not for 'mere animal propagation', but for 'men's nutrition, their education and their establishment', and for answering all the purposes of a rational and moral being. Men, he pointed out, were well-qualified for propagation before they were sufficiently qualified by 'mental prudence and by acquired skill in trades and professions for the maintenance of a family'. Surely, to allow someone 'to introduce citizens into the Commonwealth before a rational security can be given that he may provide for them and educate them, as citizens ought to be provided for and educated, is totally incongruous with the whole order of society'.[40] And he called on the House of Commons to have mercy on the youth of both sexes and protect them from their youth and inexperience. Ten years earlier, in a debate on divorce, having declared that 'the foundation of all the order, harmony, tranquillity and even the civilisation that is amongst us turns upon two things, the indissolubility of marriage and the freedom of the female sex', he strongly but unsuccessfully supported the proposal that a clause should be inserted in all divorce acts forbidding the marriage of adulterous parties and providing that their children should not be legitimized. This, he said, would not punish adultery but make it inconvenient. The stronger the marriage tie, he explained, the more easy it was 'for women to move freely in polished society'.[41] Naturally, then, at the end of the century he denounced both the French National Assembly for declaring that marriage was a civil contract, dissoluble by mutual consent and on a number of other grounds, and the assembly's successor, the convention, for placing bastards on the same footing as legitimate children. The new French approach to divorce aimed not at 'the relief of domestic uneasiness' but at 'the total corruption of all morals, the total disconnection of social life'.[42]

At a late stage in his political career, Burke, who in early manhood had turned away from the Bar, found himself playing the role of a prosecuting counsel as the leader of the managers appointed by the House of Commons to conduct the impeachment of Warren Hastings. From the early 1780s Burke had been intensely interested in Indian affairs, and, having examined a vast mass of manuscript and printed material and having questioned a number of witnesses, he had decided that Hastings, the Governor-General, a man actuated by 'avarice, rapacity, pride, cruelty, ferocity, malignancy of temper, haughtiness and insolence', was 'the scourge of India',[43] and Burke pledged himself 'to God, to his country and to the unfortunate and plundered inhabitants of India that he would bring to justice the greatest delinquent that India ever saw'. There were, he explained to the House of Commons, three modes by which state delinquents could be proceeded against – a bill of pains and penalties, which Burke rejected as unfair to the accused; a prosecution in the King's Bench which, as it would involve a very large indictment, would overwhelm the court, blocking all its normal work; or an impeachment, the prosecution of a great state offender by the House of Commons, 'the great inquest of the nation', before the House of Lords, 'the most high and supreme court'.[44]

Impeachment, an historic and impressive process, was, according to Burke, 'the cement that binds the constitution together'.[45] But though the threat of impeachment was still part of parliamentary rhetoric and was in 1787 imbedded in the American constitution, it was falling into disuse. Viewed retrospectively, most impeachments had in their inception and progress reflected violent partisanship, and better methods for bringing ministers and high officials to account were being developed. By the mid-nineteenth century a great legal historian could refer to impeachment as 'a cumbersome and unsatisfactory mode of proceeding', and, having Hastings in mind, add that it was 'monstrous that a man should be tortured, at irregular intervals, for seven years, in order that a singularly incompetent tribunal might be addressed ... by Burke and Sheridan, in language far removed from the calmness with which an advocate for the prosecution ought to address a criminal court'.[46] But in 1788 Burke was convinced that an impeachment accorded with the status of the offender and the magnitude of the cause – involving as it did grave crimes, relations between Great Britain and India, and the principles that should govern imperial policy.

There was, too, a practical reason for proceeding by impeachment. The House of Lords, Burke argued, in a cause within its original jurisdiction, should follow 'the laws and usage of parliament' and should not feel obliged to follow the rules of pleading observed in the inferior courts at Westminster or indeed the rules of Roman civil law. At the beginning of his opening speech, he reminded the house that 'Your lordships are not bound by any rules whatever, except those of natural, substantial and immutable justice', and he hoped that 'the liberality and nobleness of the sentiments to which you were born' would not, by any abuse of the forms and technical course of the proceedings, deny justice to India.[47] But the peers, conscious perhaps that they were living in an enlightened age and that most of the precedents relating to impeachment were drawn from periods of ruthless civil strife, readily consulted the judges when legal issues arose during the Hastings impeachment, and the judges delivered their opinions privately to the House. The managers bitterly complained that this practice left them in doubt about matters on which they desired to have every light; but, of course, by not stating their opinions publicly, the judges deprived the managers of opportunities for challenging them – probably at interminable length.[48] Burke indignantly pointed out that by allowing the judges to decide what evidence should be admitted, the lords were reducing themselves to the level of mere jurors, seriously upsetting the constitutional balance. In 1789 Burke boldly asserted that, though the House of Lords was a supreme court of justice, the

House of Commons, 'the watch, the inquisitor, the purifier of every judicial and executive function', had a degree of control over the upper house in its judicial capacity – 'one of the seeming paradoxes of our constitution', he remarked.[49] Wisely, however, he refrained from attempting to express this paradox in action, an attempt which would presumably have led to a major clash between the two Houses.

In a long defence of the managers' conduct of the Hastings prosecution, Burke pleaded eloquently for a flexible approach to the rules of evidence, paying particular attention to the rules relating to circumstantial evidence.[50] In the civil law, he pointed out, many attempts involving much subtle reasoning had been made 'to reduce to rule the principles of evidence or proof', and in ancient times the English common law courts had tended to observe 'a rigid strictness in the application of technical rules'. But, as Burke was quick to point out, human actions were not of 'a metaphysical nature' and could not be 'subjected (without exceptions that reduce it to almost nothing) to any certain rule'. Fortunately, 'the genius of the law of England' permitted 'the general moral necessities of things and the nature of the case' to override even those rules that 'seem to be the very strongest'. Rules which savour of the schools, Burke argued, should yield to experience, observation, good sense, manly reason and human sagacity. He commended Hardwicke and Mansfield for their readiness to enlarge the rules of evidence and disregard useless technicalities, Mansfield being outstanding for his efforts to make the law 'keep pace with the demands of justice'. In short, the need to track down and punish crimes that were difficult to detect 'superseded the theoretic aim at perfection and obliged technical science to submit to practical experience'.[51]

Besides deploring an uncritical and unreasonable adherence to the rules of evidence, Burke also warned against an excessive deference to precedent. Precedents, he stated, should have been created in 'good constitutional times' and be agreeable to the general tenor of legal principles, and he denounced lawyers as 'hunters after precedents' and 'scratchers of parchment'. 'In a question which concerned the safety and welfare of the people', he declared, 'every consideration except what has a tendency to promote these great objects became superseded, *salus populi suprema lex*' (a maxim he would have heard with distaste if advanced in defence of Hastings).[52]

Legal reformers would have highly approved of Burke's fervent concern that legal forms, sometimes archaic, should not obstruct the quest for truth. Unfortunately, however, his reasoned and erudite plea for a common-sense approach to the laws of evidence and the use of precedent was seriously weakened by his disregard for the rights of the accused and his passionate determination to secure Hastings' conviction. During the impeachment years Burke, much as he esteemed and respected the law, displayed at times a degree of contempt for the English Bar. Though he declared in the House of Commons that he had for the legal profession 'a degree of veneration, approaching almost to idolatry', he went on to say that he could not help feeling that its members were 'very apt to be influenced by a very natural prejudice, which the French called *esprit de corps*'. This, for instance, explained the antipathy of lawyers to impeachment, a procedure by which those who 'called all others to account' might themselves be brought to trial.[53]

In fact, he approved of the country being governed by law, but not by lawyers.[54] Writing to Lord Hailes, the well-known Scottish judge, historian, antiquarian and Christian apologist, Burke remarked that he never thought 'of some of you Scotch gentlemen of the robe without being a little ashamed for England. Our bar does not abound in general erudition – and I am every day more and more convinced that they are not the better professional men from not being more extensively learned'.[55] Two years later he characterized Chief Justice Kenyon, a learned if limited lawyer and a strong supporter of Hastings, as 'a violent, hot-headed vulgar man, without the least tincture of liberality or generous erudition and, though of some low acuteness, is void of anything like enlarged sense'.[56] A few years later, chatting with a young Irish barrister with intellectual inclinations, Burke discussed the legal profession in more general terms. He thought that the law as a profession was 'not calculated to develop the highest powers of the human mind', though he granted that there were several exceptions to this. A barrister's work and studies might sharpen his understanding and give a degree of logical precision to his thinking; but the general effect was 'to reduce the mind from a wholesale to a retail dealer in subordinate and petty topics of information'.[57]

There is an embarrassed fascination in observing Burke, an admirer and ardent defender of historic institutions and well-established corporations, appearing in the guise of an exasperated critic of traditional legal procedures and of the English Bar. Burke, of course, could insist that he always distinguished between reform, which was good, and innovation, which would probably prove disastrous. But his attitude in the late 1780s and nineties to the legal profession and their procedures can, of course, be largely explained by the course of the Hastings impeachment. The House of Lords in its judicial capacity 'corrupted by the Indian malady', the judges whom it consulted, some lawyers in the Commons, Hastings' powerful legal team and Thomas Erskine, the great Whig advocate who had appeared for the defence when a pamphleteer was prosecuted for his support of Hastings – all were, in Burke's eyes, leagued to preserve Hastings, 'the head, the chief, the captain general in iniquity',[58] from the punishment he so richly deserved, and consequently to deny justice to the people of India.

It is also possible that Burke may have been influenced by memories of a somewhat domineering, if generous, father, pressing him to enter a profession which, if seriously pursued, would have to a great extent cut him off from enthralling intellectual interests. Moreover, towards the end of his life, he was saddened and puzzled by the 'astonishing and unmerited want of success' at the Bar of his brother and his son.[59] Family feeling rendered him oblivious to defects, which must have interfered with their careers. Richard, his brother, though undoubtedly intelligent, was convivial and feckless, the very model of a cheerful but almost briefless barrister. His son, though able, industrious and high-minded, was opinionated, overfluent and rather insensitive to other people's reactions.

Finally, even in a man of outstanding intellectual gifts, personal set-backs can colour ratiocination. In 1784 Burke took an action for libel against the *Public Advertiser*, which had accused him of misapplying public money, claiming £5000 damages. The jury, because they thought 'my only view was to clear myself of the imputation which had been thrown upon me', awarded him only £100. 'A more direct encouragement', he exclaimed, 'could not be given to such practices. £100 is as nothing to the stock of that paper.' In 1797, when he was suing a printer for literary piracy, he angrily complained that the courts 'seemed to be in league with every kind of fraud and injustice', proceeding as if they had an intricate settlement of £10,000 a year to discuss when dealing with 'an affair which might be as well decided in three weeks as in three hundred years'.[60]

Circumstances, in fact, provoked Burke at times to pronounce that the law was an ass.[61] But though he may, during short bouts of irritation, have impulsively expressed intense exasperation with lawyers, their practices, procedures and prejudices, Burke nevertheless remained convinced that the law, with all its limitations, must be regarded with reverence, and that lawyers, with all their faults, performed functions of the utmost value to the community.

NOTES

1. H. Boulter, *Letters Written by His Excellency Hugh Boulter ... to Several Ministers of State* (Oxford 1769), i, p. 226.

2. *The Correspondence of Edmund Burke*, ed. T.W. Copeland (Cambridge 1958–78) [hereafter referred to as *Correspondence*], i, p. 274.

3. J. Mackintosh, *The Miscellaneous Works of the Right Honourable Sir James Mackintosh* (London 1840), i, p. 355.

4. C. Kenny, *King's Inns and the Kingdom of Ireland: The Irish 'Inn of Court' 1541–1800* (Dublin 1992), p. 179.

5. W. Holdsworth, *A History of English Law* (London 1922–66), xii, p. 24.

6. *Correspondence*, i, p. iii.

7. *The Writings and Speeches of Edmund Burke*, ed. P. Langford (Oxford 1981–) [hereafter referred to as *Writings and Speeches*], i, pp. 323–4.

8. *Ibid.* p. 323.

9. *Writings and Speeches*, ix, pp. 453–8, 462.

10. *Correspondence*, iv, p. 85.

11. *Writings and Speeches*, viii, p. 109.

12. *Writings and Speeches*, vi, p. 350.

13. *Writings and Speeches*, viii, pp. 81–4.

14. *Writings and Speeches*, ii, p. 65, and viii, p. 220; *Correspondence*, vi, pp. 42–4.

15. *Writings and Speeches*, viii, p. 221.

16. *Writings and Speeches*, iii, p. 195.

17. *Writings and Speeches*, ix, pp. 248–9.

18. *Writings and Speeches*, vii, p. 317.

19. *The Parliamentary History of England from the Earliest Period to the Year 1803* (London 1806–20) [hereafter referred to as *Parliamentary History*), xxii, pp. 228–30.

20. *Writings and Speeches*, viii, p. 74, and ix, p. 250; *Correspondence*, vi, p. 317.

21. *Writings and Speeches*, viii, pp. 49, 5–96.

22. *Writings and Speeches*, ii, p. 225.

23. *Correspondence*, ii, p. 187.

24. *Correspondence*, i, p. 22; *Parliamentary History*, xxi, p. 388.

25. *Parliamentary History*, xxx, p. 981.

26. *Correspondence*, iv, p. 134.

27. *Parliamentary History*, xxviii, p. 146.

28. *Writings and Speeches*, iii, pp. 338–9, 614.

29. *Correspondence*, viii, p. 328.

30. *Correspondence*, iii, p. 252.

31. *Correspondence*, viii, p. 328.

32. *Correspondence*, iii, p. 231; *Writings and Speeches*, iii, p. 636; *Parliamentary History*, xxix, pp. 512–13.

33. *Writings and Speeches*, iii, p. 618.

34. *Correspondence*, iv, p. 255.

35. *Writings and Speeches*, iii, p. 612–18.

36. *Ibid.* p. 225; *Correspondence*, iii, p. 141; *Parliamentary History*, xviii, pp. 1298–302.

37. *Writings and Speeches*, iii, p. 585.

38. *Parliamentary History*, xxv, pp. 391–2.

39. *Parliamentary History*, xxix, p. 512.

40. *Parliamentary History*, xxii, p. 410.

41. *Writings and Speeches*, ii, pp. 357–8.

42. *Writings and Speeches*, ix, pp. 243–5.

43. *Writings and Speeches*, vi, p. 275, and v, p. 476.

44. *Parliamentary History*, xxv, pp. 1060–8; *Writings and Speeches*, vi, pp. 51, 56–5; W. Blackstone, *Commentaries on the Laws of England* (5th edn, Oxford 1773), iv, p. 259.

45. *Writings and Speeches*, vi, p. 272.

46. J.F. Stephen, *A History of the Criminal Law of England* (London 1883), i, p. 160.

47. *Writings and Speeches*, vi, p. 276. For an authoritative account of the impeachment, see P.J. Marshall, *The Impeachment of Warren Hastings* (Oxford 1965).

48. *Parliamentary History*, xxxi, p. 315.

49. *Parliamentary History*, xxviii, pp. 1032–4.

50. The report of the committee of managers, which was very largely or wholly the work of Burke, is printed in *Commons' Jnl*, xlix, 504–37, and in *Parliamentary History*, xxxi, pp. 287–373 (and see also *Correspondence*, vii, p. 540).

51. *Parliamentary History*, xxxi, pp. 326–42.

52. *Parliamentary History*, xxviii, pp. 1130–3.

53. *Parliamentary History*, xxviii, p. 1234.

54. *Ibid.* p. 1169.

55. *Correspondence*, vi, p. 468.

56. *Ibid.* p. 3.

57. S. Prior, *Memoir of the Life and Character of ... Edmund Burke* (2nd edn, London 1826), ii, p. 531.

58. *Writings and Speeches*, vi, p. 276.

59. *Correspondence*, vii, p. 590.

60. *Correspondence*, v, pp. 159–60, 165; ix, pp. 245–6.

61. Mr Bumble's particular grievance (see Charles Dickens, *Oliver Twist* [1838], chapter 51) was removed by the Criminal Justice Act 1925, s. 47.

VIII John Hely-Hutchinson (1723–94)

The extent to which a politician could with decency look for personal advantages presented a difficult problem in eighteenth-century ethics. To procure an adequate reward for one's public services – and perhaps incidentally to provide for one's family – was regarded as reasonable and even commendable. But it was also recognized that a man should exercise restraint in pursuing his private objectives, and an opponent's efforts to recompense himself were commonly described as jobbery. A few politicians showed a high-minded disregard for the conventional profits of the game. Many combined a genuine desire to serve the state with enlightened self-interest. Some were noted for their greedy determination to grasp all the glittering prizes and even the minor perquisites of public life. In this last category Hely-Hutchinson was outstanding. Able and public-spirited, he was so eager to get paid for his services and so tasteless in emphasizing his claims at every opportunity, that he became a by-word even among his contemporaries. 'If England and Ireland were given to him,' Lord North remarked, 'he would solicit the Isle of Man for a potato garden.' But in the end he over-reached himself. The bold stroke by which he gained for himself an unexpected place, the provostship of Trinity, landed him in a tiring and ludicrous situation. The price he had to pay for this secure and lucrative post was that he was to become involved in a series of academic battles, which absorbed his energies, sharpened his temper and rendered him the laughing-stock of Dublin.

Born in 1723, the son of Francis Hely, Generosus, of Cork, he entered Trinity College in 1740 and graduated in 1744 after a respectable but undistinguished undergraduate career. He rapidly built up a large and lucrative practice at the Irish Bar and in 1751 he improved his prospects by marrying Christina Nickson, who in 1757 inherited the extensive estates of her uncle Richard Hutchinson. In 1759 Hely-Hutchinson (as he henceforth called himself) entered parliament for Lanesborough and in 1760 he was returned for Cork, a great independent constituency which he was to represent for thirty-four years. Within a few months of entering the house he came to the front as a strenuous advocate of economy and a pertinacious critic of the government. By 1761 he had become one of the government's debating mainstays, and he was appointed prime sergeant (with special financial advantages) in 1761, alnager in 1763, secretary of state in 1766 and provost of Trinity College in 1774. Gossip insisted that he tried to secure a major's commission (admittedly with the object not of serving but of selling). Until he became provost he was a strong candidate for the attorney generalship, and he toyed with the possibility of becoming lord chancellor. For years he urged the claims of his wife to a peerage, and in 1783 he secured for her the barony of Donoughmore, thus crowning his political career in the conventional manner by ennobling his family and at the same time holding on to his seat and influence in the House of Commons. His outlook on titles was crystallized in a letter written to his son a month or so before he died: 'The degree of a viscount accepted or obtained by a baron was never yet and never will be imputed to him as vanity. The rejection of it if offered would be so considered by any reasonable man.'

Alert, self-assured, urbane, indefatigable, Hutchinson had a mastery of economic fact, parliamentary procedure and legal precedents. His debating style was 'neat, flowing, smooth and copious' and, as an opponent said, he was invaluable in debate because he was always ready to go out in all weathers. An adept in forming advantageous friendships, in council he was downright and level-headed. More than once his career was endangered by his bold if not disinterested bearing in a political crisis. In 1767, when the Viceroy had a heavy legislative programme to carry through parliament, Hutchinson suddenly placed his services at the disposal of the great Shannon-Ponsonby alliance, which was in opposition. But after a year or so he was enticed back to lead the government party, and the Viceroy, after emphatic prompting, was wondering how he could be placed in some post 'where by applying more of his time to public business his uncommon abilities might be rendered more useful to the government'. Ten years later, when nationalist sentiment was mounting, Hutchinson, who was genuinely concerned for Ireland's economic interests and who was at last in a post from which he could not be dislodged, became notably tepid in his support of the administration and published an able, if ponderous, pamphlet against the trade restrictions. The Lord Lieutenant, Buckinghamshire, considered making a striking example by dismissing him from his official posts. But Buckinghamshire's recall saved Hutchinson from political martyrdom, and the new lord lieutenant was soon flattering him by 'attentions to the College'. Finally, in 1788, Hutchinson gambled in political futures by supporting the Whigs in the regency dispute. Again, a lord lieutenant urged his dismissal; again Hutchinson was saved, this time by joining a strong knot of office-holders who had all blundered in the crisis, but who by hanging together, managed to elbow their way back into the government's ranks.

In his later days Hutchinson adopted the air of an elder statesman, an authority on parliamentary good breeding. He was active both in public and behind the scenes in preparing schemes for the promotion of Irish trade; advised by John Howard, he advocated penal reform; he tried to secure adequate postal facilities for Cork; a foe to 'prejudice', he tackled the tithe question and eagerly advocated Catholic Emancipation; and he favoured a moderate measure of parliamentary reform (though he once incautiously admitted that, were the plan of reform he proposed adopted, his influence, from the type of property he possessed, would be increased). His conception of his own political career is presumably enshrined in a speech he made near its close, when pressing the House of Commons to facilitate the admission of Trinity undergraduates to its galleries: 'It is to observe and admire great talents and ability, to behold and adore the radiant forms of wisdom and virtue, that I wish the gentlemen of the university may attend this house.'

One of his earliest political friends was Gerard Hamilton ('Single-Speech Hamilton'), who had built up a great oratorical reputation on a remarkably slender output. Hamilton and Hutchinson shared two interests: politics (which they seem to have regarded largely as a matter of exerting blackmailing pressure on the government) and oratory. Oratory was a subject to which an aristocratic society, reared on the classics and pre-occupied with parliamentary life, devoted earnest attention. Hamilton composed *Parliamentary Logick*, a crudely practical manual of debating tactics. Hutchinson introduced into the Irish parliamentary debates 'a classical idiom', a more formal, consciously modelled, and highly decorated style than had hitherto prevailed. 'He enlarged and expanded every thought to its fullest extent', as one critic put it, and 'rendered a Billingsgate brawl into dictionary language.' But there was a great gap between the polite accomplishments befitting a gentleman and the learning expected from a pedagogue; and in spite of his interest in *belles lettres*, no one would have associated Hutchinson with the headship of a house.

But the path had been prepared for his translation by his immediate predecessor as provost of Trinity, Francis Andrews, a *bon vivant* and social climber. Andrews, though a fellow, was not in holy orders (being a jurist), and after being appointed provost in 1758 he entered parliament, became a leader of the government party, posed as a cynical man of the world, and lived sumptuously in the elegant new provost's house, which he had built. The spectacle of a provost carving out a political career for himself would obviously tempt a politician to think of becoming provost. The government, for its part, was keenly interested in the political value of every piece of Crown patronage, and shortly after Andrews' death, North discussed with the Lord Lieutenant the possibility of securing Flood's support by offering him the provostship. On the whole, the Prime Minister was against the proposal. He doubted if 'Mr. Flood, whose early principles and practice have led him to oppose British government, can with safety and propriety be trusted with such a place for life, which, besides rendering him totally independent, gives him in a manner the disposal of a borough and the means of forming the principles of the young nobility and gentry of Ireland'. Hutchinson was less likely to display an awkward independence, and his promotion to the provostship involved his resignation of the prime sergeancy and the alnagership. The former, it was decided, could be given to Dennis, a protégé of the importunate Lord Shannon; the latter the Chief Secretary collared for himself. When it was rumoured that Hutchinson was going to be appointed provost, a determined effort was made to prevent it from happening. Charlemont, a prim and public-spirited nobleman, Robinson, the Archbishop of Armagh, 'who hated a job', and Tisdall, the Attorney General, a member for Trinity who must have resented Hutchinson securing a strong foothold in his constituency, all favoured for provost Thomas Leland, a senior fellow and the author of a dry, lucid history of Ireland and of a stilted academic work on oratory. Tisdall took up Leland's cause in London; Charlemont tried to mobilize the literary world, led by Dr Johnson's circle, and Leland himself tried to get Burke to use his influence in his favour. But in spite of all their efforts Hutchinson attained his objective and held the provostship from July 1774 to his death in September 1794.

As provost, he was from the start severely handicapped. He was an intruder into a close-knit society and his appointment robbed most of the fellows of the automatic step, which would have followed the elevation of a senior fellow. Furthermore, besides injuring their material prospects, Hutchinson at an early stage offended the fellows' professional pride by telling the Board that the classics were not properly taught at Trinity and, with a father's vanity, contrasted the undergraduates' attainments with those of his son at Eton. Not only was he an educational amateur whose pretensions to accurate scholarship were said to rest on an easy acquaintance with English translations and an Eton cram-book, but he was particularly at sea in the Trinity tradition, which assigned a firmly established predominance to mathematics. Thirdly, constitutional developments in College placed Hutchinson in a position that a man of his temperament was almost certain to abuse. By the naturally authoritarian Laudian statutes the provost had power to relax in individual cases many of the College regulations (which by the middle of the eighteenth century were often irritatingly archaic). In addition, it had been successfully maintained by Hutchinson's immediate predecessors that the statutes empowered the provost to veto any decision of the Board and in certain cases to nominate fellows and scholars. Finally, as Hutchinson himself remarks, a contest which 'sprang from the bitter root of electioneering … spread through the whole society and disturbed its tranquillity'. The cause of this was the new Provost's determination to secure one of the university seats for his family. At the elections of 1776 and 1790 he put forward a son as a candidate. On each occasion the Provost's son was declared by his father, acting as returning officer, to be elected. In the first instance an election committee declared Richard Hutchinson's election invalid and at the subsequent by-election he was defeated by John Fitzgibbon (later Earl of Clare). On the second occasion an election committee by one vote sustained the return of Francis Hutchinson. Each contest led to a disgraceful amount of bickering, browbeating and scandal-mongering in College. On each occasion the Provost installed an agent in College, used his disciplinary powers to distress his opponents, and encouraged his supporters by lavishing hints of favours to come – it was even rumoured that a candidate for fellowship was offered in return for his vote a preview of the questions in the subject in which the Provost was examiner. At the polling the Provost exercised his duties as returning officer with such gross partiality that in 1790 'a bulrush chair was torn into two parts and the greater part of it, in which some nails were sticking, was thrown at his head'.

The first contest led to at least three sensational and unedifying episodes. The Court of the King's Bench had to decide whether the Provost had challenged the Attorney General or whether 'the words that passed between the two gentlemen were words common to lawyers on different sides of a question'. The printer of the *Hibernian Journal*, which published a series of violent satirical attacks on the Provost, was seized by a gang of students, dragged into College, and 'pumped'. Berwick, a scholar who was expected to vote with the opposition, was deprived of his scholarship for contumaciously refusing to obey the Provost's order respecting residence – which would have prevented him earning his living as a private tutor. Berwick appealed to the visitors and, in the great hall of the College, a tumultuous undergraduate audience heard the Archbishop of Armagh (the Senior Visitor) continually interrupting the Provost's voluble defence of the sentence. On technical grounds the visitors decided that the sentence was invalid. The Provost appealed to the Chancellor and Berwick unsuccessfully tried to get the courts to intervene. In the end the affair petered out inconclusively, largely owing to the Chancellor's disinclination to commit himself, and Berwick retired to an Ulster living to become in later years a literary ornament of Irish Whig society.

About the time of the second election contest Hutchinson was immersed in conflicts with the fellows over academic policy, and in 1791 an appeal was made to the visitors on three issues – the provost's power to assign pupils, the distribution of tutorial fees, and the provost's negative (his veto). The Provost spoke for three and a half hours in his own defence, 'with a degree of ability and good temper which reflected on a man of seventy high honour'. He certainly retained his tactical skill, for, having mixed 'particular facts with abstract discussion' on the legal points at issue, when Magee, a junior fellow (later Archbishop of Dublin), attempted to follow his example, the Provost at once rose 'and stated the impropriety of suffering young gentlemen to use such language; it would induce an end to all subordination'. Fitzgibbon, who delivered the visitors' opinion, found for the provost on the first two issues, but on the vital constitutional question he decided that the provost did not possess power to veto the actions of the Board and in fact was only *primus inter pares*.

These quarrels, and in particular the election of 1776, inspired a large output of prose and verse mainly directed against Hutchinson and characterized by patent unfairness, heavy facetiousness and strained academic scurrility. Unluckily for Hutchinson the controversial dust stirred up by his explosive career has obscured his real services to the College. A versatile man of the world, he was anxious to widen the College curriculum. Though deferring to the orthodox academic view that a sound education was based on 'a union of classical knowledge with the more solid and useful attainments of science', he emphasized, as might have been expected, the importance of literature both classical and modern which, he asserted, tended to 'elevate and enlarge the mind and humanize and refine the manners'. Shortly after his appointment he secured from the Erasmus Smith Board, of which he was treasurer, an annual grant for entrance prizes in composition. In the same year he was responsible for the foundation of professorships in Italian and Spanish and in French and German. These he promised to endow, if necessary out of his own pocket, but by a well-managed application to the government he obtained an annual grant for their salaries from the Crown. As a more direct method of improving the undergraduates' manners he suggested the erection of a riding-house, arguing that the teaching of modern languages and horsemanship would encourage young men of fashion to substitute the Trinity College course for the Grand Tour and fit the less fashionable undergraduates for tutorships. His attempts to add some polish to the rude energy and self-assured simplicity of the Trinity undergraduates of the period highly amused his critics:

> For Locke and old Newton are thrown aside now,
> To push carte and tierce and make a fine bow,
> And Chesterfield's graces on Alma shall shine
> To give *bon ton* to each rustic divine.

Hutchinson was on less controversial ground in the problems of organization presented by the medical school. Up to his time the teaching of medicine in Trinity had been scrappy, and the relations between the university and the powerful College of Physicians had been uncertain and even, at times, hostile. Hutchinson's political acumen and parliamentary skill were of the greatest value in drafting and pushing through the Act of 1785, which may be said to mark the effective foundation of the present medical school. On one issue, however, he was defeated. He was anxious to open the professorships in the new school to men of all nations and religions. The bigotry of the episcopal bench in the Lords ensured that only Protestants should be eligible.

Finally, he left one massive monument to his provostship. Believing that 'great public buildings raise the reputation of a seminary of learning, and attach the students to the place of their education and the country in which they have received it' he obtained, both from the Erasmus Smith Board and parliament, grants that enabled the College to complete Parliament Square and erect the Public Theatre.

Near the close of his career, with his accustomed industry, he prepared another memorial to his provostship – a history of Trinity College based on vigorous research into masses of unpublished material and obviously meant to be a vindication of his career. But his heirs failed to publish it. Possibly they were reluctant to revive old quarrels, possibly they were completely uninterested in academic antiquarianism, perhaps even they realized that the work revealed only too clearly its author's aptitude for shouldering his way to success, with a determination unvitiated by any doubts as to the righteousness of his aims and methods. Hutchinson, in short, is one of those historically unlucky men who are remembered for their faults. For if his vicarious generosity, administrative skill, sustained industry and good intentions could have overshadowed his overbearing arrogance, contentiousness, and unceasing and shameless attention to his own interests, he might have been remembered as a constructive politician and a great provost.

SOURCES

Donoughmore MSS, HMC [the papers are now in the Dept. of Manuscripts, TCD].

Fortescue MSS, HMC, i, ii.

J. Hely-Hutchinson, 'History of Trinity College, Dublin' (TCD, MSS 1774, 1774a, 1774b).

An Account of some Regulations Made in Trinity College, Dublin Since the Appointment of the Present Provost (Dublin, 1775).

Pranceriana, Poetica, or Prancer's Garland, with an appendix (Dublin 1776).

Lacrymae Academicae, or the Present Deplorable State of the College of the Holy and Undivided Trinity of Queen Elizabeth near Dublin (Dublin 1777).

J.R. Scott Falkland, *A Review of the Principal Characters of the Irish House of Commons* (Dublin 1789).

An Enquiry how far the Provost of Trinity College, Dublin is Invested with a Negative on the Proceedings of the Senior Fellows (Dublin 1790).

A Full and Accurate Report of the Proceedings in the Case of the Borough of Trinity College, Dublin (Dublin 1790).

The Harcourt Papers, ed. E.W. Harcourt, ix, pp. 198–200.

The Correspondence of the Rt. Hon. Edmund Burke, eds Lord Fitzwilliam and Sir R. Bourke, i (1844), pp. 457–64.

IX Edward Carson (1854–1935)

The Irish unionists have received less historical attention than they deserve. For years they were solidly established in power, so they fail to appeal to the romantic who instinctively sympathizes with the weak against the strong; in the end they were unsuccessful, so both the victorious nationalist and those who consider that the inevitable is obviously right, eye them with contemptuous indifference. The result is that the strength and importance of the unionist element in Irish and indeed in British history is often underestimated. For over a century the Irish supporters of the Union included the bulk of the landed interest, the Protestant clergy, very large sections of the professional and business classes and practically the whole Protestant community of the North. Their political, social and economic power was immense. Their intellectual strength was by no means contemptible and they were thoroughly convinced that their cause was righteous and rational. They believed the Union offered to Irishmen a fuller and richer social life, while it enabled them to make a valuable contribution to the common development of the two islands. If their nationalist opponents accused them of treachery to the national cause, they considered they were fighting for larger loyalties against the onset of a stifling provincialism. For, in their own eyes, they were the most intelligent and progressive element in Irish life.

For over a century the unionist point of view was expounded and defended in parliament by a succession of able and eloquent lawyers, Fitzgibbon, Whiteside, Napier, Cairns, Plunket and Carson. Edward Carson, the last of this line, was born in 1854. His father, a competent academic architect, was a successful Dublin professional man; his mother, Isabella Lambert, was a member of a Galway landed family. At school at Portarlington and later at Trinity College Dublin, his record was respectable rather than distinguished. Possibly he was handicapped by the chronic ill health which was a drag on his energies until the end of his long and active life. Probably his abilities were of the kind which mature slowly and which are called out by the demands of practical life rather than by those of abstract speculation. The only way in which his future was foreshadowed was in the part he played in the College Historical Society, where, a tall, lean, assured youth, he debated frequently and held office. In 1877 he was called to the Irish Bar. Ten years later he became junior counsel to the attorney general, in 1889 he became a QC and in 1892 Irish solicitor-general.

The reasons for this rapid rise were twofold. Carson possessed great forensic abilities and the Irish executive needed his services – for during the eighties in Ireland law and politics were inextricably mixed. After the defeat of the first Home Rule bill in 1886 the land agitation had entered on a new phase, with the adoption of the Plan of Campaign. The tenants on each estate where the new tactics were employed combined to offer their landlord a sum which they considered to be a reasonable equivalent of their annual rents. If this was not accepted, no rents were to be paid. The Nationalist party, sympathizing with the tenants and anxious to embarrass the Unionist government, threw all its weight behind the agitation. On the other hand, Lord Salisbury's Cabinet had taken office deeply committed to the view that what Ireland needed was twenty years of resolute government, which, they believed, would bring peace and contentment. Both parties used all the resources at their disposal. There were evictions, often accompanied with violence, mass meetings, arrests, proclamations, prosecutions, riots, boycottings, intimidation and even libel actions. Men on both sides threw themselves into the fray with gusto; the atmosphere was tense; sensation followed sensation. There were some tragic episodes and a fair amount of what verged on farce. On the whole, the battle was fought, to a remarkable extent, within legal limits. The government, though it secured special powers, was of course compelled to fight by the rules laid down by the law, and its opponents, though they denounced the law and its instruments frequently and vehemently, nevertheless took quick-witted advantage of every legal device and quirk which could be used in their own favour. The government would have been rendered powerless and ridiculous if it could not secure adequate legal help. Fortunately for the government it had the assistance of several able lawyers – Atkinson, the future lord of appeal, the popular Peter O'Brien, celebrated for the care he was said to have taken over the composition of juries, and Edward Carson.

Though Carson was the youngest of the group, he became, in the eyes of the public, the most outstanding. To begin with there was his appearance. Thin, tall, angular, with a straight nose, curving, mobile mouth, long jaw and jutting chin, he provided for his opponents a cartoonist's conception of the upholder of autocratic and alien law. The same face and figure were of course in later days to be, for his friends and followers, symbolic of an indomitable determination to maintain the right. The quixotic Scawen Blunt, who was conducting an exuberant crusade on behalf of the Irish tenantry, referred to Carson as a 'Castle bloodhound', adding, however, that he almost felt pity for Carson, which presumably showed he detected some signs of humanity behind the prosecutor's mask. William O'Brien spoke of Carson as a liverish young man, with the complexion of one fed on vinegar and with features as inexpressive as a jagged hatchet. But he too added a qualification – Carson's features were a libel on the real man. Carson himself in later days looked back on his work with quiet satisfaction. He believed he was upholding order against anarchy, and individual liberty against mass tyranny. Balfour, who during the most critical period was chief secretary, declared years later, 'I made Carson and Carson made me ... No one had courage. Everybody right up to the top was trembling ... Carson had nerve however. I sent him all over the place, prosecuting, getting convictions. We worked together.' And Carson admired Balfour for his readiness to back up his officials and for his efforts to improve conditions in the poorer parts of Ireland.

In 1892 Carson was rewarded for his services by being appointed solicitor-general, and this appointment set in train a series of events which had an unexpected and decisive effect on his professional career. As a result of the legal changes that had led amongst other things to Carson's promotion, one of the two Dublin University seats in parliament was vacated. The government naturally wanted to have the Irish law officers in the house and the opportunity of bringing in Carson for the only constituency in the South of Ireland that could be relied on to return a Unionist was too good to be missed. So in the general election of 1892 he was persuaded to stand for the university. Surprisingly enough, he was opposed. An influential section of the constituency strongly objected to the university seats being made stepping-stones by which ambitious barristers via parliament attained the bench. It was alleged, too, that Carson was a liberal Unionist, and therefore unfit to represent a conservative university. A North of Ireland colonel was selected to oppose him, but after a short and rather absurd contest – for, as the political differences between the candidates were infinitesimal, personal issues, including comparisons between their very meagre undergraduate academic records, playing a leading part – Carson was returned for the constituency he was to represent for a quarter century.

Now, if he was to perform his duties to his constituents honestly and adequately, he had to reside for a substantial portion of the year in London, and this meant almost abandoning his practice at the Irish Bar from which he derived most of his income. Admittedly, he could look forward to being offered a seat on the bench when the Conservatives returned to office; and Carson's conception of his future in 1892 seems to have been a few years in parliament and then an Irish judgeship. But as the result of a chance conversation in a club – or so at least tradition asserts – Carson decided to be called to the English Bar and to join a set of chambers in the Temple. Always rather a pessimist, particularly when his own affairs were concerned, he did not expect to get much or any work, but his Irish reputation, the influence of his few but powerful English friends, Arthur Balfour and Lord and Lady Londonderry, as well as his own outstanding skill in handling the work he was given, stood him in good stead.

So it was in 1893, after having been a brief year at the English Bar, that he was able to apply for silk, and a year later a somewhat sulky and reluctant Liberal lord chancellor agreed to call him to the Inner Bar. For the next twenty-five years, until 1921, when he was appointed a lord of appeal, Carson was one of the leaders of the English Bar. In fact, it could be argued that after Charles Russell became a lord of appeal in 1894, he was the greatest advocate of his day. And that at a time when competition was keen and when it would probably be true to say the activities of the law received more attention than at any other period, with the press giving ample space to the *cause célèbre*, which, in a placid age, satisfied the public demand for excitement.

Carson possessed in a superlative degree several of the qualities that make a great advocate. To begin with, he was extraordinarily conscientious; he did not allow a ready tongue to take the place of adequate preparation. He worked up his cases thoroughly and refused firmly to take more briefs than he could handle properly. Then he had the great gift of seeing swiftly what were the essential points in any problem confronting him. Both in law and in politics he had the instinct which directs a man to disregard irrelevances and side issues and make straight to the hard core of a question. This enabled him to attain one of his ideals: compression. His speeches derive much of their strength from being closely packed with essential argument, and thus being relatively short as well as remarkably forceful. To the end of his days he was easily irritated by prolixity and he spoke comparatively seldom in parliament.

His speeches, besides being relatively short, were exceedingly lucid and gained immensely in strength from their apparent unstudied simplicity of style. His language was always deliberately matter-of-fact, indeed sometimes scornfully colloquial, but the short, clear, clipped sentences, and the ordinary words selected with a flair for the truly emphatic, hammered his meaning home with a stark, undecorated force. Moreover, when his sympathies were completely engaged, his speeches, in form and content, carried a terrific conviction of the righteousness of his cause. Even the printed word gives some indication of the weight they must have possessed when delivered in the famous flexible brogue backed by all the power of a masterful personality.

Finally, though a man of firm convictions, he was neither dour nor dull. His contemporaries frequently refer to his charm. This elusive quality can be even now sometimes detected in his speeches and in the fragments of his conversation that survive. He could surprise, by an outburst of almost boyish frankness or by sudden good humour. A vehement hard-hitting partisan, he could, when party feeling was running high, make an unexpectedly restrained speech or drop a remark infused with generous friendliness. In fact, he was a man of very strong emotions, which he expressed with a spontaneity unusual in politics.

His place in politics was, in one respect, a strange one. Though a strong party man (a Unionist front bencher, four times in office and twice in the Cabinet), he was in many respects a solitary, isolated figure. He had not begun life as a Conservative. We know that, as an undergraduate, the general pattern of his thought was liberal. In the College Historical Society, though he had approved of the existing Irish land system and of Pitt's Irish policy and of the House of Lords, he had supported the abolition of capital punishment, of the political disabilities of women and of the connection between Church and State. And in the intellectual sphere he was prepared to oppose the view that contemporary dramatic taste showed marked signs of degeneracy. Later, like many leading Irish Unionists, for some years after 1886 he called himself a liberal unionist. And traces of this liberalism remained in his political composition and cropped up unexpectedly. For instance on the Irish university question, he differed from many of his party in arguing that the Irish Catholics should be given the type of university education they wanted. This, from the standpoint of most Unionists was not the ideal solution, but Carson thought it was the only practical one. And he supported Birrell's University bill of 1908 in a generous speech in which he wished the new universities success. Twelve years later he emphatically declared that people who wanted to economize on education were talking rubbish – a view which must have startled and irritated some of the strong Conservatives with whom on other matters he was then co-operating. Again, in the Archer-Shee case he attacked unsparingly a great British institution, the Admiralty, for the way in which it was treating a cadet accused of theft.

As a lawyer Carson may have been shocked at the methods employed by the authorities to establish the truth, and he may well have been amazed at their simple inability to weigh evidence scientifically. But he seems to have been immensely stimulated in his persistent and ultimately successful fight for justice by the fact that he was battling against the state machine and trying to overcome the stubborn reluctance of public officials to admit they might have been mistaken. Lord Beaverbrook indeed argues that Carson was a natural revolutionary, always happiest when 'against the government'. And in support of this theory it can be pointed out that Carson twice abruptly resigned office, and early in his parliamentary career quarrelled publicly with his party over the Irish land question, declaring angrily that the ministers had changed their views when they crossed the House. Most significantly of all, of course, he threatened to oppose by main force an act of parliament, prospectively defying the law. This theory has the attraction that it places Carson in the Irish revolutionary tradition, labelling him as a physical force man in the Unionist camp. But as in fact he never did resist the law, it would probably be better to say that he was in politics a courageous individualist, a man who by temperament and long professional training was prepared to take momentous decisions on his own. Moreover he tended to be 'a single issue man', and therefore was bound to be a lonely figure with a simple creed in a political world which was concerned about a multiplicity of questions and which accepted that each party had something to offer to the wellbeing of the community. But he was not a blind fanatic. Besides being capable of generosity he was a shrewd tactician, well-aware of the balance of forces and able to execute a feint or a strategic retreat.

The Union was first seriously threatened in Carson's political lifetime when in 1886 the Liberal party was converted to Home Rule. But Gladstone's decision to introduce a Home Rule bill split the Liberal party; the bill was rejected by the House of Commons, the Unionists won the ensuing general election, and shortly afterwards the Irish Home Rule party was rent by dissensions. When the Liberals again achieved office in the early nineties and again introduced a Home Rule bill, the House of Lords threw it out by an overwhelming majority. And a year later the electorate endorsed the Lords' decision. Thus, for the first fifteen years of Carson's parliamentary career, the Union seemed almost unbreakable. Unionists' Cabinets were in office backed by big majorities, their opponents

were unhappily quarrelling amongst themselves, the Irish land question was being solved and Ireland was prosperous, peaceful, and it
could be assumed contented, all the surface ruffles being dismissed
by Unionists as the work of agitators. And if the Liberals did return
to office there was always the House of Lords to block a Home Rule
bill until the next general election. Admittedly, there were Unionists
who were not altogether comfortable and who felt that the process
of killing Home Rule by kindness should include a judiciously measured grant of administrative autonomy. But when it was discovered
that the Chief Secretary seemed to be involved in negotiations for
devolution, the Irish Unionists emitted an angry growl.

When, however, Carson was elected leader of the Irish Unionist
parliamentary party in February 1910, Unionist fortunes were seriously declining. As a result of the general elections held at the beginning and end of 1910, the Liberals remained in office; but from January 1910 onwards they were dependent on the support of the Irish
and Labour parties. Liberals asserted that the two general elections
of 1910 had given them a mandate for a Home Rule bill. And the
Irish party was now in a position to strengthen the Liberals' conviction that Home Rule was desirable by emphatic prodding. Moreover, the House of Lords, by recklessly using its long dormant powers against Lloyd George's budget, had laid itself open to a smash-
ing counter-stroke. And in 1911 the Liberal government was able to
compel the upper house to accept a bill which drastically reduced its
power to delay legislation. Once the parliament act was on the
statute book it was clear that if a Home Rule bill was introduced in
the Commons early in 1912 it would, if certain conditions were fulfilled, be presented for the royal assent about the middle of 1914,
even if the House of Lords refused to pass it. And as parliament had
a life of five years, the government, if all went normally, was under
no obligation to go to the country until some time in 1915. In April
1912 the government did, as might have been expected, introduce a
Home Rule bill, and Unionists were forced to consider seriously if
it were possible to defeat it. They were saved from utter despair by
one fact. They believed that the next general election would almost
certainly result in a Unionist victory. For 1886 and 1895 were
cheering precedents, and at any rate it seemed that the swing of the

pendulum to the right could not be long deferred. Therefore, if the government could be compelled to go to the country before the bill was on the statute book, or if it were possible to prevent the bill coming into operation for a year or so, the Unionists would probably be in a position to reverse the Liberals' Irish policy.

The Unionists had one important advantage. In the north-east of Ireland there was a community nearly a million strong which was thoroughly hostile to Home Rule. The Protestants of the North, whose own religious feelings were strong enough to make them aware of the dangers inherent in *odium theologicum*, had no desire to find themselves a religious minority in an independent Ireland. They thought it was to Ireland's economic advantage to be closely connected with Great Britain, and above all they did not want to be thrust out of the United Kingdom.

If such a community, clergy and people, landed gentlemen, farmers, business men and artisans, was united in its detestation of Home Rule and was prepared to obstruct the working of the Home Rule Act by every means in its power, it would obviously be a most formidable obstacle. Needless to say, the whole development of the Anglo-Saxon political tradition is condemnatory of the use of force in politics. But in this instance Unionists felt that their strongest feelings were being outraged. They considered they were being deprived of their rights, which is even worse than being denied them. And they believed that by showing their readiness to use force they would demonstrate the strength of their feelings – probably without having in fact to use it. And they tried to provide that if force had to be employed in opposition to the law, it would be disciplined and controlled by open and known authority.

From 1911 the Ulster Unionists were making well-advertised preparations to resist Home Rule. A provisional government with an executive committee and administrative departments was planned, and dramatic arrangements were made for its protection. The Ulster Volunteer Corps was formed, a private army which drilled and paraded, boasted of its military efficiency and later armed itself. All this constituted a brutal departure from the accepted traditions of British politics, and the Ulster Unionists were very fortunate at this time to have Carson as their spokesman and leader. For in addition to having a great professional reputation, he was a shrewd tactician, and, what was far more important, he had the right personality for conducting an unorthodox political campaign. His raw, almost frightening sincerity, his curt defiance and biting contempt for the government, the nationalists and his critics in general, delighted his Ulster audiences and impressed, in time, even his English opponents. A sense of showmanship or the regal instinct made him ration his appearances and his words in the North so that each visit, and indeed each speech, was an occasion which presented the community with an animated symbol of their resolute rebelliousness.

But as the Home Rule bill made its weary and repetitive way through parliament, it became clear that strenuous stone-walling would not suffice. As the Ulster Unionists began to prepare their resistance, Unionists as well as Liberals and nationalists were compelled to reassess their attitude to the Irish problem. As early as 1912, when the Cabinet was considering the draft of the Home Rule bill, the suggestion was that Ulster (or some area in it) should be excluded from its operation. And though it was decided not to start by giving special treatment to the North, the possibility of making concessions later was not ruled out. Later, as tempers hardened and manners worsened, moderate men in both the Conservative and Liberal parties began to consider exclusion of some area in the North. This was to be the basis of a compromise which might provide an agreed solution to a problem which was bedevilling English politics at a time when labour unrest and Anglo-German relations were exceedingly disquieting. Churchill suggested to Austen Chamberlain that Northern Ireland should have Home Rule within Home Rule or be excluded from the scope of the bill. And Bonar Law, though strident in public, admitted to Liberal ministers that if the North was excluded, he was prepared to consider Home Rule for the rest of Ireland. By 1914 the Liberals had reached the stage of making concessions, which would certainly influence moderate opinion in England, and a section, at least, of the Conservatives was prepared to examine the government offer.

What attitude in these circumstances was Carson to adopt? A downright adherence to the status quo would offend English opinion, and weakening would disturb his supporters and might encourage his opponents. He early made his standpoint clear. In June 1912, when an English Liberal moved an amendment excluding four Northern counties from the operation of the Home Rule bill, Carson supported him on the grounds that it was a simple act of justice. And in March 1914 he announced that if six counties were permanently excluded from the Home Rule bill, he and his followers would not indeed cease to oppose Home Rule with the utmost vigour – but they would confine themselves to constitutional methods.

Thus by the summer of 1914 it was an open question: would the Irish crisis terminate in a compromise (disagreeable to everybody, but feasible) or in civil war? In the event, the outbreak of the Great War for the moment thrust the Irish question into the background and prodded Carson with the greatest opportunities of his life. During the war he was thrice in office, as attorney general in the first coalition Cabinet, as first lord of the admiralty from December 1916, and as a member of the War Cabinet between July 1917 and January 1918. It would be foolish to claim that he showed himself to be a great administrator.* He had little previous experience of departmental work, and Lloyd George contrasts Carson's administrative methods with his own, much to Carson's disadvantage. For Carson lacked that combination of toughness and agility which enabled Lloyd George to hustle higher civil servants. Nevertheless he made a contribution of supreme value. His sense of urgency, his earnestness, and his quick perception made him realize early that a system perfected over years of peace was ill-adapted for the pace of modern war. His ruthless disregard of forms made him a dominant, hard-driving member of the group, which during 1915 and 1916 pressed hard for changes in both men and in the machinery by which the government was carried on. And it can be claimed for Carson that he was one of the architects of the War Cabinet, a constitutional embodiment of the will to victory.

But throughout, the Irish question remained in the background, more embittering and more perplexing than ever. Carson could never escape it. English politicians were more anxious than ever to

---

* Carson was a popular and inspiring first lord, but his deference to expert professional opinion weakened his effectiveness (see A.J. Marder, *From the Dreadnought to Scapa Flow*, iv [1969], pp. 54–5).

get it out of the way, and Irish Unionist opinion in the South, confused and disheartened, was splitting in three. The Northern Unionists were coming to accept the exclusion of six counties, which they had almost won by 1914, as a safe if unattractive solution. The Southern Unionists were divided between those who still hoped to defeat Home Rule and those, who feeling that Home Rule was inevitable, were determined to try and keep Ireland in the empire and whose policy was summed up in the famous phrase that the coercion of Ulster was unthinkable and that the partition of Ireland would be disastrous. Carson had not lost his detestation of Home Rule, by which, as he said in 1920, Ireland would be cut off from the greatest kingdom that ever existed. But he tended to emphasize more and more the importance of safeguarding the special position won by the North of Ireland.

The key to his attitude can be found in his belief that there was no halfway house between union and complete separation. If Home Rule was granted, paper safeguards would be worthless and there would be an irresistible tendency towards Irish independence. Therefore *faute de mieux* he accepted the exclusion of the North. The indignation and despair with which he saw the fulfilment of his prophecies were voiced in the strange and moving speech, partly philippic, partly apologia, which he delivered on the treaty in the House of Lords. The complacency with which Curzon, in polished periods, blandly expounded the Conservative leaders' faith in their very recently discovered Irish policy, stung him to the core. Speaking as an idealist, Carson protested violently against political opportunism. As the Ulster leader, he fought fiercely for the fragment of the Union which survived. But his last important speech was fundamentally that of an Irish Unionist, a member of a deserted garrison, a Conservative facing defeat and seeing the close of a great tradition.

X Trinity Cameos

1. Murder in the Rubrics

Violence, though perhaps frequently contemplated, is fortunately rarely employed in academic life, and Edward Forde is the only fellow of Trinity known to have been murdered. The general outline of the story is familiar. But in 1932 the British Museum acquired a manuscript (now British Library Add. MS 40851) that has been photostatted for the College library, and which adds many details. It consists of a verbatim report of the trial of the alleged murderers, made by John Crawford of the Middle Temple, who was present, and 'in spite of the great crowd pressing', took voluminous notes, which cover 117 folio pages.

The rude vigour that characterized Anglo-Irish society during the early eighteenth century often led in Trinity to a contemptuous disregard of collegiate restraints. A small band of hard-worked fellows, relying largely on inadequate penalties and their uncertain prestige, struggled to maintain academic discipline in a closely packed community containing many high-spirited, extravagant and wild young men.

Outstanding amongst the upholders of authority was Edward Forde, a son of an Archdeacon of Derry, who had been elected to fellowship in 1730 at the age of twenty-four. When the rooms of one of his colleagues, Hugh Graffan, who had 'fallen under the displeasure of the scholars' for his disciplinary activities, were wrecked, Forde exerted himself to track down the perpetrators of the outrage, with the result that he was sent several threatening letters. Between midnight and one o'clock on the night of 7–8 March 1734 there was a scuffle at the Front Gate, the porter being badly beaten by a group of young men dressed in white. At about the same time

Forde's windows in number 25 were smashed by a volley of stones from the Mall (the portion of the College Park at the back of the Rubrics). Forde, who had a brace of pistols, fired at the assailants, and then going out on the staircase ordered a couple of undergraduates, Roan and Hansard, who lived beneath him, to summon a porter. Roan, apparently a hard-headed Northerner, advised him to come downstairs, but Forde, turning back into his room, picked up his second pistol. The ensuing events are best described in Roan's own words. Having 'not had time', he later explained, 'to put on my clothes, I went down to my room to do it, and immediately ran up again to Mr. Forde's room as did Mr. Hansard. I then heard a confused noise in the Mall under Mr. Forde's windows. Mr. Forde stood near the window and looking to the Mall said to me, "there they are". I endeavoured to prevent Mr. Forde being hurt himself or shooting at the persons in the Mall by importuning him again to retreat, but he would not, and taking up a pistol advanced again towards the window and pointed the pistol downward at the persons in the Mall through a broken pane of glass. I immediately heard the shot from the Mall and Mr. Forde was wounded. Hansard and I got him down to Hansard's room, where he lay some time speechless, and then spoke for a surgeon ... We asked Mr. Forde if he knew who shot him, who answered, "I do not know, but God forgive them, I do." He lay pretty easy about ten minutes. Mr. Dobs came in and endeavoured to bleed him, but he was dead.'

Eighteenth-century journalism contrived to produce a more embellished account of the scene. The Dublin correspondent of the London *Daily Courant*, after giving a full account of the events leading up to the fatal shot, went on to describe how Forde, 'being refreshed by a draught of water and his sense of pain growing less exquisite by the decay of his spirits', exclaimed to some of those about him, ' "Tell the scholars that I beg pardon for the offences I have committed against them and that I sincerely forgive them." '

Some hours later the fellows met, 'and having been informed that Mr. Cotter had company the day before and [was] all night drinking in his chamber, had a just and reasonable suspicion of that company'. So a posse of five fellows, led by John Whetcombe, a member of the Board who was shortly afterwards to be denounced by Swift for planning a gross piece of ecclesiastical jobbery, marched over to Cotter's rooms, which were at the library end of the Rubrics. Here they found Boyle, a graduate of two years' standing, and three undergraduates, Cotter himself, Crosbie and Scholes. On the table were an empty punch bowl, some bottles and glasses. Cotter and his companions were sent to the Vice-Provost, Boyle being 'got out of bed with difficulty', and the fellows collected a large assortment of clues – powder, guns (one of which had apparently just been fired), white clothes, footprints under Cotter's windows into which a dirty pair of Crosbie's shoes fitted, a bent water-spout near Cotter's windows, and a pocketbook, possibly Crosbie's, found in the Mall.

At the beginning of July 1734 the four suspects were put on trial for murder before a commission of Oyer and Terminer for the city of Dublin. Before the trial began it was alleged by the prosecution that William Tisdall, who had recognized the persons who were in the Mall when the fatal shot was fired, had been prevailed on to abscond, and it was shown that owing to his erratic movements through Carlow and Kildare it had been impossible to serve a summons on him. Moreover, another undergraduate, Josiah Paine, alleged that Benjamin Barrington, a Master of Arts, had vehemently pressed him to make an untrue affidavit in favour of the prisoners, telling him that if he did so 'he would gain to himself very good friends and a good interest'. Naturally the prosecution wanted a postponement. But after carefully considering the point, the commission divided equally and the trial went on. During the proceedings the prosecution met with a series of setbacks. The porter at the Front Gate, having been 'a little in liquor', professed to be unable to recognize the men who assaulted him. Another porter was worthless as a witness; for during the disturbances his aim had been 'to keep out of the way for fear of harm'. One of the fellows, on being asked how he knew a gun was recently fired, became badly flustered and it was ruled that the pocketbook could not be received in evidence. And Hansard insisted that he was certain from their voices that the persons in the Mall were not the prisoners but three other students, Lee, Dee and Campbell. Given the available evidence, it is scarcely surprising that the Lord Chief Justice summed up in favour of the prisoners, and the jury, after a short withdrawal, found them not guilty. Though the Board showed its opinion of the verdict by promptly expelling Cotter and his companions, the incident does not seem to have seriously affected their later careers. Cotter became an MP and a baronet, and Crosbie, after succeeding his father, the first Lord Branden, was created a viscount and an earl. The officious Benjamin Barrington married an heiress and ended a highly successful ecclesiastical career as Dean of Armagh.

2. *Primary Accumulation*

John Barrett, sometime fellow, Vice-Provost and librarian, is still the outstanding eccentric in College history. In many respects he was the popular or cartoonist's conception of the don. Erudite in strange fields (he published works on palaeography, archaeology, eighteenth-century biography and astrology), he was archaic in speech, careless in dress, and immersed in his books with a childlike unawareness of the realities of life. But there was an important facet of his character, which was neither childlike nor peculiarly donnish. He was a miser who, in accumulating a fortune, displayed pertinacity and self-sacrifice on a heroic scale. Fortunately there are preserved amongst the College manuscripts four small notebooks, which contain a considerable amount of information about his financial affairs.[1] In three of them, financial details are scribbled down among miscellaneous notes and book lists. The fourth is devoted entirely to his personal finances. In it, in a minute, clear hand, covering the minimum possible amount of paper, he records from 1793 to 1821 a quarterly statement of his affairs, together with, for some years, an exhaustive account of his receipts and expenditure.

He began with some capital, inheriting from an uncle house property in Dublin worth about £2000. This included a house in Merrion Square (number 20), which yielded a rent of £60 per annum. And from 1791, when he became a senior fellow, his College income must have always amounted to at least £1000 a year. As early as 1797 his capital amounted to £12,500. In ten years it had rather more than doubled (he was worth £29,000 in 1807). In another ten years it had risen to £63,000, and a few months before he died, when he listed his assets in a hand that showed signs of physical decline, he calculated he was worth £83,000. Then, as throughout his life, he held a surprisingly large sum in an easily negotiable form, his cash and bank notes amounting to £5000 (during the disturbing period 1799–1802 he had kept between £10,000 and £13,000 in these forms). The bulk of his fortune, however, was in government stock (the age of safety in equities had not yet dawned). But though over five-sevenths of his holdings were in government securities, he had a small amount invested in Dublin city stock and about £20,000 in Grand and Royal Canal stock. And when, a few months before he died, he was estimating the yield from his securities, he had to append to his canal holdings the depressing note 'uncertain'. It must be added that he seems to have over-valued his securities, since his will was proved for under £70,000. However, even taking this figure, his achievement was an impressive one, and it may well be asked how he accomplished it.

The answer is simple. He seems for years to have lived extraordinarily below his income. Unfortunately, we do not possess figures for his pioneering days. But in 1804, when his habits must have been fixed, he enjoyed an income of just over £2000. His expenditure in that year amounted to about £114. Five years later, when his income had risen to £3200, his expenditure had risen to £275. Thus there was a substantial margin for investment. It should be added at once that Barrett's expenditure was not, by contemporary standards, abnormally low. After all, many a Dublin clerk, married and with a family, lived on a middle-class level on less than £100 a year. What is noticeable is the enormous disproportion between income and expenditure.

Barrett's accounts show how resolutely and watchfully he kept expenditure within bounds. Service cost him less than £1 per quarter. For years he was looked after by the devoted Katty. Anecdotage preserves a remark of Barrett's addressed to her. On one occasion, when out with a penny to buy a halfpenny worth of milk for her master, Katty fell and broke her leg. Barrett, who was obviously a man of real kindness, hurried to visit her in hospital. He was anxious to console her but he didn't lose sight of practical considerations. He realized the jug was broken but he at once asked, 'D'ye see me now, where's my halfpenny change?' It must, however, be quickly added that his accounts show that when Katty was dying he was careful to see she was well looked after.

For the rest, his expenditure was what one might expect for a College bachelor. Heat and liquor loom large. He ordered plenty of coal (at £1 a ton) and wine, brandy, 'cyder' and whiskey. His one extravagance was books. His library at his death amounted to 3000 volumes, including a large section devoted to 'fiction and romance'. He also bought pictures and, it was rumoured, framed them himself, refusing to waste money in employing a carpenter, with the result they hung at odd angles on the walls of his scantily furnished rooms.

As has been said, Barrett was a kindly man and the frequent references in his accounts to small sums given to poor people show that his charitable impulses were strong if well-controlled. In his will, after leaving small legacies to his servants and family, he directed his executors, Kyle (the Provost) and Bartholomew Lloyd (the future provost), to use the residue for 'the relief of the sick and indigent poor and naked', and a number of Dublin hospitals and charities received large donations.

3. The Rivals

During the eighteenth and early nineteenth centuries the parliamentary constituency of Dublin University was often vigorously contested; for the electorate, the fellows and scholars, were an alert and independent body. Nevertheless, at the general election of 1818 an unopposed return might have been expected; for the sitting member, William Conyngham Plunket, was one of the outstanding forensic and parliamentary orators of the day. He may not have possessed a profound knowledge of the yearbooks (his eulogistic biographer tactfully explains that 'he was averse to intellectual drudgery') but he had a masculine intellect and his speeches, massive and luminous, had tremendous persuasive force. Moreover, his politics (he was a very moderate Whig) were eminently suited to an academic constituency. His commanding abilities and stately geniality had won him a circle of firm and admiring friends. And to two of them, William Magee and Peter Burrowes, he had largely owed his return as Member for Trinity in 1812. Burrowes, a barrister whose political honesty and over-abounding good nature had made him one of the most popular men in Ireland, had for Plunket 'an affection bordering upon idolatory'. Magee, one of the most brilliant of the junior fellows, was a staunch upholder of the Establishment. But so great was Magee's admiration for Plunket that he was prepared to support his candidature in spite of his advocacy of Catholic Emancipation (which Magee attributed to an excess of generous compassion).

But in 1813 Magee became Dean of Cork, and when the next general election occurred two other influential academic men, Provost Elrington, and Lloyd, the future provost, had another candidate, John Wilson Croker, ready to come forward. Croker did not lack temerity – one of his first publications was a satirical attack on the easily irritated Dublin theatrical world – and he was by 1818 well embarked on a career characterized by many-sided aggressiveness. Entering parliament shortly after the Union, he had shown himself to be a dependable, hard-hitting Conservative and had been appointed secretary to the Admiralty. Wilson Croker is now usually remembered as the unfortunate victim of Disraeli's unsparing ridicule, of MacAulay's erudite scorn and of Thackeray's quiet contempt. But he was also the friend of Peel and Wellington (and the author of a poem on Talavera which Wellington had read with satisfaction), the moving spirit in the foundation of the Athenaeum, a civic improver (he wanted the managers of the Wellington Testimonial to erect a triumphal arch of vast dimensions in the College Park), a pioneer in the study of French revolutionary and English literary history, and, for years, a mainstay of the *Quarterly*, for whose readers he regularly provided an orthodox Tory interpretation of current affairs. But if his critics were unfair, it is easy to see why. Croker, even when well-intentioned, was domineering and hectoring. As a controversialist (and much of his time was spent in controversy) he was unsparing, relying on the savage stoke supported by a masterly command of minutiae. Though in 1818 he still had forty years of activity ahead, his reputation and experience made him a formidable candidate as we can see from his letters to

Peel, which give a day-to-day account of his campaign in Trinity.[2]

There were no real political differences between the candidates. If Croker was in office, Plunket's friends were on the point of coalescing with the government. Consequently Liverpool, the Prime Minister, seems to have been reluctant to endorse Croker's candidature, and when Peel, the Chief Secretary, finally wrote a commendatory letter to the Under-Secretary its effect was delayed, since the Viceroy, from ignorance or pique, refused to accept this intimation of the government's wishes.[3] Thus Croker had the annoying experience of being tackled by Plunket in the square and being asked if he had the government's backing. Croker was reduced to the dignified but ineffectual retort that such a question ought not to be put to him.

But College politics, in the narrowest sense of the term, certainly did play a part in the election. A few years earlier the regulations enforcing celibacy of the fellows had been tightened, and already a number of them were looking for the abolition of the requirement or for generous individual dispensations. And several of the fellows were prepared definitely to support the candidate who they believed would be the better able by his influence to secure these objectives. Moreover, Plunket's friends argued that Croker's candidature should be seen as part of the Provost's policy, which was a compound of personal ambition and academic and political reaction. Elrington was undoubtedly a fussy and testy if well-meaning Tory, and had rendered himself unpopular by driving out of College 'that glorious flame fanned by the panting eloquence of warm youth', the College Historical Society. In addition, according to his critics, he was an apostate Whig and a tuft-hunter, had Orange sympathies, and was a patron of 'the mummery and buffoonery of undergraduate theatricals'. And of course 'his head was aching for a mitre'. As for Croker:

> ... this secretary whose every feature
> Foretells the talent of the creature,
> Lively and vulgar, low and pert –
> He plays *au vif* the courtier-flirt.[4]

He was a hired, pensioned, purchased placeman, who had so little influence with his own employers that those electors who intended to vote for him merely in the hope of getting rid of the Provost were warned that Croker would undoubtedly be unable to get Elrington a bishopric.

Needless to say, Croker was shocked by Plunket's electioneering methods. 'The very face of the country is covered by his [Plunket's] supporters,' he wrote. 'One scholar had ten letters from friends of Plunket.' The Dean of Cork, 'with the vision of a mitre on his head,' endeavoured to induce Croker's supporters to ignore their promises, and Mr Justice Day for two hours used all the resources of casuistry to induce a poor Kerry scholar to break his word. As for the fellows, if Sadleir was coldly calculating, Hincks was also a nuisance. 'A very simple man', Hincks could not be persuaded to withdraw his support from Plunket because he had secured him a dispensation. But it was Dr Wray who aroused Croker's wrath. 'I have never seen or heard of in all my election practice', he wrote, 'so much of filthy venality as in this Doctor of Divinity.' Needless to say, Croker's own tactics were not dissimilar. He went to immense epistolary trouble to get the support of a Sligo country gentleman and of the Surgeon-General. The former employed a scholar as a private tutor; the latter could presumably influence a military surgeon whose brother was a scholar.

At the election the fellows were equally divided, but the scholars turned the scale and Plunket was returned by a majority of 3 on a poll of 65. Speeches justifying their votes were made by several of the electors, including Sadleir and Wall. Sadleir's was long and suave, Wall's short and rude. When the result was announced, Plunket was chaired to his house in Stephen's Green by a crowd, 'none of whom were not in the garb of a gentleman'.[5]

Croker found a seat at Yarmouth and remained in parliament until the passing of the Reform bill, which he fought tooth and nail, before retiring, disgusted, from parliamentary politics. Plunket had earlier been given a peerage. Elrington and Magee were both placed on the episcopal bench, and Plunket secured for Peter Burrowes, who was rumoured to be in financial difficulty, the office of judge of the Insolvent Debtors' Court.

4. Riot at the Gate

The 12th March 1858 was a wet, dreary day, but during the morning large crowds had collected between Westland Row and the Castle to see the state entry of the new Viceroy, Lord Eglinton. Winton Eglinton, during his previous tenure of office, had been popular and the procession included not only the Viceroy himself on horseback, but the Lord Mayor's state coach (the Lord Mayor having just laid the city's keys, mace and sword at the Viceroy's feet on Westland Row arrival platform) and an escort of the first Dragoons and the Scots Greys, who three and a half years before had taken part in the Charge of the Heavy Brigade at Balaclava.

In College Green the crowds were thick, and behind the College railings, which then bulged in a great semi-circle into the Green, there were hundreds of undergraduates. They passed the time by throwing eggs, oranges and squibs. Two policemen who were regarded as officious were dragged behind the railings and severely buffeted. Subsequently, an immense amount of evidence was to be given about the atmosphere which prevailed. Some of the witnesses were impressed by the cheerful high-spirits of the undergraduates and genial good humour displayed on all sides. Others were irritated by the noise and disorder and noticed how horses were being dangerously alarmed by the fireworks. The Junior Dean, the Rev. William Stubbs, now remembered as the author of a solid history of College, after a time arrived and confiscated a large bag of eggs, some walking sticks carried by undergraduates, and 'a bundle of sticks such as they use in hurling'. Having tried to disarm one party, he attempted to conciliate the other by advancing to the railings and saying to the police, 'Boys, I hope we will give and take with good humour today.'

After the procession passed at about two o'clock, the noise and disorder continued and Colonel Browne, a Dublin police commissioner, the brother of Mrs Hemans and a brave Peninsula veteran, rode up to the railings and good-naturedly asked the undergraduates to desist. His expostulations had no effect and suddenly Browne (who had been struck by an orange) decided to take strong measures. He recited the Riot Act and ordered the foot police, supported by fifteen mounted police, to clear the enclosure. Moreover, he asked a detachment of Scots Greys who were in the Green to move up in support. But their commanding officer cautiously refused to act until the police were repulsed. A few minutes of wild confusion followed. The undergraduates, some with sticks, resisted the foot police, but the mounted men with drawn sabres soon swept through the enclosure. There were numerous scuffles and several young men received severe blows from batons (injuries which rumour, at first, exaggerated). The Junior Dean, 'dodging' the police, managed to reach Browne and said to him, 'I pledge my honour to get the students into the College if you withdraw the police.' Other gentlemen remonstrated with Browne, and the enclosure being almost clear, the police were called off.

Immediately a wave of indignation swept through a section of Dublin society. The Board put up a notice asking undergraduates who had witnessed the conduct of the police to come forward. A petition was drawn up and received numerous signatures requesting the Viceroy to hold an inquiry into the conduct of the police, and a large identification parade was held in Dublin Castle yard, undergraduates and policemen picking out persons they regarded as guilty of assault. The viceregal inquiry was held in private, but there were protracted and well-reported proceedings in the College Green police court, both undergraduates and policemen making charges of assault. Browne appeared, and a pathetic dialogue occurred between him and MacDonough, a QC representing the College. When Browne had concluded his evidence, MacDonough remarked, 'The engagement was over.'

> BROWNE: Yes, the field was lost and won.
> MACDONOUGH: Lost and won? You won it.
> BROWNE: No. I lost it.
> MACDONOUGH: You lost it?
> BROWNE: Yes I lost more by it than any other man. I have lost peace of mind. I have endured a great deal of anxiety and felt great regret, and will always regret it as long as I live.
> MACDONOUGH: I am happy to hear the word regret.
> BROWNE: I shall regret it to the end of my life.

As Browne retired there was loud applause in which the students in court joined.

Browne, some students and some policemen were all returned
for trial at the assizes, and the whole affair came under the scrutiny
of one of the ablest judges on the Irish Bench, Christian, who was a
subtle, aloof, clear-headed, judicial individualist, and in his charge
to the grand jury he made it clear that he thought they should reject
the bill against Browne. However, a true bill was found and Browne
was put on trial. He was magnificently defended by O'Hagan;
Christian, when summing up, emphatically reminded the jury that
it was the duty of those entrusted with the preservation of the public peace to prevent disorder. He commented severely on the failure
of the College authorities to enforce order and he referred to the
'melodramatic' character of some of the evidence for the prosecution. The jury, after an absence of five minutes, found Browne not
guilty, and as he left the court he was loudly cheered by a large body
of students. The next day the Solicitor-General issued a *nolle prose
qui* in the other cases. The whole affair cost only one serious casu-
alty. Browne's career was finished. He resigned and died twenty
years later in Folkestone.[6]

5. Letter from R.B. McDowell and Conor Cruise O'Brien to the Editor of T.C.D.: A College Miscellany, 16 June 1938

Dear Sir,

Recently we have carried out an investigation as to the opinions and
habits of the male students of the College, the results of which may
be of some interest to your readers. Since we examined only about
a hundred people, selected haphazardly, we do not claim that our
deductions are based on completely satisfactory data, but they are
perhaps more valuable than the generalizations often made in College conversation.

Our first question was: 'Why did you enter College?' Nearly half
the people we examined came to College to be prepared for some
definite profession. Forty per cent of the remainder were anxious to
secure the supposed advantages of a university education – e.g., they
came to study some definite subject; 'for general cultural preparation';

'out of pure interest in work'; 'to meet people of different types'; 'to broaden the mind,' or 'to get a college education'. The rest drifted into College either 'at the instigation of parents' or 'as a means of putting in some time'; 'to put off working as long as possible'; 'because I was brilliant academically and not much good at anything else'; or 'because I was vacillating and entered College to postpone my decision'.

Question Number Two was: 'Did you regret coming into College?' We received an almost universal negative.

Our next question was: 'What games do you play?' We found that there were 18 per cent who took no form of exercise except walking, while the remaining 82 per cent indulged in at least two forms of sport per year.

Turning to more intellectual forms of amusement, the average attendance at the cinema was 4.8 visits per month, and to the theatre 1.9 visits. It further appears that among the people we examined, the average number of novels read per annum was 24, and of non-fiction works, 18.

Nearly everyone reads *The Irish Times* and some read *The Irish Press*, but mainly for sport. Thirty-one per cent read *The Times*, but in many cases in a superficial or fragmentary manner. As regards periodicals, the *New Statesman* and the *Spectator* are widely read, the former being much the more popular. The expensive Society weeklies and the more sensational American periodicals also receive wide attention.

University work, exclusive of lectures, takes up, under normal conditions, on the average 2.21 hours per day. Before examinations, this rises to an average of 7.18 hours per day. It is interesting to note that there is a considerable proportion who do no work whatever except before examinations.

As regards association with women, there are 30 per cent who have no interest in them. Thirty-two per cent (to use a medical student's expression) 'specialized' in a particular lady, while the remainder were Catholic in their affections.

When asked whether they desired any changes in College, most people showed concern for material comforts only. It is true that there were a few 'progressive' individuals who wished to reform the fellowship system; to distribute the wealth of the College in a more equitable form; to remove the Divinity school, and to promote research.

The chief subjects of complaint, however, were compulsory Night-Roll and Chapel, cleanliness of rooms and sanitation. It was deplored that there were not more opportunities for men and women students to meet; but as regards the question of women on the Buffet, 52 per cent were hostile to their admission; 22 per cent were in favour; 8 per cent were uninterested, 15 per cent had no objection, provided there was room; and 3 per cent saw 'social and economic difficulties'.

The figures for compulsory Chapel were: For, 28 per cent; Against, 52 per cent. Twenty per cent gave no opinion. For Night-Roll our statistics are: For, 49 per cent (9 per cent being Freshmen); Against, 30 per cent (14 per cent being Freshmen).

To the question: 'Do you read *T.C.D.*?' and 'What do you think of it?' all but 5 per cent of the people we approached read it, at least occasionally; but not by any means all buy it. Of the sixty-four people who expressed a definite opinion, thirty approved of it in varying degrees; thirty-four despised it. By far the most popular section is Campanilia: even one or two gentlemen who considered it 'vulgar and objectionable' were forced to admit that they read it regularly and with pleasure. The most common objections to your paper were that it is produced by a small and snobbish clique, and that its scandal is restricted too exclusively to what one gentleman called the 'upper ten' – i.e., the hierarchies of the Hist. and the Phil. Several gentlemen objected to your anonymity, which one defined as 'saying things you wouldn't dare if you had to sign your name'.

Concerning opinion on College Societies, of the people we questioned, 54 per cent were members of the College Historical Society, 24 per cent belonged to the University Philosophical Society, and 22 per cent were unattached.

Some regretted that the minor societies aped the forms, and borrowed the dignity (or pomposity) traditionally associated with the two major bodies; while the officers of these two bodies were accused of having an undue sense of their own importance, and of being cliquish. Indeed, they were actually compared to Nazis.

The existence of the Philosophical Society does not seem to impinge on the consciousness of Hist. members. On the other hand, it was remarked by members of the Phil. that the Hist. rooms were rather too noisy, and that it produced a rougher and more biased type of personality.

To turn from College affairs to those of the wider world, of the group we surveyed, 26 were completely apathetic when it came to politics. Fianna Fáil has 14 supporters, twice as many as Fine Gael; 11 people were 'vaguely pink'; 9 were definitely Labour. Five Republicans were balanced by seven Unionists. Nine gentlemen had British, rather than Irish, political interests. Of these one opposed the National Government, four are Conservatives, and four Liberals. There were only four professed Pacifists. Among the oddities are: a Conservative, Socialist and three anti-Fascists, of whom one was also an anti-Communist. We also found two archaic survivals: a Home Ruler and a supporter of Cumann na nGaedheal.

Apart from a few members of the Irish Labour party, nobody appeared to take any active part in politics; or, we venture to say, has any coherent system of political thought.

In religious matters, the great majority (so far as we can tell) were professed Christians.

In conclusion, we wish to thank all who were approached for their willing co-operation; though, in passing, it may be said that the contemptuous geniality of many of our victims failed to conceal their delight in talking about themselves.

The following gentlemen assisted us in tabulating our returns: Mr G.D.P. Allt, Mr D.W. Greene, Mr D.M. Kennedy and Mr W.R. Smyth.

> We remain,
> Sincerely yours,
>
> R.B. McD.
> D.C.C. O'B.

NOTES

1. TCD, MSS 2369–72.

2. British Library, Add. MS 40784.

3. British Library, Add. MS 40794.

4. *An Address to the Undergraduate Scholars of Trinity College* (Dublin 1818) and *Crokeriana* (Dublin 1818).

5. *Dublin Evening Post*, 27 June 1818; Freeman's Journal, 26 June 1818.

6. The riot and the proceedings in the police court and at the assizes were reported at length in the press – for instance in *Saunder's Newsletter*, 13 March–13 April 1858, and 18–22 June 1858.

Appendix

Persons Known to Have Been Admitted Members of the Dublin Society of United Irishmen, 1791–4

INTRODUCTORY NOTE

The authority for the inclusion of a name in the following list is the Collins' letters and the summons-papers enclosed in them (Rebellion Papers, 620/19–21; see above, pp. 116–17).

'Admitted' means 'admitted to membership of the Dublin Society of United Irishmen'. 'Proposer' means 'proposer of someone for membership of the Dublin Society of United Irishmen'. The authority for particulars of this kind is as stated above. 'Freeman' means 'freeman of the city of Dublin'. The authority for the admission of freemen is *An Alphabetical List of the Freemen of the City of Dublin, Commencing January 1774*, and ending 15 January 1824 (copy in the National Library of Ireland).

A list of members of the Catholic Convention (Nov. 1792–April 1793) is contained in *A Full and Accurate Report of the Debates in the Parliament of Ireland, in the Session of 1793; on the Bill for the Relief of His Majesty's Catholic Subjects* (Dublin 1793). For booksellers and printers see M. Pollard, *A Dictionary of the Members of the Dublin Book Trade* (London 2000).

The particulars given below have been selected for their value as evidence of social and economic circumstances, and of religious identity.

It is probable that the following pairs of entries each refer to the same individual: (20, 21), (50, 52), (51, 52), (60, 306), (61, 62), (95, 144), (127, 129), (174, 175), (219, 221), (249, 250), (255, 256), (282, 283), (297, 298), (313, 314), (369, 370), (405, 406). The net total of persons named in the list may therefore be no more than 407.

AUTHORITIES CITED

Manuscript Material*

Cath. Qual. Rolls	Catholic Qualification Rolls, National Archives of Ireland
Reb. Papers	Rebellion Papers, in N.A.I.
SP I	620/20/36
SP II	620/54/12
SP III	620/54/13
SP IV	620/54/13 [a second list]
SP V	620/54/18
SP VI	620/54/20

* Manuscript citations are given as in the 1940s; in some cases (e.g. the Sirr Papers in TCD) the press-marks have been changed.

SP I is the alphabetical list of names and subscriptions referred to above (p. 117). SP II–VI are the lists of members compiled by Collins (see p. 117). 'J.W.' signifies a letter from Leonard McNally, 'Higgins' a letter from Francis Higgins, in the Rebellion Papers.

Reg. Deeds	Registry of Deeds, Dublin
Sirr Papers	Sirr Papers, in TCD, MS 868
SP I–VI	See Reb. Papers
St. Pr. Pt.	State Prisoners' Petitions, N.A.I.

PRINTED MATERIAL

DC	*Dublin Chronicle*
DEP	*Dublin Evening Post*
DG	*Dublin Gazette*
DWJ	*Dublin Weekly Journal*
FDJ	*Faulkner's Dublin Journal*
HJ	*Hibernian Journal*
SNL	*Saunder's Newsletter*
VJ	*Volunteers Journal*
WD	*Wilson's Dublin Directory*

Dublin Society of United Irishmen, 1791–4

1. ADAMSON (William). Great Strand Street. Merchant. Took test 1 Feb. 1793. Admitted freeman Mich. 1791. Went bankrupt (*DG*, 9 Dec. 1794). [*WD*; SP I]

2. ALLEN (Christopher). Pimlico. Dyer. Admitted and took test 3 Feb. 1792. Went bankrupt (*DG*, 23 Oct. 1794). [*WD*; SP I]

3. — (William). [SP I]

4. ALLEY (Peter). Barrister. Took test 8 Feb. 1793. In 1790 spoke at aggregate meeting which passed resolutions criticizing conduct of aldermen (*DWJ*, 24 July 1790). Author of *Public Spirit: A Poem* (1793). [Burtchaell & Sadleir; SP I]

5. ANDOE (John). Cork Street. Tanner. Admitted 7 Dec. 1792. On Cath. Qual. Rolls. His wife's marriage portion was £400 (Reg. Deeds). [*WD*; SP I]

6. — (Matthew). High Street. Woollen-draper. Took test 14 Dec. 1792. On Cath. Qual. Rolls. Under his wife's marriage settlement, she was to receive £200 if she survived him (Reg. Deeds). Twice at least he advertised for an apprentice (*DEP*, 9 Oct. 1790, 22 Sept. 1803). [*WD*; SP I]

7. ARNOLD (William). Usher's Quay. Silk-weaver. Admitted 27 April 1792. Proposer 23 Nov. 1792. Supported parliamentary reform in 1784 (*DEP*, 9 Jan. 1784). [*WD*; SP I, II]

8. ASHENHURST (John Talbot). Dame Street. Public notary. Admitted freeman Christmas 1811. A very prominent reformer in the early eighties. Secretary to Reform Congress. Secretary to Reform Club of Ireland (*DEP*, 30 May 1786).

In charge of volunteers when in 1793 they had a brush with the police (*FDJ*, 26 Feb. 1793). Advertised in the *Press*. Dealer, apparently on a large scale, in mortgages and government securities (*HJ*, 27 Aug. 1801; *SNL*, 26 May 1800). Secretary to Dublin Insurance Company. In an obituary notice he is described as 'an upright, kind-hearted, brave and amiable man' and 'a gentleman who, during the proudest period of Irish history, had been a major in the Dublin Volunteers, that spirited and un-bought association' (*SNL*, 21 March 1818). [*WD*; SP I, II, IV, V]

9. ASKIN (Matthew). Pimlico. Clothier. Admitted 21 Dec. 1792. On Cath. Qual. Rolls. His wife's marriage portion was £800, and if she survived him she was to receive £1000 out of his estate (Reg. Deeds). [*WD*; SP I]

10. ATKINSON (John Wray). Admitted and present on 20 May 1794, the night the Society was dispersed. It was rumoured that Fitzgibbon was going to oppose his admission to the Bar but he was called. Militia Colonel. [J. Agnew, *Drennan-McTier Letters*, ii, p. 64; BLG (1958); SP I]

11. — (William). Pimlico. Clothier. Proposer 28 Dec. 1792. Admitted freeman Mich. 1792. Advertised his wholesale and retail warehouse (*HJ*, 16 Dec. 1801). [*WD*; SP I]

12. AYLMER (Peter, *Esq.*). Seneschalstown, Meath. Admitted 21 Dec. 1791. Second son of Richard Aylmer, landowner, who appears on Cath. Qual. Rolls, and whose eldest son, on his death in 1794, left an estate said to be worth £1500 (Reg. Deeds; *DEP*, 6 Nov. 1794). Not named as a son of Richard Aylmer of Seneschalstown in F.J. Aylmer, *The Aylmers of Ireland* (1931), but may have been omitted by mistake.

13. AYLWARD (James). Francis Street. Woollen-draper. Proposer 11 Oct. 1792. Partner of Robert Dillon. In 1789 let a house at corner of Tighe Street and Queen Street at rent of £66 per annum (Reg. Deeds). Was member of the Catholic Convention. Died 1794 (*HJ*, 30 July 1794). [*WD*; SP I–IV, VI]

14. — (Patrick). Queen Street. Grocer. Admitted 14 Dec. 1792. Went bankrupt (*DG*, 15 Feb. 1800). Secretary to meeting of Catholics of St Paul's parish which passed an address regretting removal of Lord Fitzwilliam (*HJ*, 18 March 1795). [*WD*; SP I]

15. BACON (Thomas). Ship Street. Tailor. Proposer 4 Jan. 1793. Admitted freeman Mich. 1784. Common council man. Signed resolutions in favour of non-importation (*VJ*, 16 July 1784). Major and secretary of Goldsmiths' corps (*VJ*, 14 May 1784; *DEP*, 25 Aug. 1785). In June 1798 he was arrested, disguised as a woman, convicted on the charge of having been elected an officer of the rebels and executed. He was reported to have said 'that he did not know he was elected an officer until informed by the meeting, and that he did not imagine that the party instigating the present rebellion would have gone to any such length as they have done' (*HJ*, 6 June 1798). [*WD*; SP I–V I]

16. BEASLY (Samuel). Dollymount, Co. Dublin. Admitted and took test 1 Feb. 1794.

17. BELL (John). Strand. Proposer 4 Jan. 1793. Probably the 'John Bell, Gent.' who in 1792 sold for £99 a plot of land at Fairview, on Strand Road (Reg. Deeds). [SP I]

18. — (William). Mary's Abbey. Tailor. Admitted 4 Jan. and took test 8 Feb. 1793. A Common council man. Signed resolutions in favour of non-importation (*VJ*, 16 July 1784). In 1795 complained of six Catholic votes being illegally rejected in an election for the Common council (*HJ*, 23 Dec. 1795). [*WD*; SP I, V, VI]

19. BENNET (Thomas). Bridge Street. Very probably a cotton-merchant. Admitted 28 Dec. 1792. Proposer 8 Feb. 1793. Possibly admitted freeman Mich. 1786. [WD; SP I]

20. BERFORD (John). Coombe. Stuff-manufacturer. Possibly on Cath. Qual. Rolls. Took test 11 Oct. 1792. [WD; SP I]

21. BESFORD (John). Proposer 7 Dec. 1792.

22. BETAGH (Matthew). High Street. Woollen-draper. Admitted 28 Dec. 1792. [WD; SP I]

23. BINNS (George). Dame Street. Ironmonger. Admitted freeman Mich. 1782. Went bankrupt (DG, 8 Oct. 1801). Capt. of 8th company Royal Dublin Volunteers (HJ, 21 Nov. 1796). Possibly elected keeper of Newgate (DEP, 13 May 1809). [SP I, V]

24. BLENNERHASSET (Harman). Aungier Street. Barrister. Admitted 4 Jan. 1793. [DAB; SP I, V, VI]

25. BOND (Oliver). Bridge Street. Wholesale woollen-draper. In 1785 advertised for a man who understood carding machines and jennies (DEP, 13 Dec. 1785). Later declared that he had formed a connection with one of the first manufacturing and printing companies in Ireland (DEP, 20 Oct. 1792). Collins described him as 'a firebrand'. [DNB; WD; SP I–VI]

26. BRADY (Hugh). Oldcastle, Co. Meath. Apothecary. Admitted 14 Dec. 1792. On Cath. Qual. Rolls. By his marriage contract, he received £400 and in return settled on his wife's lands worth £40 per annum (Reg. Deeds). In May 1805 Wm. Corbet reported that 'Brady the apothecary, who has been sometimes very useful to me, has been in the county Meath for some time past, and reports that the peasantry there, a great number of whom he intimately knows, were perhaps never more indifferent about politics' (Reb. Papers, 620/14/188/22).

27. — (Peter). West New Row. Cardmaker. Admitted 21 Dec. 1792. In 1784 a Peter Brady, as secretary to the Knights of St John, signed their resolutions in favour of protection (VJ, 30 April 1784). Member of the Catholic Convention. [WD; SP I]

28. BRASSINGTON (Richard). Great Britain Street. Land-surveyor. Admitted 8 Feb. 1793. May have collaborated in producing a survey of Carton demesne. [J.H. Andrews in Bull, Irish Georgian Society, xviii, pp. 97–8; WD]

29. BRAY (Robert). Francis Street. Poplin and stuff-merchant. Admitted 7 Dec. 1792. Admitted freeman midsummer 1792. Went bankrupt. (DG, 4 March 1800). [WD]

30. BRENNAN (Edward). Francis Street. Silk and worsted-manufacturer. Took test 31 Aug. 1792. Proposer 14 Dec. 1792. On Cath. Qual. Rolls. Advertised that he had in stock 'a large assortment of Morines and Paragons of the best quality and colours, superior to any imported' (DEP, 15 Oct. 1785). Acted as secretary to Catholics of parish of St Nicholas Without, when they met to express regret at the removal of Fitzwilliam (DEP, 18 March 1795). He was said to be member of a group whose object was to persuade all denominations to join the revolt (Higgins, 31 Dec. 1796). In Sept. 1798 an informer reported that Jeffers, who had led 2000 men in the Rebellion, was hidden in his house (Reb. Papers, 620/18a). [WD; SP I]

31. BROOKE (Edward). Meath Street. Silk-dyer. Admitted 10 Feb. 1792. [WD; SP I, IV]

32. BROWN (Henry). Meath Street. Merchant. Admitted 14 Dec. 1792. Proposer 8 Feb. 1793. [SP I]

33. BROWNE (George). Rutland, Harold's Cross. Linen and silk-printer. Admitted 1 June 1792. Admitted freeman Mich. 1777. [*WD*]

34. — (George Joseph). Chancery Lane. Barrister. Admitted 27 Jan. and took test 3 Feb. 1792. Seems from the newspaper reports to have had a good practice. Was a member of the aggregate committee that convened the Reform Congress (*DEP*, 11 Sept. 1784). In Feb. 1792, at meeting of Aldermen of Skinners' Alley, he moved a resolution approving of the public conduct of Simon Butler and Napper Tandy (*FDJ*, 9 Feb. 1792). An obituary notice referred to him as a gentleman of 'acknowledged great ability in public life, and tried sincerity in private', who was rapidly advancing to an eminent position in his profession (*DEP*, 25 May 1793). [SP II–IV]

35. BROWNE (John). Vicar Street. Silk and cotton-manufacturer. Admitted freeman Mich. 1789. [SP I]

36. — (Patrick). [SP I]

37. BROWNLOW (James). Thomas Street. Shoemaker. Admitted 13 Jan. 1792. [*WD*; *VJ*, 15 Oct. 1784]

38. BURGESS (Edmund). Gardiner Place. Attorney. In 1797 made over his lease of house in Linenhall Street (Reg. Deeds). [*WD*; SP I, III, IV]

39. BURKE (Edmund, *Esq.*) Limerick. Admitted 10 Feb. 1792.

40. — (John). Meath Street(?). Attorney. Admitted 23 Nov. and took test 7 Dec. 1792. [SP I]

41. — (John). Stephen's Green. Physician. Proposer 3 Feb. 1792. Regarded by Collins as 'an agitator'. A number of persons who wished to defend the state prisoners met at his house, and it was said that the answer of the Leinster committee, to the effect that they would not rise as the chances of success were slight, was drafted by Drs Burke and McNevin (Higgins, 27 Sept. 1796, 17 Oct. 1797). [*WD*; SP I–VI]

42. — (Michael). Mary's Lane. Grocer. Admitted and took test 31 Aug. 1792. Proposer 16 Nov. 1792. [SP I]

43. — (Robert). Cork. Merchant. Admitted 31 Aug. 1792. Appointed assignee of a bankrupt's estate in 1799 (Reg. Deeds).

44. BURROWES (Peter). Barrister. For admission, see *Drennan Letters*, p. 62. [*DNB*]

45. BURY (George). Church Street. Chandler and soap-boiler. Admitted 9 March 1792. Admitted freeman Easter 1789. [*WD*]

46. BUSBY (John). New Street. Silk-throwster. Admitted 4 Jan. and took test 8 Feb. 1793. Admitted freeman midsummer 1788. In 1790 let a small parcel of ground in the Liberties of St Thomas (Reg. Deeds). [SP I]

47. BUTLER (Nicholas). Clarendon Street and Grafton Street. Jeweller. Proposer 27 Jan. 1792. In an advertisement, he declared himself to be the original maker of patent sword-canes, whose 'beauty, colour and shape exceeds any real Dragon Cane ever imported ... and what should be a further recommendation, they are really Irish invention and execution' (*DEP*, 16 Aug. 1783). In 1784, with the approval of the Dublin Volunteers, he advertised emblematic buttons, to be worn with Irish cloth, of which the design was two hands clasped (*VJ*, 10 May 1784). Later he informed the public he could supply them with plated buckles 'of Irish manufacture, superior in quality to any imported, and the prices less' (*DEP*, 6 Jan. 1787). According to Collins, a papist and a mad Jacobin. In the chair at a meeting of the Independent Dublin Volunteers (*VJ*, 10 May 1784). [*WD*; SP I–VI]

48. — (*Hon.* Simon). Barrister. [*DNB*; SP I–VI]

49. BYRNE (Frederick). Francis Street. Woollen-draper. Admitted 16 Nov. and took test 23 Nov. 1792. Probably a Catholic. Appeared twice as a witness in criminal cases. In the first instance, the accused had bought £1 13s. worth of cloth at his shop. In the second, he was a witness for the defence in a case of wife-beating. When the judge stated that he had never heard such shocking perjury, he was probably referring to Byrne's evidence (DWJ, 29 Oct. 1791; DEP, 1 March 1803). [WD; SP I]

50. BYRNE (John). Abbey Street. Biscuit-baker. [WD; SP I]

51. — (John). Church Street. Chandler. Admitted 29 March 1793. On Cath. Qual. Rolls. Went bankrupt (DG, 28 July 1803). [WD; SP I]

52. — (John). Mullinahack. Probably the son of Edward Byrne of Mullinahack. Proposed 13 April 1793. Present 1 Feb. 1794. James Tandy, in his examination in Oct. 1803, declared that he had paid a visit to France twelve months previously with Mr John Byrne, eldest son of Byrne of Mullinahack (Reb. Papers, 620/11/188/34). [Reb. Papers, 620/20/78; SP II, V, VI; The Irish Catholic Petition of 1805, ed. B. MacDermott (1992), pp. 12, 176]

53. — (John, Esq.). Admitted 27 April 1792.

54. — (Joseph). New Row. Merchant. Took test 27 Jan. 1792. Proposer 7 Dec. 1792. On Cath. Qual. Rolls. In 1789 let a house and yard in Monasterevan at a rent of £30 per annum (Reg. Deeds). Went bankrupt (DG, 14 Oct. 1800). [WD; SP I]

55. — (Patrick). Grafton Street. Bookseller and lottery-office-keeper. Proposer 27 Jan. 1792. On Cath. Qual. Rolls. Member of the Catholic Convention. In 1793 his house collapsed, and after a lawsuit he secured £1000 from an insurance company (DEP, 24, 26 Jan. 1793; HJ, 28 July 1794). In 1797, he was described as printer to the Catholic Committee and a distributor of libels (Higgins, May 1797). In May 1798 he was committed to Newgate. While he was there, according to himself, he suffered greatly from sickness, his wife died, and his property was scattered. In petitions to the government, he emphasized that he had helped to improve the art of printing in Ireland and had given employment to a great number of industrious families (Two memorials of Pat. Byrne to the Irish government, St. Pr. Pt., VI/30/2). Banished by 38 Geo. III c. 38. Emigrated to Philadelphia. Died 1814 (HJ, 7 Feb. 1806). [WD; SP I, II, IV, V]

56. — (Robert). Church Street. Chandler. [SP I]

57. — (Walter). Abbey Street. Merchant. Proposed 30 Dec. 1791. Was member of the Catholic Convention. [WD; SP I, II, IV, V]

58. — (William). Admitted 16 Nov. 1792.

59. CALDWELL (Nathaniel). College Green. Bookseller. In Jan. 1798 Higgins stated that there were some Northerners, whose behaviour was suspicious, staying at Caldwell's house, that he had gone to Scotland 'to cultivate the people' there, and was a Northern provincial representative (Higgins, 16 Jan. 1798). In June 1798 Pollock spoke of him as 'the chap that got the addresses from the United Britons to the United Irishmen' printed, and as a commissioner for managing the rebel lottery (Reb. Papers, 620/38/182a). [WD; SP II]

60. CALLAGHAN (J.). Proposer 4 Jan. 1793. Possibly the same as James O'Callaghan.

61. CAREY (Edward). Greencastle, Co. Donegal. Possibly a mistake for George Carey. An Edward Carey inserted an advertisement in the Dublin Evening Post to the effect that the account of a riot near Greencastle, which had appeared in a Strabane paper, was 'pregnant with falsehood and malignancy'. He had been represented as carrying on a malicious prosecution against the revenue

officers. In fact, he had been supporting the laws of his country against wanton attacks on the lives of innocent people, as he should always consider himself bound to do whenever power or influence was used to suppress justice (*DEP*, May 1791). [SP II, IV]

62. — (George). Camden Street. During 1793–9, a George Carey of Green-castle, Co. Donegal, was mortgaging or selling an estate of well over 1800 acres (Reg. Deeds). [SP I]

63. — (William Paulet). Engraver and editor of the *National Evening Star*. Was expelled from the Society and appeared as a Crown witness against Drennan. [*DNB*; Carey, *An Appeal to the People of Ireland*; SP I]

64. CARPENTER (Richard). Francis Street. Apothecary. Proposer 28 Dec. 1792. Admitted freeman Mich. 1777. In 1796 leased a house and three acres of land in Crumlin (Reg. Deeds). [*WD*; SP I]

65. CARR (Charles). Charles Street. Dyer and cotton-manufacturer. Admitted 28 Dec. 1792. [*WD*; SP I]

66. CAROL (William). Mary's Lane. Chandler. Admitted 7 Dec. 1792. Possibly the Carroll, a chandler in Ash Street, who was described by an informer as being 'very active in that part of the town' (Reb. Papers, 620/7/74/21).

67. CARROLAN (Edward (?)). Carrickmacross. Took test 10 May 1793. Was the son of a distiller and was apprenticed to an attorney, but his political views prevented him from qualifying. As a young man he was well known in east Ulster, being active in the defence of United Irishmen and Defenders (Norman Steel to Marsden, 30 Sept. 1800, Reb. Papers, 620/49/59). After the '98 Rebellion, he was in Hamburg, and when he returned to Ireland the government kept a watch on his movements (Higgins, 19, 25, 30 Sept. 1800, Reb. Papers, 620/49/38, 620/49/54a, 620/67/58). In 1809 the death was announced of an Edward Carolan of Carrickmacross, 'a young gentleman of most agreeable manners and excellent heart' who had been carrying on the brewing business on an extensive scale (*DEP*, 4 Nov. 1809).

68. CARROLL (Francis). Pill Lane. Woollen-draper. Admitted 5 Oct. and took test 11 Oct. 1792. Admitted freeman midsummer 1790. [*WD*; SP I]

69. CARTLAND (Nathaniel). W. Park Street. Silk-dyer. Admitted 4 Jan. 1793. Admitted freeman Christmas 1789. In 1784 signed the resolutions of the Amicable Club of Dublin in favour of the non-consumption of foreign manufactures (FJ, 14 April 1784), and in 1786 those of the Aldermen of Skinners' Alley expelling Alderman Warren (*DEP*, 9 Feb. 1786). He also signed a unanimous resolution of the Aldermen of Skinners' Alley criticizing the sub-committee of the Catholics of Ireland (*FDJ*, 6 Sept. 1792). [*WD*; SP I]

70. CARTON (Patrick). Pill Lane. Hardware-merchant. Admitted 22 June 1792. A collector for repairs to St Mary's Chapel (Reb. Papers 620/34/39). [*WD*; SP I]

71. CASSIDY (Luke). Parliament Street. Hatter and laceman. Admitted 23 Nov. 1792. On Cath. Qual. Rolls. Advertised that he was manufacturing hats and gold lace (*DEP*, 23 June 1787). In 1786, in his marriage contract, he promised that if his wife should survive him, she would receive either £1200 and an annuity of £60, or £1500 (Reg. Deeds). He was said, in 1797, to have been one of a committee for suborning Crown witnesses, and to have been heard boasting that the officers of the Fraser Fencibles had been sworn United Irishmen, and in 1798 to have been one of a party who were to seize the Castle (Higgins, 17 Oct., 11 July 1797; 24 May 1798). [*WD*; SP I; *Cox's Irish Magazine*, Feb. 1814]

72. CASSIN (Denis). Fleet Street. Flour-merchant and dealer. Member of the Catholic Convention. A wine importer (*DEP*, 20 July 1790). Luke Cassin, with whom he was in partnership, went bankrupt (*DG*, 11 May 1797). He owned a flour mill in Cloghan (King's County) and farmed about 100 acres of land. Politically hostile neighbours declared, *c.* 1804, that he was 'a most Bigotted Popish gent', had served in the Austrian army, and that it was rumoured he had been major general of the rebel army of King's County. About March 1804 he was arrested on the charge of organizing a conspiracy against the government under the cloak of forming a yeomanry corps. The authorities were apparently unable to secure sufficient evidence to bring him to trial, but he was imprisoned until October 1805, the victim, he complained, 'of malice and Bigotted prejudice'. On his release he demanded compensation, including £309 for law-costs incurred through not being able attend the courts in connection with Luke Cassin's bankruptcy (Reb. Papers, 620/13/171, 178; 620/14/183/12; 620/14/186/14, 16). [*WD*; SP I–V]

73. CHAMBERS (John). Abbey Street Printer and bookseller. Proposer 23 Nov. 1792. Master of his gild in 1793. About 1792 rebuilt his house, constructing behind it 'the completest printing office ever erected in Ireland' (*DEP*, 10 Jan. 1792). In 1797 opened an establishment for the sale of merchants' and traders' account books on the scale and plan of those in London (*Press*, 30 Dec. 1797). In Jan. 1797 he led the party in the old Independent Volunteers who were against offering to assist the government, and in February he was deputed by the radicals to sound the sheriffs about summoning an aggregate meeting (J.W., 1 Jan., 25 Feb. 1797, Reb. Papers, 620/36/227). In May 1797 he was reported to be leading a committee of fifteen, all men of letters, and a month later to have been admitted into the United Irishmen's 'cabinet' (J.W., 29 May, 21 June 1797, Reb. Papers 620/10). Near the end of 1797 he was reported to be in London, where he was having frequent conferences with people from France (J.W., 11 Sept. 1797, Reb. Papers, 620/10). He was banished by 38 Geo. III c.78. After three years in France he went to America. Died 1837. (J.W., 16 Nov. 1802, 10 June 1805, Reb. Papers, 620/10 and 620/14/188/13). [*WD*; SP I–VI]

74. CLARKE (John). Pill Lane. Silk-manufacturer. Admitted 7 Dec. and took test 14 Dec. 1792. Admitted freeman Easter 1789. In 1794 settled on his wife £150 per annum, charged on two houses which he owned, as well as £500 out of his estate (Reg. Deeds). Went bankrupt (*DG*, 1 Nov. 1798). [*WD*; SP I]

75. CLINCH (John, *Esq.*). Rathcoole. Admitted 16 March 1792. May have been the Joseph Clinch of Rathcoole hanged in 1798. [*Kildare Arch. Soc. Jnl*, v, p. 74]

76. COCHRAN (Henry). Pill Lane. Silk-manufacturer. Admitted 28 Dec. 1792 and took test 4 Jan. 1793. Admitted freeman midsummer 1792. Went bankrupt (*DG*, 19 Feb. 1791). In 1798 was imprisoned for being member of a group which aimed at exciting sedition in the ranks of the Liberty Rangers. From prison he wrote to Cooke begging to be released, emphasizing that he had given himself up and confessed all he knew (Reb. Papers, 620/52/147; St. Pr. Pt., VI/29/2). [*WD*; SP I]

77. COLE (William). Lower Ormond Quay. Boot and shoe-manufacturer. On commencing business, he announced that he was 'determined to use the best materials and have his work carried on by the best workmen' (*DEP*, 24 March 1788). In 1796 he surrendered his lease of a piece of ground for £20 (Reg. Deeds). According to Collins, a real Jacobin. [*WD*; SP I, V, VI]

78. COLEMAN (Francis). Dame Street. Mercer. Took test 21 Sept. 1792. Proposer Oct. 1792. On Cath. Qual. Rolls. In 1784, swore that he would not deal in foreign silks for four years unless protective duties were granted (P7, 7 July 1784). Advertised suits for the king's birthday-night (*HJ*, 25 Feb. 1784). [*WD*; SP I, V]

79. COLGAN (James). College Green. Woollen-draper. Admitted 28 Dec. 1792. In 1793 advertised his English, Irish and Scotch carpets (*DC*, 11 May 1793). In 1794 announced that 'to keep Irish artists employed' he would sell the Irish goods cheaper than any other house (*DEP*, 17 April 1794). [*WD*]

80. COLLINS (Edward). Bridge Street. Proposer 21 Dec. 1792. Probably partner of Robert Collins. [SP I]

81. — (John). Pill Lane. Silk-manufacturer. Mentioned 8 June 1792. Admitted freeman Mich. 1781. In 1796 mortgaged for £500 a piece of ground on which he had erected two brick houses (Reg. Deeds). In 1784 twenty-seven of his workpeople published an advertisement thanking him for having employed them during a time of distress, at material injury to his own interests. They added that 'all goods sold at No. 79 Pill Lane are Irish and from the sale of which Irishmen must receive employment' (*VJ*, 28 April 1784). Shortly afterwards Collins published an affidavit to the effect that he would not sell any goods as Irish which were not really so, and that he would not deal in any manufactured article of foreign origin while the non-importation agreement lasted. He also announced that he sold by wholesale only, and that Belfast cotton goods were sold at his place (*VJ*, 10 May 1784). In 1797 it was reported that he had been paid 'a smart sum' for preparing 10,000 green stocks and handkerchiefs (Higgins, 9 April 1797). [*WD*; SP I, IV, V, VI]

82. — (Robert). Bridge Street. Woollen-draper. Admitted and took test 23 Nov. 1792. Proposer 21 Dec. 1792. Admitted freeman midsummer 1792. Went bankrupt (*DG*, 20 April 1793). [SP I]

83. — (Thomas). Capel Street. Commission-mercer and linen-merchant. Gave information to the government about the Society's proceedings. Was appointed naval officer in Dominica, a position said to be worth £600 a year. Died 1814 (Ainslie to Lord Bathurst, 8 July 1814, PRO, CO.71/49). [Fitzpatrick, *Secret Service Under Pitt* (2nd edn), pp. 163–72; SP I, IV, V]

84. COLLIS (John). Barrister. Took test 23 April 1793. According to Collins, was secretary when the Society was dissolved by the sheriff. May possibly have been the John Collis of Tralee who, much to his indignation, was arrested in June 1798 on account of information being received that he was carrying on correspondence with the enemy. The general commanding the district declared that Mr Collis was supposed to have made a fortune smuggling (Reb. Papers, 620/38/100, 145a). [Burtchaell & Sadleir; SP I, V]

85. COMYN (Andrew, *Esq.*). Ryefield, Co. Roscommon. Admitted 8 June 1792. Described on Cath. Qual. Rolls as 'farmer'. Signed a Catholic address in support of the general committee (*HJ*, 31 Jan. 1792). In 1788 sold for £270 his lease of lands in Roscommon (Reg. Deeds). [SP I]

86. CONNOR (Patrick). Cook Street. Wine-cooper. On Cath. Qual. Rolls. Went bankrupt (*DG*, 13 Nov. 1788). In 1792 leased a warehouse and stable (Reg. Deeds). When he died, it was said that 'the widow and orphan have lost a general benefactor' (*DEP*, 10 March 1803). [*WD*; SP I, VI]

87. CONWAY (Matthew). Merchants' Quay. Merchant (grocer). Admitted 28 Dec. 1792. Proposer 29 March 1793. In 1796, in return for £85, let a house at a rent of £68 (Reg. Deeds). [*WD*; SP I]

88. COOKE (Alexander). Mary's Abbey. Attorney. Admitted 2 March and took test 1 June 1792. Proposer 14 Dec. 1792. [WD; SP I, IV]

89. COOMBES (Robert). 'Of the College'. Admitted 21 Feb. 1794 and took test April 1794. Secretary to the Dublin Medical Society (DC, 11 April 1793). [Burtchaell & Sadleir]

90. COOPER (James). Pill Lane. Woollen and haberdashery-warehouseman. Took test 11 Oct. 1792. Proposer 28 Dec. 1792. Went bankrupt (DG, 4 Oct. 1798). [WD; SP I]

91. — (Samuel). Wexford, Attorney. Admitted 7 Dec. 1792. 'A Mr Samuel Cooper an attorney is said to have signed Councillor Bagnel Harvey's summons to the town of Ross, as secretary to the Army' (FDJ, 16 June 1798). [SP I]

92. COPELAND (John). Francis Street. Silk-manufacturer. Proposer 16 March 1792. On Cath. Qual Rolls. His petition for freedom of weavers' gild was rejected on religious grounds (HJ, 3 Oct. 1794). In 1794 sold his interest in a house for £35 (Reg. Deeds). [WD; SP I–V]

93. COROLAN (John). Carrickmacross. Apothecary. Admitted 28 Dec. 1792. [WD; SP I]

94. CRAWFORD (James). W. Arran Street. Attorney. Admitted 10 Feb. 1792. Proposer 26 Oct. 1792. According to Collins, ' very bad'. [WD; SP I–VI]

95. CREHALL (John). Chamber Street. Dyestuff-merchant. Took test 13 April 1792. On Cath. Qual. Rolls. [WD; SP I]

96. CREIGHTON (Abraham). Capel Street. Tailor. Admitted 4 Jan. 1793. A Common council man. In 1784 eight journeymen published an advertisement complaining that Mr Creighton (who made his men work on Sunday) had discharged them, on the ground that he would not employ any man who contributed to a sick or burial fund. In his reply, in which he made a vigorous attack on what he considered the tyranny of combinations, Creighton declared that he had recently given employment to several industrious tailors, and that thereupon his former journeymen refused to remain unless the newcomers were discharged. As for the insinuation that he was a friend to foreign manufactures, he had not imported a yard of them since the non-importation agreement took place (VJ, 6, 10, 13 Dec. 1784). It was said that he and Chambers refused to drink Lord Camden's health at a city dinner (Higgins, 3 Feb. 1797). [WD; SP I, V, VI]

97. CROSBIE (Henry). Parliament Street. Woollen-draper. Proposed 11 Jan. 1793. In June 1783 leased a mill and land in Finglas with the intention of becoming a cotton-spinner. But in Sept. 1784, deciding to devote himself entirely to the woollen business, he sold the machinery for £347 and let the premises at a rent of £31 per annum. In 1788 let them for thirty-one years for £200. In 1797 leased a house at a yearly rent of £100 (Reg. Deeds). In 1784 published an affidavit that he would not sell any goods as Irish which were not truly so, and that he would not import any English goods for ten months unless protection was granted [VJ, 7 July 1784). [WD; SP I]

98. — (Matthew). New Row. Wholesale linen-draper. Admitted 19 Oct. 1792. About 1798 an informer stated that an oath was administered to him by an apprentice of Mr Crosbie, the linen-draper of New Row (Reb. Papers, 620/38/179). [WD; SP I]

99. CROSS (Richard). Bridge Street. Bookseller. Proposer 21 Sept. 1792. On Cath. Qual. Rolls. A member of the Catholic Convention. Published an edition of the Fathers under the patronage of Maynooth (VJ, 29 July 1796). [SP I–V]

100. CUNNINGHAM (Robert). Pill Lane. Woollen-draper. Proposer 14 Dec. 1792. Went bankrupt (DG, 4 April 1793). [WD; SP I]

101. DALTON (John). Leixlip. Admitted 27 April 1792. Obituary notice in
DEP, 31 March 1804.

102. D'ARCY (Thomas). Abbey Street. Merchant. Took test 24 Feb. 1792.
On Cath. Qual. Rolls. A member of the Catholic Convention. In 1796, for
£445, he let a house at a yearly rent of £113 (Reg. Deeds). [*WD*; SP I–IV]

103. DAVOCK (James). Pill Lane. Silk-manufacturer. Admitted and took test
30 March 1792. Proposer 22 June 1792. Collector for repairs to St Mary's
Chapel (Reb. Papers, 620/34/49). His petition for the freedom of the weavers'
gild rejected on religious grounds (*HJ*, Oct. 1794). According to Collins, 'a
Jacobin'. Probably the Davock who attended Lord Edward FitzGerald when he
was moving from place to place before his arrest (Madden, *United Irishmen*
[2nd edn], ii, 406). [*WD*; SP I–V]

104. DAWSON (John). Castle Street. Woollen-draper. Proposer 3 Feb. 1792.
In 1784 he announced that it was not in his power 'to have so great a variety
of superfine Irish cloths as will serve his customers, for while the manufacturers
retail by public bounty they will not sell to the shopkeepers on such terms as
will give them an adequate profit'. He promised not to import from England for
the next six months, and hoped that 'his generous countrymen' would consider
his stock on hand as equivalent to Irish manufactures (*VJ*, 4 June 1784). In
1792 he mortgaged certain lands in Louth for £4000 (Reg. Deeds). Went bankrupt (*DG*, 8 March 1792). Presumably the Mr John Dawson who went on a
mission to a society at Ardee (*FDJ*, 30 Oct. 1792). [*WD*; SP I–V]

105. — (William). Beresford Street Attorney. Admitted 3 Feb. 1792. [*WD*;
SP I]

106. DELANY (Francis). Mullingar. Brewer. Admitted 4 Jan 1793. Took test
8 Feb. 1793 [Reg. Deeds].

107. DERMOTT (Hw. [*sic*] Hill). [SP I]

108. DEVOY (Thomas). In May 1798 a Thomas Devoy of Cole's Lane, vict-
ualler, in a letter to Cooke, stated that he had been arrested on the charge of
being a United Irishman. He was willing to take the usual oaths if released (St.
Pr. Pt., VI/29/2). [SP I]

109. DILLON (Edmund). Possibly a mistake for Edward Dillon, or the
apothecary of Ormond Quay who appears on the Cath. Qual. Rolls. [SP I]

110. — (Edward, *Esq.*). Hollymount, Co. Mayo. Took test 23 April 1793.
On Cath. Qual. Rolls. A member of the Catholic Convention.

111. — (Martin). Smithfield. Salesmaster. Admitted 16 Nov. 1792. In 1790
settled £1500 on his wife. In 1794 sold a piece of ground for £100 (Reg. Deeds).
[*WD*]

112. — (Richard). Bridge Street. Wholesale linen-merchant. Admitted 21
Sept. 1792. Proposer Oct. 1792. On Cath. Qual. Rolls. Went bankrupt (*DG*, 29
Nov. 1803). He was secretary to a meeting of Catholics of St Audeon's parish
which expressed regret at Fitzwilliam's withdrawal (*HJ*, 18 March 1795). Higgins speaks of him as 'one of the most Violent and Bloodthirsty' amongst the
discontented, and refers in 1796 to the Catholic Committee, and in 1797 to 'the
Pill Lane King Killers' as meeting at his house (Higgins, 15 March 1798, 30
Sept. 1796, 29 Jan. 1797). About the beginning of 1798, through Mr Charles
Ryan, Cooke sent him advice as to his 'publick conduct and deportment'. From
then on, he declared to Cooke, he avoided conversing on politics, sent a dona-
tion to a fund for the widows and orphans of soldiers, gave £20 to the volunteer
loan, and tried to enroll in the Liberty Rangers (Reb. Papers, 620/38/92). He
was banished under 38 Geo. III c. 78, and went to Paris (Miles Byrne, *Memoirs*

[1907 edn], ii. 363). [*WD; SP I*]

113. — (Robert). Francis Street. Woollen-draper. Took test 13 Jan. 1792. Proposer 27 Jan. 1792. On Cath. Qual. Rolls. Partner of James Aylward. A member of the Catholic Convention. [*WD; SP I–VI*]

114. DIXON (James). Kilmainham. Tanner. Admitted 7 Dec. 1792. On Cath. Qual. Rolls. A member of the Catholic Convention. In 1796, as he was security for the gaoler, he was allowed to visit the Northern prisoners in the county gaol (J.W., 26 Sept. 1796, Reb. Papers, 620/10). In March 1797 Higgins, after referring to him as treasurer of the party, remarked that 'without a ray of understanding he assumes the most violent principles'. In April he paid for handkerchiefs for republican clubs, but in October, according to Higgins, he was deposed from his office (Higgins, 14 March, 9 April, 30 Oct. 1797). In June 1798 he was imprisoned in Ennis gaol, where he was allowed a pint of port and a bottle of porter daily (Reb. Papers, 620/40/87, 149). On his release, much to the indignation of Higgins, he went about boasting that, through his friends in the castle, he would obtain compensation for the losses (estimated at £1000) which he had sustained when his house was occupied by the military (Higgins, 20 Jan. 1799). He was again in prison in 1803, though according to himself he had 'purposely confined himself to a domestic life' (Reb. Papers, 620/12/141/24; 620/13/174/2). [*WD; SP I, V, VI*]

115. DODD (William). Smithfield and Queen Street. Distiller. Admitted 8 Feb. 1793. In February 1796 erected a distillery in Westmeath. Spent £5000 on the buildings and paid £2700 per annum in excise. In June 1797 a party of militia attacked and fired his premises. This, he declared, was done not because of disloyalty on his part, but from a spirit of rancour. His utensils were seized by the revenue authorities, and as a result of being unable to meet other creditors he went bankrupt and was flung into gaol. He repeatedly petitioned the government for compensation (Reb. Papers, 620/36/160, 620/47/14, 620/64/182; St. Pr. Pt., VI/39/2). [*DG*, 5 May 1803; *WD; SP I*]

116. DONOVAN (John). Peter Street. Barrister. Admitted and took test 28 Dec. 1792. Was appointed attorney general of the Gold Coast in 1816, and after a few months' residence died of fever. An obituary notice referred to him as 'an upright, honourable, and kind-hearted man' (*DEP*, 21 Nov. 1816). [Burtchaell & Sadleir; *SP I, V, VI*]

117. DORAN (Thomas). Francis Street. Woollen-draper and rectifier. Admitted and took test 11 Oct. 1792. A member of the Catholic Convention. Owned his premises and a house in Brunswick Street (Reg. Deeds). [*WD; SP I, V, VI*]

118. — (William). Cork Street. Tanner. [*WD; SP I*]

119. — (William, *Gent*.). Patrick Street. Admitted 29 March and took test 31 May 1793.

120. DOWDAL (Patrick). Engine Alley. Oil, flour and wool-factor. Admitted 21 Dec. 1792. [*WD; SP I*]

121. DOWLING (Frank). Fishamble Street. Chandler. Admitted 16 Nov. 1792. Proposer 8 Feb. 1793. His obituary notice spoke of him as 'a man of mild & inoffensive manners' (*DEP*, 6 Aug. 1807). [*WD; SP I*]

122. — (James). George's Quay. Grocer. Admitted 29 March 1793. Possibly the James Dowling who, in May 1797, having received an invitation to a United Irishmen's meeting, wanted to give the government information (Reb. Papers, 620/30/18). [*WD; SP I*]

123. — (Joseph). Great George's Street. Ironmonger. Admitted 8 Feb. and took test 15 Feb. 1793. [*WD; SP I*]

124. — (Matthew). Great Longford Street. Attorney. Lord Cloncurry's agent (Reb. Papers, 620/34/39). Accompanied Tandy in a professional capacity to the Dundalk trial (*DC*, 21 March 1793). Captain in Goldsmiths' corps (Reb. Papers, 620/53/179). Secretary to an aggregate meeting of the citizens of Dublin (*DEP*, 5 Aug. 1790). Fought a duel (*DC*, Dec. 1792). According to Higgins, he had a room opposite the sessions house, where witnesses were dressed and instructed (Higgins, 29 Jan. 1798, Reb. Papers, 620/36/226). Condemned to banishment by 38 Geo. III c. 78. [*WD*; SP I–VI]

125. — (Thomas, *Gent.*). Longford Street. Admitted 4 Jan. 1793. [SP I]

126. DOYLE (James). New Market. Possibly the grocer of New Row. [*WD*; SP IV]

127. — (James). Ormond Quay. Chicken-butcher. According to Collins a papist. [SP III, VI]

128. — (Michael). 23 Fisher's Lane. Poulterer. Present 14 Dec. 1792. On Cath. Qual. Rolls. In 1788 leased the ground in Fisher's Lane on which he had built a house, undertaking to pay a rent of £50 a year (Reg. Deeds). [SP I, V]

129. — (Nicholas). New Market. Possibly a corn-factor, or may be a mistake for James Doyle. [*WD*; SP II]

130. — (Richard, *Esq.*). Lemonstown, Co.Wicklow. Balloted for 30 Nov. and took test 7 Dec. 1792. Member of the Catholic Convention. (SP I]

131. DRENNAN (William). Physician. [*DNB*; *Drennan Letters*; SP II, IV–VI]

132. DROUGHT (Thomas). Kildare. A Thomas Drought of King's County was a witness for the defence in the Sheares trial. He had been a magistrate for his county, but had been dismissed, apparently on account of the scandal caused by his domestic affairs. In 1792 he made a bet that Ireland would be a republic in four years. [SP I]

133. DRUMGOOLE (Christopher). Weavers' Square. Clothier. Admitted 14 Dec. 1792.

134. DRYE (Thomas). Weavers' Square. Clothier. In 1791 he and his brother sold a plot of land in Wicklow for £30 (Reg. Deeds). In 1796 agents from Belfast visited him, but he refused to deal with them as their credentials were insufficient (J.W., 9 July 1796, Reb. Papers, 620/36/227). In 1795 appeared for trial on charge of high treason, but was discharged (*HJ*, 1 Jan. 1796). In May 1798 it was reported that among those arrested in Cork, was Drye, who was said to be a delegate from the Northern United Irishmen (J.W., May 1798, Reb. Papers, 620/10). He was condemned to banishment by 38 Geo. III c. 78. [*WD*; SP I]

135. DUDGEON (John). Pill Lane. Woollen-draper. Admitted 22 June and took test 6 July 1792. [SO I, II]

136. — (Samuel). Pill Lane. Woollen-draper. Admitted 22 June and took test 31 Aug. 1792. Admitted freeman Mich. 1792. Said to be publishing O'Connor's *Address* in 1797 (J.W., 12 Feb. 1797, Reb. Papers, 620/10). [*WD*; SP I, II]

137. DUFF (John). Thomas Street. [SP I]

138. DUIGAN (John). James's Street. Tanner. Took test 8 March 1793. [*WD*; SP I]

139. DUIGENAN (Miles). Grafton Street. Grocer, wine and spirit-merchant. Admitted 3 May 1793. In 1792 advertised for an apprentice and tried to let furnished lodgings on his first floor (*DEP*, 9 Feb. 1792). In 1793 was charged with shouting 'Liberty, Equality' and 'No King'; pleaded that he must have been drunk (*FDJ*, 5 March 1793). Later sentenced to six months' imprisonment for insulting an officer (*FDJ*, 6 May 1794). Was a leading organizer in the period

before the Rebellion but was considered 'rash and weak' (Sirr papers, N 4. 12; Reb. Papers, 620/29/224, 620/52/160; J.W., 24 May 1797, Reb. Papers, 620/10). *The Union Star* was said to be printed in his house (J.W., undated, Reb. Papers, 620/10). In 1797 his arrest alarmed many, but he himself was 'up and alive', for he was certain that the only witness against him was discredited (J.W., 27 May 1797, Reb. Papers, 620/10). After nine months' imprisonment, he was discharged. On the outbreak of the Rebellion he was again arrested, though according to himself, he was trying to take the oath of allegiance. His house and stores were plundered and creditors served writs amounting to £600 (Reb. Papers, 620/51/285; 620/4/29/53). Was attainted by 38 Geo. III c. 80, but released at the end of 1801 (*HJ*, 11 Dec. 1801). [*WD*; SP I, V, VI]

140. ELLIOT (James). Church Street. Slater. [*WD*; SP I]

141. ELLWORTH (J.). Proposer 1 Feb. 1793.

142. EMMET (Thomas Addis). Barrister. Admitted 7 Dec. 1792. (*DNB*; SP I, V, VI)

143. ENNIS (James). Bridge Street. Wholesale linen-draper. Proposer 23 Nov. 1792. In 1793 mortgaged a house in Bridge Street (Reg. Deeds). [*WD*; SP I]

144. ERCHALL (John). Chamber Street. Admitted 16 March 1792. Probably a mistake for John Crehall.

145. ESMOND (John). Cutpurse Row. Laceman. Took test 13 Jan. 1792. Proposer 27 Jan. 1792. On Cath. Qual. Rolls. [*WD*; SP I–IV]

146. — (John). Co. Carlow. Admitted 9 March 1792. Probably John Esmond MD, 2nd son of Sir James Esmond Bt. and a member of the Catholic Convention. Married a co-heiress. According to a conservative journalist, on marriage he gave up his profession and devoted himself to 'objects of the most dangerous sort'. Convicted of treason and executed 1798 [*FDJ*, 2, 16 June 1798]

147. EUSTACE (Rowland). Pill Lane. Malt-distiller and spirit-merchant. On Cath. Qual. Rolls. In 1786 took a mortgage on a house, and in 1790 a parcel of ground in Pill Lane (Reg. Deeds). Went bankrupt (*DG*, 2 Feb. 1797). [*WD*; SP I]

148. EVANS (Hampden). North Gt. George's Street. Admitted 21 Dec. 1792. Was said to have had a fortune of £8000 to £10,000 (Miles Byrne, *Memoirs* [1907 edn], ii, 336). A reformer in the 1780s. Arrested in July 1798 on a charge of treason (*HJ*, 23 July 1798), and banished by 38 Geo. III c. 78. [SP I, V, VI]

149. — (Thomas). Lower Coombe. Pump-borer and turner. Admitted 9 March and took test 1 June 1792. [*WD*; SP I, IV]

150. EWING (Patrick). James's Street. Flax-dresser. A Common council man. Collins described him as 'a wicked fool', and Higgins referred to him as the bosom friend of Napper Tandy. In 1796 subscribed to the defence of the Northern prisoners (Higgins, 27, 30 Sept. 1796). [*WD*; SP I–VI]

151. FAIRFIELD (John). Werburgh Street. Woollen-draper. Admitted 21 Dec. 1792. On Cath. Qual. Rolls. A member of the Catholic Convention. In 1790 sold two houses (Reg. Deeds). In 1784 promised not to deal in imported goods for two years unless protection was granted (*VJ*, 19 July 1784). [*WD*; SP I]

152. FARRELL (Michael). Cork Hill. Grocer. Proposed 27 April 1792. On Cath. Qual. Rolls. [*WD*; SP I, 11]

153. FAWCETT (Robert (?)). Capel Street. Attorney. Admitted 6 July 1792. [*WD*; SP I, II, V]

154. FAY (William). James's Street. Merchant. Admitted 12 April 1793. [*WD*; SP I]

155. FEGAN (—). Proposer 5 Oct. 1792.
156. FITZGERALD (David). Suffolk Street. Attorney. Admitted 13 Jan.
1792. Probably went bankrupt (*DG*, 9 June 1796). [*WD*]
157. FITZSIMMONS (Christopher). Crow Street. Surgeon. [*WD*; SP I, II, IV]
158. FITZSIMONS (James). Abbey Street. Merchant. Admitted 21 Dec.
1792. On Cath. Qual. Rolls. A member of the Catholic Convention. [*WD*; SP I]
159. FLANAGAN (—). Took test 27 April 1792. 'Dr.' Possibly the Dr
Bernard Flanagan of Athlone who died 1795 (*DEP*, 10 Sept. 1795). [SP II–V]
160. FLANAGAN [or O'FLANAGAN] (Lewis, *Esq.*). Abbey Street. Admitted
9 March 1792. A member of the Catholic Convention. [SP I]
161. FLOWER (Edward). Pill Lane. Pin-maker. Admitted freeman Mich.
1783. [*WD*; SP I]
162. FLYN (Patrick). Old Church Street. Linen-draper. Admitted 21 Dec.
1792. Went bankrupt (*DG*, 10 Nov. 1801). [*WD*]
163. FOLEY (David). Youghal. Apothecary. Admitted 3 Feb. 1792. On
Cath. Qual. Rolls. In 1791 sold the townland of West Newport (Reg. Deeds).
164. FRANKLIN (Anthony). Pill Lane. Builder. Admitted 7 Dec. and took
test 14 Dec. 1792. Admitted freeman Mich. 1789. In 1793 sold a plot of ground
on Summerhill (Reg. Deeds). [SP I]
165. FRAZIER (Henry). Grafton Street. Bookseller. Admitted 9 March and
proposer 19 Oct. 1792. According to Collins, 'a mad Jacobin'. [SP I–VI]
166. FULLAM (Patrick). New Row. Woollen-draper and trimming-mer-
chant. Proposer 4 Jan. 1793. In 1784 signed resolutions in favour of protection
(*VJ*, 16 July 1784). Went bankrupt (*DG*, 14 July 1795). [SP I]
167. FYANS (Robert). Thomas Street. Yarn and cotton-merchant. Took test
24 Feb. 1792. Apparently an acquaintance of Carrolan's (Higgins, 25 Sept.
1800). [*WD*; SP I, II, V]
168. GANNON (Bartholomew). Corn Market. Linen-draper. Proposer 19
Oct. 1792. In 1790 let shop at a rent of £20 (Reg. Deeds). Lord Edward Fitzgerald was concealed in his house (Madden, *United Irishmen* [2nd edn], ii, 406).
[*WD*; SP I]
169. GAVIN (—). Took test 23 Nov. 1792.
170. GELLING (David). Dame Street. Hatter and umbrella-manufacturer.
Proposed 2 Nov. and took test 16 Nov. 1792. Proposer 14 Dec. 1792. [*WD*; SP I]
171. GILDEA (Anthony, *Esq.*). Co. Mayo. Admitted 9 March 1792. Possibly a high sheriff of Mayo.
172. GILL (Henry). Skinners' Row. Woollen-draper. [*WD*; SP I]
173. GILLIGAN (Valentine). Francis Street. Linen-draper. Admitted 21 Dec.
1792. On Cath. Qual. Rolls. [*WD*; SP I]
174. GILTENAN (Edward B.). Francis Street. Poplin and stuff-manufacturer.
Proposed 2 Nov. and took test 16 Nov. 1792. Proposer 10 Dec. 1792. On Cath.
Qual. Rolls. Had a wholesale and retail warehouse. Twice advertised for an
apprentice (*DEP*, 26 May 1789; *HJ*, 14 Nov. 1798). President of a division of
the Sick and Indigent Room-Keepers Society (*HJ*, 23 July 1800). Higgins
reported that he was 'a somewhat violent man with the R.C. party', and that,
though he had several times compounded with his creditors, he had always supported a fair character in trade (Higgins, 26 May 1797). [*WD*; SP I]
175. — (J.B.). Proposer 4 Jan. 1793. Probably a mistake for E.B. Giltenan.
176. — (William). Castlecomer. Merchant. Admitted 4 Jan. 1793. The
trustees for the creditors of E.B. Giltenan, deceased, announced for sale a mortgage on a large plot of ground in the marketplace of Castlecomer, on which

were two houses and several town parks, all in the possession of W. Giltenan, the mortgager (*HJ*, 23 July 1801).

177. GORMAN (Thomas). Queen Street. Builder. Admitted 8 Feb. 1793. On Cath. Qual. Rolls. In 1785 sold house for £45 10s.; between 1788 and 1793, mortgaged two houses, a piece of ground in the city, and – for £350 – several plots of ground in the suburbs (Reg. Deeds). Went bankrupt (*DG*, 8 Aug. 1795). [*WD*; SP I]

178. GRAHAM (Francis). Church Street. Grocer. Took test 21 Sept. 1792. Admitted freeman Christmas 1790. Went bankrupt (*DG*, 12 Aug. 1794). [SP I]

179. GREEN (John, *Esq.*). Carrickmacross. Admitted 21 Dec. 1792.

180. GROGAN (John, *Esq.*). Heathfield, Co. Wexford. Admitted 10 May 1793. Probably commanded Heathfield Cavalry in the Rebellion (Miles Byrne, *Memoirs* [1907 edn], i, 62). [SP I]

181. HAM (Paul). Pill Lane. Clover and skinner. Admitted 22 June and took test 6 July 1792. Went bankrupt (*DG*, 12 April 1788). In 1787 let a house at a rent of £30; in 1789 let a skin-yard and house at rent of £11; and in 1787 for £30 down let a plot of ground at a rent of £20 (Reg. Deeds). [*WD*; SP I, II]

182. HARRISON (Jervis). Saul's Court. Woollen-factor. Went bankrupt (*DG*, 10 June 1797). [SP I]

183. HARVEY (Beauchamp Bagenal). Barrister. Admitted 22 June 1792. [*DNB*; SP I, V, VI]

184. — (James). Wexford. Probably a brother of B.B. Harvey. Admitted 3 June 1793. [Burtchaell & Sadleir; SP I]

185. HATTON (William). Proposer 10 May 7793. For a time, lieutenant in the XVIIth Dragoons. Owned land and house-property in Wexford (keg. Deeds). Was a member of the committee of the Independent Electors of County Wexford (*DEP*, 20 May 1790). According to Barrington, he was one of the rebel directory of Wexford, and unaccountably escaped (Barrington, *Personal Sketches*, i, 270). [SP I)

186. HAWKESWORTH (Amory). Bride Street. Barrister. Took test 8 June 1792. In 1798 was a member of the lawyers' corps (Sirr Papers, N 4. 12). [Burtchaell & Sadleir; *WD*; SP I, II, VI]

187. HAY (Philip). King Street. Attorney. Admitted 4 Jan. 1793.

188. HENRY (Alexander). Clover Hill, Ballymoney, Co. Antrim. Admitted 7 Dec. and took test Dec. 1792. Admitted freeman Christmas 1793. Apparently a man of property (Reg. Deeds). [SP I]

189. — (Lodovick). Queen Street. Attorney. [*WD*; SP I]

190. HICKEY (Marcus). Simpson's Court. Attorney. [*WD*; SP I]

191. HINCKS .(—). Linen Hall. Probably a ship-broker. Did considerable business with America (e.g., *HJ*, 14 Feb. 1801; *DEP*, 8 Jan. 1803). [*WD*; SP II, IV]

192. HOEY (Peter). Ormond Quay. Bookseller. Proposer 30 Dec. 1791. On Cath. Qual. Rolls. Elected churchwarden of St Michan's, but Dr Duigenan refused to admit him (*HJ*, 2 Feb. 1795). Was active in the reform movement in the eighties (PRO, H.O. 100/14). About 1798 an informer reported that he was 'ill disposed' (Reb. Papers, 620/51/203). [*WD*; SP I–VI]

193. HOGAN (John). Usher's Quay. Attorney. Took test 11 Oct. 1792. [*WD*; SP I]

194. — (Patrick). Queen Street. Attorney. Admitted 4 Jan. 1792. [*WD*; SP I]

195. HOWARD (Leonard). Gt. Ship Street. Attorney. Admitted 4 Jan. 1793. [SP I]

196. HOWIE (Thomas). 9 Bridge Street. Scots-merchant. Admitted 11 Oct. 1792. Admitted freeman Easter 1792. [*WD*; SP I]

197. HUBAND (Joseph). Peter Street. Barrister. Director for many years of Grand Canal (Ruth Delany, *The Grand Canal of Ireland* (1973); SP I)

198. — (Josuah, *Esq.*). Charlemont Mall. Admitted 1 June 1792. [SP I]

199. HUGHES (James). High Street. Woollen-draper. Admitted 14 Dec. 1792. On Cath. Qual. Rolls. [*WD*; SP I]

200. — (James). Usher's Street. Brewer. Admitted 25 Nov. 1792. 'J. Hughes' was a proposer 28 Dec. 1792. On Cath. Qual. Rolls. [*WD*; SP I]

201. HYLAND (William). Back Lane. Leather-seller. Admitted 7 Dec. 1792. A member of the Catholic Convention. Took test 7 Dec. 1792. On Cath. Qual. Rolls. In 1790 let a tenement at a yearly rent of £26; in 1792 mortgaged a piece of ground for £653 (Reg. Deeds). [*WD*; SP I]

202. HYNDMAN (Robert Augustus). Bride Street. Admitted 1 Feb. 1793. According to Carey, was a young man whose literary talents and independence of mind marked him for a much more superior position in life to that which he occupied (Carey, *An Appeal to the People of Ireland*, p. 189). [SP I]

203. JACKSON (Henry). Iron-founder. Old Church Street. Common council man. According to himself, having started business in 1766, by 1798 he had a foundry in Church Street 'wrought by a Steam Engine the first ever erected in Dublin'. He had another steam engine on the Quays for the purpose of slitting and rolling iron, and a third in Phoenix Street for grinding wheat. Also he had iron-mills at Clonskeagh, employing numerous people (St. Pr. Pt., VI/31/1). Banished by 38 Geo. III c. 78. [*WD*; SP I–VI]

204. JOHNSON (Henry). Meath Street. Worsted-manufacturer. Admitted 4 Jan. 1793. On Cath. Qual. Rolls. Member of the Catholic Convention. [*WD*; SP I]

205. — (James). Arran Quay. Attorney. It was said that 'Js. Johnson of the Inns Quay' was employed by Bond and Jackson as their attorney (J.W., 21 May 1798, Reb. Papers, 620/10). [*WD*; SP I]

206. — (James). Ormond Quay and Newry. [SP I]

207. JONES (Griffith). College Green. Jeweller. Admitted 24 Feb. and took test 13 April 1792. In 1737 settled £450 and a share in an annuity of £30 on his wife; in 1791 mortgaged a house in College Green (Reg. Deeds). Went bankrupt (*DG*, 15 Jan. 1793). [*WD*; SP I–IV]

208. — (William Todd). Barrister. MP for Lisburn, 1783–90. A prominent pamphleteer and one of the earliest Protestant advocates of Catholic Emancipation. [*WD*; SP I, III, IV]

209. JORDON (Thomas). Pill Lane. Hosier. Admitted Dec. 1792. Admitted freeman Easter 1782. In 1791 settled £1500 on his wife whose portion was £1000 (Reg. Deeds). Was a manufacturer as well as a merchant (*DEP*, 4 March 1790), and in 1787 advertised his Irish wares which were as cheap as similar goods imported from England. Informed the public that he never imported, so 'they might be sure what are purchased from him are IRISH MADE' (*DEP*, 4 April 1790, 6 Jan. 1787). In 1797 Higgins wanted Cooke to see him, as his information might be useful (Higgins, 24 Nov. 1797). In 1799 Jordon wrote to Castlereagh, complaining that, though he had submitted an account of the loss he had sustained when his house and concerns at Newtownmountkennedy were occupied by the military, he had received no answer (Reb. Papers, 620/56/115). [*WD*; SP I]

210. KEANE (Edward C.). Chancery Lane. Attorney. Admitted 27 Jan. and

took test 2 March 1792. Accused by an informer, in 1798, of being one of a group in the Liberty Rangers that was trying to aid the United Irishmen, and as a result was imprisoned. Writing to the government from prison, he explained that, having a number of Catholic clients, 'and it appearing to me then reasonable that the laws against them should be repealed', he had become a member of 'the old United Irishmen'. Since he opposed resolutions which he thought seditious, he was regarded in 'a very cool and suspected light'. Since acting for Hamilton Rowan, he had refused to appear for United Irishmen, and he had no concern with 'the modern United Irishmen' (Reb. Papers, 620/38/103; 52/154). He was banished by 38 Geo. III c. 78 and struck off the rolls, but remained in Dublin practising, through his clerk (Higgins, 18 May, 28 Dec. 1801). [WD; SP I, V, VI]

211. — (John). Poole Street. Clothier. Proposed 30 Nov. 1792. [WD, SP I]

212. — (Roger). Parke Street. Silk and worsted-manufacturer. Proposed 30 Nov. 1792. Proposer 4 Jan. 1793. On Cath. Qual. Rolls. [WD; SP I]

213. KEEFE (Thomas). Phoenix Street. Merchant. Admitted 27 Jan. 1792. [WD; SP I]

214. KELLY (Edward). Church Street. Linen-draper. Admitted 14 Dec. 1792. [WD; SP I]

215. — (Edward). Old Church Street. Distiller. Admitted and took test 2 Nov. 1792. [WD; SP I]

216. — (Edward). Usher's Quay. Woollen-draper. Admitted 21 Dec. 1792. [WD; SP I]

217. — (James). Old Church Street. Linen-merchant. On Cath. Qual. Rolls. Member of the Catholic Convention. His executors advertised for sale the lease of his house at a yearly rent of £40, and a profit-rent arising from another house (HJ, 12 Sept. 1800). [WD; SP I]

218. — (Joseph). Cork Street. Brewer. Admitted Nov. 1792. Proposer 7 Dec. 1792. On Cath. Qual. Rolls. Advertised in DEP, 30 May 1789. Went bankrupt (DG, 22 Jan. 1793). [WD; SP I]

219. — (Joseph). James's Street. Tanner. Admitted 7 Dec. 1792. Probably on Cath. Qual. Rolls. [WD; SP I]

220. — (Michael). Galway Walk. Tanner. Admitted 12 April 1791. [SP I]

221. — (Nicholas). James's Street. Tanner. Possibly a mistake for one of the other Kellys. [SP V, VI]

222. KENNEDY (Andrew). Patrick Street. Grocer. In 1793 sold the lease of a house and plot of land in Wicklow for £37 (Reg. Deeds). [WD; SP I]

223. — (Henry). Aungier Street. Physician. Admitted 9 March 1792. Lord Edward FitzGerald stayed with him in 1798 (Madden [2nd edn], ii, 403). [WD; SP I–IV]

224. — (Patrick). Pitt Street. 'Captain'. Admitted 24 Feb. and took test 30 March 1792. Proposer 7 Dec. 1792.

225. KEOGH (James). Pool Street. Clothier. Admitted 21 Dec. 1792. [WD; SP I]

226. — (John). Mt Jerome. Retired silk-mercer. On Cath. Qual. Rolls. Member of the Catholic Convention. [DNB; SP II–IV]

227. KIERNAN (Richard). Capel Street. Physician. Admitted 21 Dec. 1792. Member of the Catholic Convention. According to Higgins, near the end of 1797 he opposed the idea of a general rising (Higgins, 26 Oct. 1797). [WD; SP I]

228. KIRWAN (Martin). Aungier Street. Barrister. Took test 10 Feb. 1792. Proposer 21 Dec. 1792. From about 1797, chairman of sessions for Co. Mayo.

In 1805, a prisoner in Kilmainham who wished to see him spoke of him as being as loyal a gentleman as any in Ireland (Reb. Papers, 620/14/186/1). [*WD*; SP I–VI]

229. LABELLAIRE (Peter). Werburgh Street. Linen-draper. Admitted 23 Nov. 1792. Proposer 4 Jan. 1793. In 1788 sold a plot of ground for £200 (Reg. Deeds). In the following year announced that the designs on his cloth had been drawn or approved by personages 'distinguished as well for their taste as patriotic disposition to encourage the manufactures of this kingdom' (*DEP*, 17 March 1789). Went bankrupt (*DG*, 24 Dec. 1794). [*WD*; SP I]

230. LALOR (John). Templemore, Co. Tipperary. Probably the John Lalor, member of the Catholic Convention who died on 7 September 1828. [M. O'Connell (ed.), *The O'Connell Correspondence*, i, p. 310; SP I]

231. LAMBERT [or LAMBART] (Patrick). Brabazon Row. Clothier. On Cath. Qual. Rolls. [*WD*; SP I]

232. LANGAN (John). Cutpurse Row. Shoemaker. Took test 6 July 1792. On Cath. Qual. Rolls. In 1789 was paid £330 for a mortgage (Reg. Deeds). [*WD*; SP I]

233. LAW (Richard). New Market. Silk-throwster. Admitted 7 Dec. took test 14 Dec. 1792. Admitted freeman Easter 1782. [*WD*; SP I]

234. LAWLER (or LAWLOR) (Joseph, *Esq.*). Admitted 27 April 1792. [SP I]

235. LEE (Edmund). Dame Street. Music-seller and instrument-maker. Took test 27 Jan. 1792. Proposer 24 Feb. 1792. In 1785 announced that he was manufacturing on an extensive scale pianofortes and harpsichords, which were 'of such qualities of tone, as ... to be at least equal to any made in this or any other country' (*DEP*, 29 Jan. 1785). [*WD*; SP I–III, V]

236. — (Thomas). Pill Lane. Merchant. Admitted 24 Feb. 1792. [*WD*; SP I, III, IV]

237. LEW (—). Clonmel. Took test 14 Dec. 1792.

238. LEWINS (Edward Joseph). Vicar Street. Admitted 9 March and took test 6 July 1792. Secretary during May 1793. Probably the same Edward Lewens who was a member of the Catholic Convention, a cotton manufacturer in Thomas Street in 1794, and an emissary from the United Irishmen to the French government in 1797. Collins refers to Laurence Lewins, Vicar Street, as secretary to the Society on 3 May 1793. Laurence Lewins did exist, but possibly Collins was referring to E.J. Lewins.

239. LIDWILL (—). Took test 14 Dec. 1792.

240. LONG (John). Kilkenny, and the Castle Hotel, Essex Street. Took test 31 May 1793. Present 27 Feb. 1794. According to Collins, a papist, an Irishman in the Neapolitan service, and a French agent. [SP I, V, VI]

241. LUBE (John, *Esq.*). Co. Kildare. Admitted 24 Feb. 1792 and took test 2 March 1792. Probably a Catholic (Burtchaell & Sadleir). In 1787, on his marriage to a Miss Lee, who was entitled to a considerable fortune, he settled on her lands worth £180 per annum (Reg. Deeds). [SP I, V, VI]

242. LYONS (Ch., *Esq.*). Roscommon. Admitted 3 Feb. 1792.

243. — (Lewis). Arran Quay. Schoolmaster. Proposer. 11 Oct. 1792. On Cath. Qual. Rolls. Member of the Catholic Convention. Member of committee of Dublin Literary Society (*DEP*, 13 Aug. 1791). When he opened his school, he announced that he intended to adopt a plan of instruction 'at once easier ... as well as more complete and expeditious than that usually followed' (*DEP*, 6 Sept. 1787). Later he made extensive alterations in his house (*DEP*, 31 July 1794). In 1799 was said to have conveyed to Roger O'Connor a packet of letters

242   DUBLIN SOCIETY OF UNITED IRISHMEN

dealing with seditious activities (Higgins, 20 Jan. 1799). An acquaintance of
Carrolan's (Higgins, 25 Sept. 1800). [SP I, II, IV–VI]

244. LYSTER (Robert Henry, *Esq.*). Admitted 9 March 1792.

245. MCALLISTER (Randal). Grafton Street. Bookseller. Proposer 19 Oct.
1792. Admitted freeman Mich. 1786. Committed to Newgate by House of
Commons in 1793 for a libel published in *National Evening Star* (*Commons'
Jnl Ire.*, xv, 185–90; *Parliamentary Reg.*, xiii, 401). Went bankrupt (*DG*, 18
June 1793). [*WD*; SP I–IV]

246. MCBRIDE (Thomas). New Row. Ironmonger. Admitted and took test
14 Dec. 1792. According to Collins, 'a real Jacobin'. In 1797 McNally said that
he was publishing O'Connor's Address (J.W., 12 Feb. 1797). [*WD*; SP I, VI]

247. MCCANN (Michael). Bridge Street. Glover. On Cath. Qual. Rolls.
Went bankrupt (*DG*, 17 Nov. 1801). [*WD*; SP I, VI]

248. — (William). [SP IV]

249. MCCORMICK (Henry). Possibly Richard McCormick. [SP V, VI]

250. — (Richard). Mark's Alley. Poplin-manufacturer. On Cath. Qual.
Rolls. Member of the Catholic Convention. It was rumoured that he was a deist
(J.W., 26 Sept. 1796, Reb. Papers, 620/10). Attainted by 38 Geo. III c. 80. [*WD*;
SP I, II, IV]

251. MCDERMOT (Hugh). Co. Sligo. Physician. Admitted 6 July 1792.
Member of the Catholic Convention. [SP I]

252. — (James J.). [SP I]

253. — (Laurence). Old Church Street. Silk-manufacturer. On Cath. Qual.
Rolls. Member of the Catholic Convention. An obituary notice said that 'he
attained through a long life the highest reputation as a trader, and the wealth he
accumulated was acquired by the practice of the most rigid punctuality and a
scrupulous regard for the highest principles' (*DEP*, 16 Jan. 1816). [*WD*; SP I]

254. MCDERMOT (Michael). Michael McDermott of Ballymahon appears
on Cath. Qual. Rolls. [SP I]

255. — (Owen). Queen Street. Barrister. Proposed 30 Dec. 1791. Proposer
21 Dec. 1792. [SP I, V, VI]

256. — (—). Ballymahon. Took test 27 April 1792. Probably Michael
McDermot.

257. MCDONNEL (James). Rossbegg, Co. Mayo. Admitted and took test 21
Dec. 1792. Member of the Catholic Convention. A leader of the Connacht insur-
gents in 1798. [SP I; R. Hayes, *The Last Invasion of Ireland* ... (1937), p. 336]

258. — (John). City Quay. Merchant. Admitted 24 Feb. 1792. Imported
timber from the Baltic and flax from St Petersburg (*DEP*, 18 Oct. 1791). When
he died he was described as 'an eminent, enterprising and successful merchant,
and a young man of the fairest character' (*HJ*, 31 July 1797). [*WD*]

259. — (Thomas). Essex Street. Printer and bookseller. On Cath. Qual.
Rolls. Member of the Catholic Convention. On 26 April 1793 resigned from the
Society. Was the proprietor of the *Hibernian Journal*, and when he died it was
said that 'in the stormy and agitated periods which have passed away' he never
'stimulated to sedition or tumult' (*DEP*, 9 March 1809). [*WD*; SP I–IV]

260. MCEVOY (John). Francis Street. Silk-manufacturer. Admitted 29
March 1793. In 1788 was paid £147 by the Wide Street Commissioners (Reg.
Deeds). [*WD*]

261. MCGUIRE (Constantine). Patrick Street. Grocer (?). Proposer 29
March 1793. On Cath. Qual. Rolls. Probably member of the Catholic Convention. [*WD*; SP I, V, VI]

262. — (John). Francis Street. Distiller. On Cath. Qual. Rolls. [*WD*; SP I]

263. MCKENNA (Theobald). Physician. Resigned from the Society 26 April 1793. Member of the Catholic Convention. [*DNB*; SP I, II, IV]

264. MCKENZIE (William). Gt Strand Street. Attorney. Admitted 21 Dec. 1792. [SP I]

265. MCLAUGHLIN (John). Usher's Quay. Merchant. On Cath. Qual. Rolls. Member of the Catholic Convention. An informer in 1799, referring to an attempt to form an executive committee in Dublin, spoke of McLaughlin of Ushers Island as being concerned in it (Reb. Papers, 620/7/74/8). [SP I]

266. — (Patrick). Francis Street. Woollen-draper. Admitted 2 Nov. 1792. A sheriff's peer. Promised in 1784 not to import for two years unless protection was granted (*VJ*, 19 July 1784). [*WD*; SP I, V, VI]

267. MCMAHON (James). Aungier Street. Apothecary. Admitted 30 March 1792. Admitted freeman Easter 1790. In 1791 sold for £300 the residue of the lease of a piece of ground in Merrion Square. (Reg. Deeds). In 1793 had a row with the Aldermen of Skinners Alley (Reb. Papers, 620/19/88; Barrington, *Personal Sketches*, i, p. 249). In 1797 Higgins reported that McMahon, who three years before had been compelled to quit Dublin, had returned. 'He thought he might have carried on his seditious practices at Swansea, but a London newspaper, the *Sun*, developed his designs and he was obliged to quit South Wales. On his return home he has been much caressed by many of the leaders,' (Higgins, 7 June 1797). [*WD*; SP I–VI]

268. MCMANUS (Patrick). New Market. Clothier. Took test 31 Aug. 1792. Proposer 21 Sept. 1792. On Cath. Qual. Rolls. In 1796 settled £2000 on his wife whose portion was £1000 (Reg. Deeds). [*WD*; SP I]

269. MCNALLY (Leonard). Barrister. [*DNB*; SP I–VI]

270. MCNAMARA (Daniel). Merchants' Quay. Merchant. Admitted and took test 21 Dec. 1792. According to Collins, a papist. [SP I, VI]

271. MCNEVIN (William James). Jervis Street. Physician. On Cath. Qual. Rolls. Member of the Catholic Convention. In 1794 paid £80 for lands in Galway (Reb. Papers, 620/48/48). [*DNB*; SP I–V]

272. MADDOX [or MADDOCKS] (William). George's Quay. Captain. Took test 11 Oct. 1792. Probably captain of the 'Draper' engaged in the Oporto trade (*HJ*, 10 July 1801). [SP I]

273. MAGRATH (Luke). Beresford Street. Attorney. Admitted 23 Nov. 1792. Admitted freeman Mich. 1800. [*WD*; SP I]

274. MAGUIRE (Simon). Bachelor's Walk. Merchant. On Cath. Qual. Rolls. Member of the Catholic Convention. In 1796 Higgins, speaking of him as a merchant who was carrying on trade with France, referred to him as having been treasurer of a fund for defraying law expenses of the Defenders (Higgins, 1 Aug. 1796). In 1796 he approached two Catholic clubs, and suggested that it would please the government if the Catholics 'of property and character' would arm. His negotiations failed and he found himself 'literally in Coventry'. It was said that, if he had succeeded, he would have received a situation in the National Bank (J.W., 13 Aug. 1796, Reb. Papers, 620/36/227). From about 1799 he appears to have been surveyor or gauger on Rogerson's Quay. [*WD*; SP I–VI]

275. MALONE (Thomas). Coombe. Grocer. Admitted 15 Feb. 1793. [*WD*; SP I]

276. MANGAN (Thomas). Thomas Street. Grocer. Admitted 29 March 1793. On Cath. Qual. Rolls. [*WD*; SP I]

277. MATHEWS (Constantine). Dawson Street. Chandler. On Cath. Qual. Rolls. In 1785 sold a house and twenty-six acres in County Wicklow (Reg. Deeds). According to Carey, he was one of the first Catholics to join the Independent Dublin Volunteers (*Appeal,* pp. 64 6). [*WD;* SP I, V, VI]

278. MAXWELL (Richard). Pill Lane. Woollen-draper. Took test 31 Aug. 1792. Proposer 5 Oct. 1792. Admitted freeman Christmas 1790. As a church-warden of St Michan's, presided over a meeting which passed resolutions in favour of reform (*DEP,* 31 Jan. 1793). [*WD;* SP I, V, VI]

279. MEEKINS (—). Vicar Street. Took test 15 June 1792.

280. MEREDITH (Jos., *Esq.*). Sligo. Admitted 27 Jan. 1792.

281. MILLER (John). Trinity Street. Attorney. Proposer 13 Jan. 1792. In 1797 an informer described him as 'a remarkable man having a large flesh mark on his face, he is a dangerous man and one of the class of United Irishmen, he is a great orator and has great abilities which he is now exerting on the subversion of the Constitution' (Reb. Papers, 620/29/57). Went bankrupt (*DG,* 12 Dec. 1795). [*WD;* SP I–IV]

282. MOLLOY [or MULLOY] (Tobias). Barrister. Author of *An Appeal from Man in a State of Civil Society to Man in a State of Nature* (1792), in which he praised the French Revolution, defended the theory of natural rights, made some contemptuous remarks about Catholics, and advocated a codification and simplification of the statute law. [Burtchaell & Sadleir; SP III]

283. MOLLOY (Tobias, *Esq.*). Ballina, Co. Mayo. Admitted 16 March 1792.

284. MOORE (Ambrose). Dame Street. Goldsmith. Proposer 16 Nov. 1792. On Cath. Qual. Rolls. Dealt extensively in house-property. In 1787 let a plot of ground at a yearly rent of £7 10s.; in 1788 let a house at a rent of £41; and in 1789 another at a rent of £45. In 1789 mortgaged to Dr Emmet for £1000 a house in Dame Street and a farm and a plot of ground (Reg. Deeds). Higgins described him as an affluent tradesman, who made money by discounting bills at 50 per cent, 'of the most avowed, wicked and Republican principles'. In Sept. 1797 was appointed secretary to the secret committee, and in Oct. treasurer (Higgins, 15 Sept., 30 Oct. 1797). After the Rebellion Higgins referred to him as 'a most active partizan … and Inciter to public commotion … holding mid-night meetings' (Higgins, 25 Sept. 1800). [*WD;* SP I–IV, VI]

285. — (James). College Green. Bookseller. On Cath. Qual. Rolls. In 1791 let to Griffith Jones, for £227 down, a house in College Green at a yearly rent of £113 (Reg. Deeds). In 1791 announced that he was the printer and proprietor of the *Encyclopaedia Britannica* 'the heaviest and most expensive work ever issued from the Irish Press, or ever before attempted in Ireland' (*DEP,* 5 March 1791). In 1802, being about to leave business, he announced that he was going to auction £20,000 worth of books (*HJ,* 11 May 1802). In 1803 he was expecting two vessels from Philadelphia with a large quantity of new American flax-seed (*DEP,* 25 Jan. 1803). In Oct. 1798 a meeting to discuss a rising was to have been held at his house (Higgins, 20 Oct. 1798). In Feb. 1803 he died, and his funeral was 'most respectably as well as numerously attended' (*DEP,* 1 March 1803). [*WD;* SP I–VI]

286. — (James). Thomas Street. Ironmonger. Admitted 16 March and took test 13 April 1792. On Cath. Qual. Rolls. Lord Edward FitzGerald, for whom his daughter carried messages, passed a weekend at his house (Madden [2nd edn], ii, 406). [*WD;* SP I, II, IV–VI]

287. MORGAN (Thomas). Pill Lane. Merchant. Admitted and took test 16 Nov. 1792. Admitted freeman midsummer 1792. [*WD;* SP I]

288. MORTON (Trevor S.). Camden Street. Attorney. Admitted 27 Jan. 1792.

289. MOSSE (James). Thomas Street. Present 1 Nov. 1793.

290. MOUARTY (—). Tralee. 'Dr.' Admitted 3 Feb. 1792.

292 MUIR (Thomas). Advocate. [MacKenzie, *Life of Thomas Muir*, p. 119; SP I]

292. MULLAY (Daniel). Abbey Street. Admitted 24 Feb. 1792. Possibly went bankrupt (*DG*, 7 Jan. 1790). [SP I–V]

293. — (James). Abbey Street. Merchant. Admitted 10 Feb. 1792. On Cath. Qual. Rolls. Member of the Catholic Convention. In 1789 let a dwelling-house at a rent of £15 (Reg. Deeds). Was said to have won a large prize in the English lottery (*HJ*, 29 March 1797). [SP I-V]

294. MULLEN (Benjamin). Chamber Street. Clothier. Admitted 21 Sept. 1792. Proposer 4 Jan. 1793. On Cath. Qual. Rolls. [*WD*; SP I]

295. — (Henry). Hanover Street. Silk-manufacturer. Took test Oct. 1792. In 1784 signed resolutions of Aldermen of Skinners Alley in favour of reform and protection (*VJ*, 12 April 1784). [*WD*]

296. MURPHY (Denis). Luke Street. Corn-broker. According to Collins, a papist. [*WD*; SP I, II, IV, VI]

297. — (Patrick). Dame Street. Mercer. Admitted and took test 1 Feb. 1793. On Cath. Qual. Rolls. Died 'universally and deservedly lamented by a numerous and respectable acquaintance' (*HJ*, 21 March 1794). [*WD*; SP I]

298. — (Patrick). Fownes Street. Probably Murphy of Weldon & Murphy's, whose premises were at the corner of Fownes Street (*DEP*, 25 Jan. 1785). [SP I]

299. MURRY (James). Exchequer Street. Physician. Admitted 10 Feb. 1792. On Cath. Qual. Rolls. In 1799 he requested permission to visit his nephew, Bartholomew Blackwell, a prisoner in Kilmainham (Reb. Papers, 620/7/80/38). [*WD*; SP I]

300. NEILSON (Samuel). Belfast. Woollen-draper. Took test 30 March 1792. According to Collins, attended when in town. [*DNB*; SP I, V, VI]

301. NEWETT (or Newit) (George). New Row. Admitted 16 March 1792. [SP I]

302. NOBLE (Arthur). Carrickmacross. Took test 30 Nov. 1792. Proposer 14 Dec. 1792. He was one of five delegates chosen to represent Monaghan in the Reform congress (*DEP*, 18 Jan. 1785). [SP I]

303. O'BERNE (Hugh, *Esq*.). Carrick-on-Shannon. Admitted 21 Dec. 1792. Member of the Catholic Convention. Worked for many years for Catholic Emancipation, and it was reported, he 'often said that the foundation of our faith, as the salvation of our country, should be laid on the broad basis of universal benevolence' (*DEP*, 13 March 1813).

304. O'BRIEN (Christopher). Francis Street. Woollen-draper. Admitted 27 Jan. and took test 24 Feb. 1792. In 1793 let a warehouse and some ground at a yearly rent of £25. In 1784 announced that in order to carry out his customers' wishes and to relieve the many starving manufacturers, he had 'laid in a large and elegant assortment of Real Irish, superfines, refines, and liberty broadcloths … of such a quality, that he has the satisfaction to say, they would do honour to any country'. At the same time he pledged himself not to sell any goods as Irish that were not really so, and drew attention to his scarlet, blue and white regimental cloths (*VJ*, 7 May 1784). In 1793 let a warehouse and some ground at a rent of £25 per annum (Reg. Deeds). Went bankrupt (*DG*, 16 May 1795). [*WD*; SP I, II, IV]

305. O'BRYAN (James). High Street. A clerk of Frazer, the army agent. According to Collins, a papist. [Reb. Papers, 620/20, 78; SP I, V, VI]

306. O'CALLAGHAN (James). Abbey Street. Merchant. Admitted 23 Nov. 1792. On Cath. Qual. Rolls. Probably went bankrupt (DG, 3 Jan. 1797). [WD; SP I]

307. — (Owen, Esq.). Coolavely, Co. Armagh. Admitted 21 Dec. 1792. On Cath. Qual. Rolls. Member of the Catholic Convention.

308. O'CONNOR (Denis). Roscommon. Admitted 24 Feb. 1792. If he was Denis O'Connor of Belanagar, elder son of the Irish historian, he took the chair at a meeting of the Catholics of Roscommon which thanked the MPs who had opposed the rejection of the Catholic petition (DEP, 10 April 1792). Another possibility is the Denis O'Conor who was son of Charles O'Conor Jr (1736–1808) and grandson of the historian. [DEP, 16 Aug. 1804; J. O'Donovan and C. O'Conor, The O'Conors of Connaught (1891), pp. 308–18]

309. — (Malachy V.). Dominick Street. Merchant. Partner and brother of Valentine O'Connor. Proposer 13 Jan. 1792. Member of the Catholic Convention. The firm sold Surat cotton, Jamaica rum, sugar and, on at least one occasion, auctioned ships (HJ, 5 July 1799; 14 Nov. 1800; 14 Sept. 1801; 21 April, 10 July 1801). In 1796, according to Higgins, Valentine O'Connor was securing cargoes of claret from Bordeaux in American bottoms and sending out provisions to the enemy via the West Indies (Higgins, 22 Aug. 1796).

In 1798 Malachy O'Connor, 'nephew of Valentine', was reported to have been present at a meeting where plans for a rising were discussed (Higgins, 20 Oct. 1798); Higgins may have mistaken the family relationship, or there may have been two Malachy O'Connors involved [WD; SP I–VI]. Collins refers frequently to Malachy O'Connor and on a few occasions to Malachy Valentine O'Connor. Valentine as well as Malachy O'Connor may have been members of the Dublin Society of United Irishmen, or Collins may have inserted 'Valentine' by mistake.

310. — (Patrick). Admitted 27 April 1792.

311. — (Thomas, Esq.). Roscommon. Admitted 13 Jan. 1792. Possibly Thomas O'Conor (1770–1855) who emigrated 1798 to the USA. [SP I, IV; The O'Conors of Connaught, pp. 303–4]

312. — (—). Cook Street. Took test 6 July 1792.

313. O'DONNELL (John). Barrister. Took test 24 Feb. 1792. In February 1793 took the place of Counsellor Powel on the committee on reform set up by the Society. [SP I]

314. — (John, Esq.). Cork. Admitted 3 Feb. 1792.

315. O'DWYER (Morgan). Barrister. Took test 23 April 1793. [SP I]

316. O'GORMAN (James, Esq.). Lakefield, Ennis. Admitted and took test 28 Dec. 1792. Member of the Catholic Convention. Although he became a yeoman in 1796, in 1799 he and his younger brother were arrested, and according to his own story, treated with great brutality. Apparently there were some grounds for his arrest, since his brother, who had been expelled from Trinity College, was suspected of treasonable practices. Author of a book on angling. [Reb. Papers, 620/8/83/3–11; 620/10/121/11; SP I; Limerick Chronicle, 30 May 1855]

317. O'HARA (Charles). High Street. Grocer. Admitted and took test 16 Nov. 1792. On Cath. Qual. Rolls. Sold tea and wine, both wholesale and retail (DEP, 1 Jan., 4 Oct. 1785). Went bankrupt (DG, 9 Oct. 1788). In 1797 was arrested on a charge of treason, but after being detained a few days was discharged (HJ, 15 Nov. 1797). [WD; SP I, V, VI]

318. — (James). Bride Street. Possibly an attorney. Admitted 1 Feb. 1793.

319. O'KEEFE (Jeremiah). S. Earl Street. Merchant. Admitted 16 Nov. 1792. [*WD*; SP I]

320. O'LEARY (Michael). Capel Street. Bookseller. Proposed and withdrawn 16 March and took test 30 March 1792. [*WD*; SP I]

321. O'NEIL (Arthur). Hoey's Court. Watchmaker. Admitted 13 Jan. and took test 24 Feb. 1792. Proposer 14 Dec. 1792. Member of goldsmiths' corps (Reb. Papers, 620/53/179). According to Collins a papist, but a member of the City Corporation in 1816. [*WD*; SP I, VI]

322. O'NEILE (Thomas). Usher's Quay. Merchant. Took test 15 March 1793.

323. OTWAY (Samuel). Crow Street. Clerk to a haberdasher. Admitted 29 March 1793. [Reb. Papers, 620/20, 78; SP I]

324. PACHE (John James). Usher's Quay. Merchant. Admitted 13 Jan. 1792. Admitted freeman midsummer 1788. [*WD*; SP I, II, IV]

325. PAINE (Thomas). Author. Admitted an honorary member 8 June 1792. [*DNB*]

326. PASSMORE (Richard). W. Park Street. Cotton-manufacturer. According to Collins, a papist. [*WD*; SP I, VI]

327. PATTERSON (John). Mary's Abbey. Saddler. Proposed 2 Nov. 1792. Advertised the 'caravans' (cases to be hung on carriages) that he had invented (*DEP*, 18 March 1786). [SP I]

328. PEEBLES (James). High Street. Wholesale woollen-draper. Admitted 23 Nov. 1792. Admitted freeman Mich. 1792. Went bankrupt (*DG*, 30 April 1793). [*WD*; SP I, II]

329. PERRY (Francis). Aungier Street. Attorney. Was deputy clerk of the rolls (*FDJ*, 24 April 1794). [*WD*; SP I, II]

330. PLUNKETT (James. *Esq.*). Roscommon. Admitted 24 Feb. and took test 1 June 1792. Member of the Catholic Convention. Probably the James Plunkett who had been in the French service, was under suspicion in 1798 and was attainted by 38 Geo. III c. 80 (Reb. Papers, 620/13/161/7; 620/53/96). [*DNB* (under Susannah Gunning); SP I, II, IV, VI]

331. — (Richard, *Jun.*). Blackhall Street. Salesmaster. Admitted 23 Nov. 1792. In 1784 an advertisement appeared signed by over 100 butchers, contradicting the malicious rumour that some butchers did not intend to buy from Mr Plunkett. They were completely satisfied with his conduct. Four months later he summoned his creditors to receive a dividend of 5s. in the £ (*DEP*, 13 July, 27 Nov. 1784). [*WD*]

332. PORTER (William). Skinners' Alley. Printer and bookseller. Proposer 8 Feb. 1793. Admitted freeman midsummer 1791. [*WD*; SP I–IV]

333. POWEL (George). Barrister. Admitted Dec. 1792. [SP I, V, VI]

334. RAINEY (Thomas). Crampton Court. Notary public. Took test 23 Nov. 1792. [*WD*; SP I]

335. RAINSFORD [or RANSFORD] (William). Chamber Street. Clothier. Admitted 13 Jan. 1792. Proposer 27 Jan. 1792. Admitted freeman Mich. 1786. Supported protection in 1784 (*VJ*, 28 July 1784). [*WD*; SP I]

336. READ (William). Dame Street. Lottery-office-keeper. Admitted 13 Jan. 1792. [*WD*]

337. REEVES (John). Queen Street. Attorney. Admitted 21 Dec. 1792. [*WD*; SP I]

338. REID (James). Pill Lane. Linen-draper. Admitted 4 Jan. 1793. [*WD*; SP I]

339. REILY (James). W. Arran Street. Carpenter (i.e. builder). Admitted 4

Jan. 1793. On Cath. Qual. Rolls. In 1790 let a house at a rent of £22 per annum (Reg. Deeds). [WD]

340. — (John). Marybone Lane. Brewer. Admitted Oct. and took test 11 Oct. 1792. Proposer 14 Dec. 1792. Went bankrupt (DG, 26 June 1794). [SP I]

341. REYNOLDS (James). Cookstown, Co. Tyrone. Physician. Died 1808. [Madden (2nd edn), ii, p. 25; Lords Jnl Ire., vii, 146; DEP, 19 Jan. 1793; SP I, V, VI]

342. RICE (Dominick). Eustace Street. Barrister. Called 1780. Proposer 4 Jan. 1793. In April 1798 an informer reported that Dominick Rice and Matthew Dowling were discussing the assassination of the Earl of Clare (Sirr Papers, N 4. 8). [SP I–VI]

343. RIDDAL (John). Rughan, Co. Tyrone. Admitted 14 Dec. 1792.

344. RIDDALL (James). Corn Market. Lace-seller. Proposer 13 Jan. 1792. Admitted freeman midsummer 1789. Advertised his English, French and Mechlin lace 'purchased from the real manufacturer' (DEP, 24 Jan. 1789, 5 March 1791). As churchwarden of St Audeon's parish, was chairman of a meeting which passed resolutions in favour of reform (DEP, 31 Jan. 1793). In Oct. 1796 the government was informed that his brother was expected back from Philadelphia with letters from Rowan, and in Dec. Sir Edward Newenham advised that letters addressed to him from Lisburn, Belfast or abroad, should be stopped (J.W., 1 Oct. 1796, Reb. Papers, 620/10; Reb. Papers, 620/26/128). A year later Higgins, who was anxious to prevent him becoming a member of the Common council, described him as 'one who had all along avowed himself an United Irishman ... was deputy Treasurer to that Society when held in Back Lane ... is one of the Committee ... was concerned in the escape of Hamilton Rowan ... and Napper Tandy is now known to have been secreted in his House' (Higgins, 21 Sept. 1797). [WD; SP I–VI]

345. RIDGEWAY (William). Bride Street. Barrister. Admitted 21 Dec. and took test 28 Dec. 1792. A relation of Tandy's. Quartermaster of the Lawyers cavalry (DEP, 7 June 1803). [DNB; SP I, VI]

346. RIKY (Elias). Chamber Street. Cotton-manufacturer and dyer. Admitted 27 Jan. and took test 3 Feb. 1792. Admitted freeman Mich. 1789. [WD; SP I]

347. ROCHE (James). Fownes Street. Wine-merchant. On Cath. Qual. Rolls. [WD; SP I, VI]

348. — (John Thomas). Youghal. Merchant. Admitted 8 March 1793. Spoke in a debate in the Society on 11 Oct. 1793 (Carey, An Appeal, p. 168). Was in the chair for a time when the Catholics of Youghal met to thank parliament for relief (DEP, 11 May 1793). Went bankrupt (DG, 23 Nov. 1793). [SP I]

349. ROE (Thomas). Mill Street. Tanner. Proposed 11 Jan. 1793 [SP I]

350. ROURKE (Thomas). 7 Christ Church Lane. Watchmaker. Admitted 27 Jan. and took test Feb. 1792. Proposer 27 April 1792. According to Collins, a papist. [WD; SP I, V, VI]

351. ROWAN (Archibald Hamilton). [DNB; SP I–IV]

352. RUSSELL (Thomas). [DNB; SP I, II, IV]

353. RYAN (Charles). Old Church Street. Apothecary. Proposer 31 Aug. 1792. On Cath. Qual. Rolls. Member of the Catholic Convention. In 1798 his son admitted to having been sworn a United Irishman but had taken no part in their activities (Reb. Papers, 620/38/178). When he died, it was said 'As a scholar and a gentleman his acquaintance was sought by men of letters ... Charles Fox esteemed him as a friend and admired him as a man of distinguished worth and talent. To the poor of his neighbourhood he was a father; in

sickness he attended them, in poverty he relieved them.' (*DEP*, 22 Dec. 1810). [*WD*; SP I–VI]

354. — (Thomas). Arran Quay. Physician. Admitted 6 July and took test 31 Aug. 1792. Member of the Catholic Convention. Higgins refers to him as one of the committee for collecting articles for the *Press* (Higgins, 24 Oct. 1797). [*WD*; SP I, II]

355. SADLEIR (Thomas). Barrister. Took test 27 Jan. 1792. Died 1815. [SP I–IV; BLG, 1950]

356. SAVAGE (Thomas). Capel Street. Tanner. Took test 5 April 1793. On Cath. Qual. Rolls. He and Joseph Kelly held a mortgage on a house in Dame Street (Reg. Deeds 475/350). Died at his country residence (*FDJ*, 2 Sept. 1809). [*WD*; SP I]

357. SCOTT (William). Exchange Court. Merchant. Admitted 16 March 1792. [*WD*; SP I, II, IV]

358. SEGRAVE (Thomas). Greek Street. Merchant. Proposed 30 Nov. 1792. Member of the Catholic Convention. Went bankrupt (*DG*, 9 May 1797). [*WD*; SP I]

359. SHANNON (Bartholomew). Kilmainham. Tanner. Admitted 29 March 1793. On Cath. Qual. Rolls. [*WD*; SP I]

360. — (Edward). Castle Street. Cloth-merchant. Admitted 14 Dec. 1792. [*WD*; SP I]

361. — (Oliver). Back Lane. Leather-seller. Admitted 1 Feb. 1793. On Cath. Qual. Rolls. [*WD*; SP I]

362. SHEARES (Henry). Barrister. [*DNB*; SP I, V, VI]

363. — (John). Barrister. [*DNB*; SP I, V, VI].

364. SHEEHY (Bryan, *Esq.*). Admitted 3 Feb. 1792. Either Bryan Sheehy of Cork or Bryan Sheehy of Limerick. Both were landowners and sat in the Catholic Convention (*IFR*, 1976).

365. SHERWOOD (Thomas Keating). Cutpurse Row. Shoemaker. Admitted 13 Jan. 1792. Admitted freeman midsummer 1789. [*WD*]

366. SIMMS (Robert). Lower Liffey Street. Merchant. [*WD*; SP I]

367. — (Thomas). Lower Liffey Street. Merchant. Proposed 30 Nov. 1792. [*WD*; SP I]

368. SLATER (Stephen). Stoneybatter. Chandler. Admitted 14 Dec. 1792. Announced in 1800 that, as he intended to retire, he wished to sell his house and concerns, where he had carried on 'soap boiling, tallow chandling, and tobacco manufacture in as extensive a manner as any other house in Dublin' (*SNL*, 19 Feb. 1800). [*WD*; SP I]

369. SMITH (Charles). Mary's Abbey. Grocer. Took test 20 July 1792. On Cath. Qual. Rolls. Went bankrupt (*DG*, 19 Jan. 1797). An informer reported, *c.* 1798, that he saw him sworn at a meeting, and heard him say: 'it was too small a split for him that night' (Reb. Papers 620/51/214). He seems to have known a good deal of what was going on and to have talked rather too freely. In 1800, after a still of his had been seized, he left suddenly for America; shortly after his departure an attorney accused him of forgery. Some years later he wrote to a friend in Dublin that he was pleased to hear that Ireland was prosperous and that a mild system of government prevailed there (J.W., 2 Jan. 1797, 17 Sept. 1800, Reb. Papers, 620/10; J.W., — 1805, Reb. Papers, 620/14/188/3). [*WD*; SP I]

370. — (Thomas). Mary's Abbey. Probably a mistake for Charles Smith. [SP II]

371. — (William Thomas). French Street. Army officer. Took test 6 July

1792. A captain in the army, lieutenant in the Battle-axe Guards, colonel and
adjutant general of the Volunteers. Owned an apparently fair-sized estate in
Westmeath (*DEP*, 9 March 1786; 31 March, 4 April 1789). Was in the chair
when the Dublin Independent Volunteers passed a resolution in favour of reform
(*DEP*, 26 April 1784). Was a candidate in the independent interest for the borough of Trim (*DEP*, 27 April 1790). Carried Napper Tandy's messages to Toler
in 1793. Offered the services of the Independent Dublin Volunteers to Pelham
in 1796 (J.W., 28 Dec. 1796, Reb. Papers, 620/36/227). [*WD*; SP I, II, IV]

372. SMYTH (Laurence). Carrick-on-Suir. Tanner. Admitted 21 Dec. 1792.
On Cath. Qual. Rolls. A member of the Catholic Convention. Signed a declaration thanking the Catholic nobility, gentry and bishops for their address to the
deluded people engaged in the rebellion (*HJ*, 8 June 1798). [Lucas, *General
Directory*, 1788]

373. SPARKS (Richard). Cutpurse Row. Hatter. Took test 27 April 1792.
Sold wholesale and retail. In 1800, announced that he was willing to sell at
reduced prices so as to keep a number of poor industrious manufacturers
employed (*HJ*, 12 May 1800). [*WD*; SP I–IV]

374. SPENCER (Robert). High Street. Woollen-draper. Took test 1 June
1792. Proposer 16 Nov. 1792. Admitted freeman midsummer 1792. Went
bankrupt (*DG*, 2 Feb. 1790). [*WD*; SP I, II, IV]

375. STACK (John, *Esq.*). Stack's Grove. Admitted 14 Dec. 1792.

376. STOCKDALE (Henry William). Abbey Street. Merchant. Admitted 16
Nov. 1792. Admitted freeman Mich. 1787. Went bankrupt (*DG*, 15 Jan. 1795).
[*WD*; SP I, V]

377. — (John). Britain Street. Printer. Admitted 27 April 1792. In 1795 let
a house in Britain Street at a rent of £33 per annum (Reg. Deeds). In 1798, as
printer of the *Press*, he was brought to the Bar of the House of Lords and sentenced to pay a fine of £500 and be imprisoned for six months for breach of
privilege (apparently for publishing a letter reflecting on the parliamentary conduct of Lord Glentworth) (*Press*, 20 Feb. 1798). On his petitioning the House
for relief, the fine was remitted (*Lords Jnl Ire.*, vii, 27–31, 117). Probably the
Stockdale from whom, in 1805, Corbet was trying to extract information. Died
1813. (Reb. Papers, 620/88/22, 35; 620/13/198/13). [*WD*; SP I, IV, V; Cox's
Irish Magazine, March 1813]

378. STOKES (Whitley). F.T.C.D. [*DNB*; SP I, II, V]

379. STOYTE (John). Kennedy's Lane. Silversmith. Admitted 14 Dec. 1792.
Admitted freeman Easter 1789. Acted as broker (*DEP*, 23 Feb. 1804). Before
the Rebellion was a leading United Irishman, and was said to have had the door
of his house painted green (Higgins, 17 Dec. 1797). Confessed to having lent his
house to Matthew Dowling, to shelter Bird, with whom he quarrelled over the
value of the latter's memoirs (Reb. Papers, 620/51/196). He was pardoned but
in 1801 was reported to be connected with a furniture club which was actually
a seditious society (Higgins, 23 May 1801). [*WD*; SP I, V, VI]

380. STUBBS (William). Francis Street. Woollen-draper. Admitted 2 Nov.
1792. Proposer 30 Nov. 1792. Went bankrupt (*DG*, 17 May 1788). Advertised
for an apprentice and had furnished apartments to let (*HJ*, 16 Nov. 1796). In
1784 published an affidavit to the effect that he would not import any goods
for twelve months, and promised that he would not sell the manufactures of one
country as those of another (*VJ*, 11 June 1784). [*WD*; SP I]

381. SULLIVAN (Jeremiah). Merchants' Quay. Paper-maker. Admitted 15
Feb. 1792. Catholic (*DEP*, 4 July 1793). Went bankrupt (*DG*, 16 Oct. 1790).

In 1795 mortgaged his house and warehouse as security for £600 which he owed. In an extremely laudatory obituary-notice, it was said that 'he had brought the infant manufacture to so high a state of perfection as almost to rival that of the sister country, with all its advantages derived from an experience of two centuries' and that 'although not as successful in trade as others of his long standing, or indeed as his exertions merited, yet his death may, in some degree, be said to be a national loss'. Also a reference was made to 'the number of workmen and their families that ever found in him a kind and patronizing employer' (*SNL*, 21 March 1818). [*WD*]

382. — (Patrick). Old Church Street. Silk-manufacturer. Admitted 7 Dec. and took test 21 Dec. 1792. [*WD*; SP I]

383. SUMMERS (John). Bridgefoot Street. [SP I]

384. — (Laurence). Bridgefoot Street. Merchant. Admitted 21 Dec. 1792. Summers was described by Collins as a papist. [SP I, V, VI]

385. SWEENEY (John). Great George's Street. Vintner. Admitted 3 Feb. and took test 24 Feb. 1792. Proprietor of the Druids Head tavern and chop-house (*DEP*, 28 Nov. 1789), where the Society dined in Dec. 1793. In 1799 sold his lease of a house for £200 (Reg. Deeds). [*WD*; SP I, II, IV]

386. SWEETMAN (Edward). Army officer. Took test 30 Nov. 1792. Member of the Catholic Convention. Strongly denounced Great Britain's conduct towards Ireland (*The Speech of Edward Sweetman ... at a Meeting of the Free-holders of the County of Wexford* [1792]). Advertised for recruits (*DEP*, 26 July 1794). [SP I, V]

387. — (John). Stephen's Green. Porter-brewer. Admitted 16 Nov. 1792. On Cath. Qual. Rolls. Member of the Catholic Convention. Was left £2500 by his uncle (Reb. Papers, 620/48/48). When he wished to let his premises, he announced they had been thoroughly repaired at a cost of £2000, and were suited to any purpose that required 'security, good air and great accommodation' (*SNL*, 1 Jan. 1800). [*WD*; *DNB*]

388. — (William). Lower Abbey Street. Brewer. On Cath. Qual. Rolls. Member of the Catholic Convention. [SP I]

389. TANDY (George). Lisburn. Admitted 3 Feb. 1792. Brother of Napper Tandy. Left £500 to his daughter and the rest of his property to his wife (copy of will, in PRONI). A leading Northern radical. Took a keen interest in the Reform Congress, and during 1784 was trying to get arms for a Volunteer company in Saintfield, and was writing to the *Belfast News-Letter* (George Tandy to Napper Tandy, 2, 6 Nov. 1784, Chatham Corresp., PRO). In 1793 presided over a reform meeting in Lisburn (*DEP*, 17 Jan. 1793).

390. — (James). Chancery Lane. Wine merchant. Son of James Napper Tandy. Admitted freeman midsummer 1787. A Common council man. He owned 'an improving property of 500–600 acres near Drogheda, and by 1803 his business was worth a rising profit of £2500 per annum (Petition of James Tandy to the Duke of Bedford, Reb. Papers, 620/14/196; Memorial of James Tandy to the Earl of Hardwick, Reb. Papers, 620/13/169/9). Was in the East India Company's service for several years, where he gained the reputation of being an excellent officer, and in fact a martinet (J.W., undated, Reb. Papers, 620/10). He joined 'the old United Irishmen', but disapproving of universal suffrage withdrew with about forty 'respectable persons'. For this he was disinherited by his father, who did not speak to him for a considerable time.

After his withdrawal, he subscribed to the Society, though he did not attend its meetings, and he supplied, at the Society's expense, the wine for Butler and

Bond when in Newgate (Petition of James Tandy to the Duke of Bedford, as above; Examination of James Tandy in 1803, Reb. Papers, 620/11/138/39; Memorial of James Tandy to the Earl of Hardwick, as above). In 1798 Higgins reported that Napper Tandy was communicating with the incendiaries through his son, and that Bacon had been concealed in James Tandy's house (Higgins, 7 March, 21 June 1798). But McNally declared that he was quite loyal, that though he was a good son 'the last man in Europe he wishes to see is his father', and that he wanted to serve in the yeomanry, but having been an officer was unwilling to serve in the ranks (J. W., undated, Reb. Papers, 620/10). In June 1798 he suggested to Pelham that the inhabitants of Dublin should be organized to patrol the streets at night (Reb. Papers, 620/38/39).

In 1803 he was arrested (much to the amusement of some extremists, who thought he always had 'a bit of the aristocrat' about him). The reasons seem to have been several trivial and probably misinterpreted incidents, the fact that he was his father's son, and that he had given certain letters to Dowdall referring to a 'scheme' which, according to Tandy, was merely for importing wine (Reb. Papers, 620/11/130/59; 138/39, 34; 620/13/169/59). After twelve months' imprisonment, he was released. By that time he complained that his business was ruined, and he was deprived of his town house by his creditors (Petition of James Tandy to the Duke of Bedford, as above). [WD; SP I–VI]

391. — (James Napper). [DNB; SP I–IV]

392. TEELING (John). Marrowbone Lane. Distiller. Admitted 7 Dec. 1792. In 1798 sold premises in Grafton Street for £86 (Reg. Deeds). [SP I]

393. THUNDER (Henry). Dame Street. Woollen-draper. Proposer 23 Nov. 1792. On Cath. Qual. Rolls. Member of the Catholic Convention. In 1784 made an affidavit that he would not sell as Irish any goods that were not really so (VJ, 21 June 1784). Ten years later, announced that his agent in England had just bought carpets, etc. (FDJ, 4 Feb. 1794). In 1795 mortgaged his house. In 1796 made over to Patrick Thunder his house, his claim to £200 and his share of his father-in-law's estate, as security for £750 which he owed him (Reg. Deeds). According to Higgins – who described him as a bankrupt – he was one of a party who were to seize the castle in 1798 (Higgins, 24 May 1798). It was also reported that a district meeting was held in his house, and that Toole, his clerk, was a leading organizer among the discontented shortly before the Rebellion (Reb. Papers, 620/52/158; Higgins, 5 June 1798). [WD; SP I)

394. — (Patrick, Esq.). Balleby (Balally), Co. Dublin. Proposed 2 Nov.; took test 7 Dec. 1792. On Cath. Qual. Rolls. Member of the Catholic Convention. In a paper of c. 1798, apparently giving a list of local leaders, he is mentioned as 'head of the Balbriggan' (Reb. Papers, 620/17/32). [SP I]

395. — (Richard). Dame Street. Woollen-draper. Took test 21 Sept. 1792. Probably a mistake for Henry Thunder.

396. TOMMINS (John). Summerhill. Merchant. Admitted 1 Feb. and took test 8 Feb. 1793. On Cath. Qual. Rolls. [WD; SP1]

397. TONE (Theobald Wolfe). Barrister. [DNB; SP I–VI]

398. TRENOR [or TRAYNOR] (Thomas). Poolbeg Street. Spirit-merchant and ship-owner. Admitted 7 Dec. 1792. Was arrested at Bond's (Sirr Papers, N 4. 12; Reb. Papers, 620/36/7). [WD; SP I]

399. TYGHE [or TIGHE] (Laurence). Thomas Street. Mead-brewer. Admitted 16 March 1792. On Cath. Qual. Rolls. In 1800 announced that he intended to retire from business and concentrate his property at his bleach-yard at Bluebell. He wanted to dispose of his house and concerns in Thomas Street, where

he had laid out several thousand pounds. He owned there a rectifying still of 140 gallons capacity (*HJ*, 16 June 1800; Sirr Papers, N 4. 8). He was said to be a stout republican, and member of a committee for assisting men to join the rebels, and of another for the subornation of Crown witnesses (J.W., 28 Dec. 1796, Reb. Papers, 620/36/227; Higgins, 11 July 1797, 30 June 1798). In 1797, Higgins reported that he had gone down to Co. Wicklow with Nicholas Butler, distributing pamphlets and swearing-in deluded people (Higgins, 27 June 1797). In 1798 he was arrested, but shortly afterwards released 'in the most honourable manner' (*HJ*, 6 July 1798). As the result of his kindness to the wounded Capt. Ryan, or in connection with the police investigations into a theft of his property, he seems to have become intimate with Major Sirr (*HJ*, 10 June 1799; Sirr Papers, N 4. 5). [*WD*; SP I, II, IV]

400. WADE (Walter). Capel Street. MD. Professor of Botany, Dublin Society. Died 1825. [*DNB*; SP I]

402. WALDRON (Laurence). Pill Lane. Wholesale linen-draper. [*WD*; SP I]

402. WALLIS (Bartholomew). Gt Longford Street. Attorney. Admitted 13 Jan. 1792. Proposer 27 Jan. 1792. [*WD*; SP I–VI]

403. WALSH (Edward). The Coombe. [SP I]

404. — (Edward). Physician and poet. Admitted 16 Nov. 1792. Possibly the same as the foregoing. [*DNB*]

405. — (James). Coombe. Merchant (grocer or coal-factor). Admitted 4 Dec. 1792. [*WD*]

406. — (James). Dame Street. Breeches-maker. Admitted 13 Jan. 1792. In 1796 he received 1000 English dressed deer-skins (*HJ*, 7 Nov. 1796). [*WD*; SP I–IV]

407. — (Michael). Henry Street. Perfume-seller. Admitted 16 Nov. 1792. In 1789 probably mortgaged a dwelling-house in Henry Street for £250 (Reg. Deeds). [*WD*; SP I]

408. — (Richard). Naul. [SP I]

409. WARREN (Thomas). Ash Street. Cotton-manufacturer. Proposer 2 Nov. 1792. On Cath. Qual. Rolls. Member of the Catholic Convention. Refused admission to the Weavers' gild (*HJ*, 2 April 1794). In 1787 paid £560 for a house, which he let for a year at £150 (Reg. Deeds). [*WD*; SP I–VI]

410. WEBB (William L.). Barrister. Admitted and took test 15 Feb. 1793. According to Collins, very violent and unsteady. [Burtchaell & Sadleir; SP I, V, VI]

411. WELDON (John). Dame Street. Mercer. Proposer 21 Sept. 1792. On Cath. Qual. Rolls. Member of the Catholic Convention. Sold wholesale and retail (*HJ*, 16 May 1794). Assisted persons imprisoned for debt (*HJ*, 22 May 1802). In 1798 an informer stated that 'Geo Weldon of 31 or 33 Dame Street' was a delegate to a baronial committee (Reb. Papers, 620/35/71). [*WD*; SP I–VI]

412. WHITE (Arthur M.). Cumberland Street. Attorney. Proposer 28 Dec. 1792. Took chair at a meeting of the Independent Dublin Volunteers (*DEP*, 2 Feb. 1793). [*WD*; SP I, V]

413. — (John). Ash Street. Factor. Admitted 14 Dec. 1792. Went bankrupt (*DG*, 30 April 1793). [SP I]

414. — (John). Fishamble Street. Haberdasher and linen-draper. Admitted 6 Nov.; took test 23 Nov. 1792. [*WD*; SP I]

415. — (Thomas). Bridge Street. Wine and spirit-merchant. Admitted 16 Nov. and took test 23 Nov. 1793. Possibly admitted freeman 1775. [*WD*; SP I, II]

416. WILDE (Michael). Dolphin's Barn. Proposer 7 Dec. 1792. On Cath. Qual. Rolls. [SP I]

417. — (Nicholas). Dolphin's Barn. Tanner. On Cath. Qual. Rolls. In 1791, sold a piece of land at Dolphin's Barn for £550 (Reg. Deeds). [WD; SP II]

418. — (Richard). Thomas Street. Ironmonger and hardware-merchant. Admitted 14 Dec. 1792. In 1785 was trying to dispose of the house he had occupied in High Street. He mentions that it had lately been fitted with marble chimney-pieces and Bath-stone grates (VJ, 10 Aug. 1785). In 1787 he entered into a partnership to manufacture plain and fancy buttons (Reg. Deeds). In 1796 he brought into another partnership for the same purpose £1600 worth of cash and merchandise (Reg. Deeds). [WD; SP I]

419. WILKINSON (George B.). Spitalfields. Silk and worsted-manufacturer. Admitted 4 Jan. 1793. Admitted freeman midsummer 1792. In 1784, when charged with having made fraudulent goods, fourteen working weavers employed by him made affidavits that this was untrue (VJ, 6 Aug. 1784). [WD; SP I]

420. — (James Tandy). Mercer Street. Physician. In 1788 let a house in Limerick at a yearly rent of £50, and twenty-six acres for £31 (Reg. Deeds). [WD; SP I, II, IV, V]

421. — (John). Phibsborough. Carpenter. Admitted 14 Dec. 1792. Seems to have possessed considerable land and house-property in north Dublin, particularly around Britain Street and Gardiner Street (Reg. Deeds). [SP I]

422. WILLAN (Jacob). Francis Street. Shag and silk-manufacturer. Admitted 30 March and took test 27 April 1792. Proposer 31 Aug. 1792. Admitted freeman Christmas 1791. In 1788 made over his rights in two cottages (Reg. of Deeds). [WD; SP I–V]

423. WRIGHT (Thomas). Gt Ship Street. Surgeon. Proposer 27 Jan. 1792. Served in America, being present at Charlestown and Yorktown. Being disabled by sickness, he relinquished his commission, which had cost £300. Purchased a post at home, but the regiment being reduced, he lost 'his money, health and home'. He then started to practice in Dublin, and, his wife admitted, 'may sometimes have spoken like a man who conceived himself injured' (Memorial of Thomas Wright to the Marquis of Cornwallis, Reb. Papers, 620/53/50; Mrs Wright to Cornwallis, St. Pr. Pt., VI/32/2). In March McNally describes him as 'completely blasted' as an informer, and later explains that his sudden rise from known poverty had aroused suspicions (J.W., 4 March, 5 May 1798, Reb. Papers, 620/10). Nevertheless in Feb. 1799 he was said to have been mixed up in an attempt to revive an executive committee of the movement in Dublin (Reb. Papers, 620/74/8; 620/14/200/1). In 1805 he was definitely both giving information to the government and trying to secure favours from it, suggesting that, as he was the only physician in Ireland who had practised in every climate, he would make a suitable secretary to the Board of Health (Reb. Papers, 620/14/188/3, 35). [WD; SP I, II, IV–VI]

425. YOUNG (Matthew). Francis Street. Woollen-draper. Admitted 10 Dec. 1792. [WD; SP I]

Sources

I. 'The Court of Dublin Castle' is hitherto unpublished.

II. 'Trinity College Dublin and Politics' appeared in *Hermathena* (1992) but is greatly revised.

III. 'The Dublin Society of United Irishmen, 1791–4' appeared in *Irish Historical Studies*, ii (1940).

IV. 'Ireland and England' appeared in *Britain and the Netherlands*, eds J.S. Bromley and E.H. Kossman (The Hague 1971).

V. 'The Anglican Episcopate 1780–1945' appeared in *Theology*, i (1947), 202–9.

VI. 'Swift as a Political Thinker' appeared in *Jonathan Swift 1667–1967: A Dublin Tercentenary Tribute*, eds R. McHugh and P. Edwards (Dublin 1967).

VII. 'Edmund Burke and the Law' appeared in *Mysteries and Solutions in Irish Law*, ed. D. Green (Dublin 2001), pp. 97–114.

VIII.'John Hely-Hutchinson (1723–94)' appeared in *Of One Company: Bibliographical Studies of Famous Trinity Men 1591–1951*, ed. D.A. Webb (an *Icarus* special 1951).

IX. 'Edward Carson' appeared in *The Shaping of Modern Ireland*, ed. C.C. O'Brien (London 1960), pp. 85–97.

X. 'Trinity Cameos' 1–4 appeared in *Trinity: A College Record*, nos 8, 2, 12, 9; '5. Letter to the Editor' was first published in *T.C.D.: A College Miscellany*, 16 June 1938.

Index